FRONTIERS

FRONTIERS

Ronald Eyre · Nadine Gordimer

Nigel Hamilton · Christopher Hitchens

Frederic Raphael · Richard Rodriguez

Jon Swain · John Wells

BBC BOOKS

Frontispiece *The US–Mexico border*

Maps by Line & Line

Designed by Alan Price

Published by BBC Books
a division of BBC Enterprises Limited
Woodlands, 80 Wood Lane, London W12 0TT

ISBN 0 563 20701 9

Set in 11 on 12 pt Bodoni
and printed and bound by Butler & Tanner Limited, Frome and London
Colour separations by Technik Limited, Berkhamsted
Jacket printed by Belmont Press, Northampton

CONTENTS

PICTURE CREDITS

*T*HE *FIRST TIME* I crossed a frontier was in 1952. The day before, my grandmother had tied a Thomas Cook label to my school raincoat and put me on the overnight ferry to the Hook of Holland. After a miserable crossing, I found myself on a train rumbling through suburbs of Utrecht with a handful of other children whose fathers were stationed with the British Army in Germany. An hour or so later, the train clanked to a halt. Two guards entered our carriage and asked to see our passports. One of them had a gun. When my turn came, the man in charge peered at me with what I fancied was particular intensity.

That moment of excitement was the highlight of a long and boring journey. It was some years before I realized that frontiers were more than marker posts on journeys abroad. That they were also things through which some people could never travel freely, and others would lose their life in the effort.

Few frontiers are natural ones. Even if they follow the course of some river or mountain range, the line is there because someone put it there. Relics of an ancient empire or scars of a modern war – they end up in the atlas like addresses of uncertain origin telling us approximately where we can find our friends and enemies. But because frontiers are man-made, they are impermanent. When I first crossed that frontier between Holland and Germany in 1952, vast chunks of the globe were still coloured pink for British. In 1987, when the television series on which this book is based was conceived, that had gone. New countries had sprung up all over the world and Europe was divided down the middle by the great ideological fault-line between communism and the democracies of the West. Now they're cutting up the barbed wire to sell it as souvenirs.

The eight films and chapters are, in a sense, snapshots taken by people who had special reason to care. Each writer undertook the journey not to find out why the frontiers were drawn in the first place, but to find out what it was like living under the shadow of a frontier at a particular moment in time. In some cases, the process of change is so slow, the concrete of prejudice so thick, that nothing has moved since the journeys were made. In other cases, the tide has rolled in, sweeping away the sandcastles and leaving us with a unique record of how it once was. And the fascination of that is not simply historical. Tides go out as surely as they roll in. People make new frontiers as easily as they dismantled the old.

GEORGE CAREY, EXECUTIVE PRODUCER
JANUARY 1990

JON SWAIN

BORDER RUN

Thailand–Cambodia

*I*N THE LAST twenty years I have crossed the frontiers of
Cambodia hundreds of times, by air, by car and by foot. And
when I have not been crossing them in fact, I have been doing
so in my imagination. Cambodia, its people, its land, its agony, has
dominated my adult life. Inside its frontiers I have seen all the worst
of the twentieth century – civil war, bombardment, famine – stalk
their cruel way through the land. Far too many countries and peoples
can claim to have witnessed unspeakable horrors: one cannot claim
that Cambodia's suffering is unique. But it has been terrible.

For all of these reasons, and many more, I was delighted to be
asked by the BBC to return once again to Thailand and Cambodia
to film the frontier. Perhaps the film would help keep public opinion
alert to the agony of this distant little country and to what remains
one of the world's major refugee crises – the thousands of people in
dead-end camps along the border. I felt, though, that it was like
filming the edge of my own life, the frontiers of myself.

I first crossed the Thai–Cambodian frontier in 1970. For some time
I had wanted very much to go to South-east Asia, and particularly
to Vietnam to see the extraordinary collision of American idealism
and Vietnamese Communism. In addition I loved France, and
wanted to see this most important part of what had once been the
French empire. The languorous beauty of Indo-China, the jungle,
the romantic landscapes and the beautiful women had woven a magic
spell on generations of Frenchmen, and now they were about to
weave a spell on me.

Jon Swain at what was once the main Thai–Cambodian border crossing where in 1975 he was expelled from Cambodia

I had, I suppose, a French connection. When I was a teenager I had run away from England to join the French Foreign Legion. I knew I did not want to work in an ordinary civilian job and felt at that time that there would be more scope for youthful action within a military framework than among the commonplace routine of civilian life. The Legion forces you to sign up for a full five-year contract, but after several months of training in a grim fort overlooking the Vieux Port in Marseilles I wanted to get out. I had discovered that, with France's colonial wars over, soldiering in the Legion offered a monotonous kind of existence, not the challenge to youth and strength I thought I wanted. I still believe, though, that at its best the Legion can offer a noble form of service. It was not easy to break my contract; but when I told the commanding officer that what I really wanted was to be a journalist, he shouted, '*Pas de journalisme ici!*' and allowed me to leave. Nevertheless my stay with the Legion had been long enough for a passion for Indo-China to be aroused in me by stories of derring-do told by veterans of France's war there.

After a short stint on a British news agency I got a job in Paris with Agence France-Presse. It was a marvellous time and I was continually fascinated by the very names of Cambodia and Vietnam: in France, of course, because of its colonial past, they exerted far more pull than in Britain. In the A F P office, where I was employed translating despatches from Saigon into English, I remember reading all the copy about the 1968 Tet offensive, when the Viet Cong invaded the grounds of the American Embassy in Saigon and so shocked the American people that President Johnson felt compelled to withdraw from the Presidential race.

One A F P journalist had already been killed in Vietnam and another would die a few years later in the twilight days of American-backed South Vietnam, shot by a Saigon policeman in sinister circumstances. None the less, I was delighted when the A F P bureau chief asked me to go to Phnom Penh early in 1970. Our previous correspondent there had been expelled for writing a story which brought him in disfavour with the unpredictable Prince Sihanouk.

In those days inter-continental flights were an altogether different business from today – they were still an adventure. I took an Air France 707 which touched down at Rome and Cairo and then flew over the Arabian desert, crossed the waist of India and came down in Bangkok. Then it was the last and best leg of all, eastwards from the sweltering Thai capital over the frontier into Cambodia.

The twice-weekly flight to Phnom Penh from Paris touched down also at Siem Reap, the gateway to Angkor in north-western Cambodia. The temples of Angkor are one of the world's greatest archaeological treasures. Their history, like that of Cambodia, has been one of grandeur and decline.

The temple complex, built in the middle of the twelfth century, is the largest known religious monument in the world. For centuries it was lost, swallowed up by the jungle, until rediscovered in 1860 by the great French explorer Henri Mouhot who saw its three towers looming out of the forest one morning. The looting and the damage that have gone on here since the war began is just one more of Cambodia's tragedies. Vandals have stolen two hundred priceless statues from the gallery of a thousand Buddhas; these sacred images were smuggled over the frontier into Thailand and sold to unscrupulous Western collectors in the art shops of Bangkok. But back in 1970 the temples still had that warm, lived-in feeling. Buffaloes grazed in their courtyards. Children bathed naked in the lotus-blossomed ponds. With war licking at Cambodia again today, their preservation still cannot be guaranteed.

After Angkor we flew on over the Tonle Sap, one of the world's

Soldiers guarding the temple complex at Angkor Wat

great reservoirs of fish, its surface glassy smooth, and on to Phnom Penh. Here I said goodbye to the Air France stewardesses and began an adventure and a love affair with Cambodia to which I have been faithful ever since.

The AFP office was in the Hotel Royal, a splendid, old-fashioned colonial-style building that had once been the French officers' club. More recently it had been a comfortable and graceful base for tourists from France who came to Cambodia for *la chasse*, to visit Angkor Wat and to taste the legendary beauty of the women. It had a smart bar with fans in the high ceilings, faded photographs of the Angkor temples on its snuff-coloured walls, and a magnificent, ornate, carved wooden staircase.

Phnom Penh, the little capital on the banks of the Mekong River, was a place where French and oriental genius fused. It captivated me straightaway, laying on me a bewildering spell unlike anything else I have ever encountered. The whole place was like a garden. It had long, tree-lined boulevards, pavement cafés, discreet opium parlours, floating brothels (*les maisons flottantes*) and some of the most beautiful and sensually innocent people in the world. Intermingled with the gilded temples topped with curved, horned roofs were spacious mansions, hiding behind flowering trees and bougainvillea. It was the most enchanting of South-east Asian cities.

When I arrived Cambodia was a picture of serenity; it was hard to imagine that a few hundred miles to the east the guns were thundering in South Vietnam. The little country was presided over with ebullient flair by the feudal genius of Prince Sihanouk, who had been installed on the throne by the French twelve years before the country gained independence in 1953. Sihanouk was more than a mere monarch: the Cambodians believed him to be a god-king with semi-divine qualities.

Since the American marines had splashed ashore in Danang in South Vietnam Sihanouk had desperately tried to keep Cambodia out of Vietnam's expanding war. But it was almost impossible. Across the western frontier Thailand was a military ally of the United States and exerted constant pressure, while only thirty miles from Cambodia's eastern frontier was Saigon. The Vietnamese Communists took over large areas of eastern Cambodia close to Vietnam, and the Americans attacked them across the border. No one liked Sihanouk's neutrality; only ordinary Cambodians profited from it.

But the violation of Cambodia's frontiers was nothing new. In the mid-nineteenth century, when the French came, the little kingdom of Cambodia was all that was left of the great Khmer empire that had flourished between the eleventh and fifteenth centuries and which had built as its capital the temple complex of Angkor. Weak and decadent, it was already slipping into Thai and Vietnamese control, and only the arrival of the French had kept its powerful neighbours out. In 1963, Cambodia had taken Thailand to the international court at The Hague over sovereignty of the twelfth-century temple of Preah Vihear on the Thai–Cambodian border, a major source of friction. To Cambodians of every political persuasion the frontiers are a serious issue.

Despite his engaging and irresponsible nature – he was a composer and film director, and enjoyed women and the good life – Sihanouk showed considerable statesmanship. By playing off the Vietnamese against the Americans and the Thais in the early sixties the Prince had just managed to keep the war from pushing too far across the frontiers, and in theory Cambodia was still a marvellous oasis of peace. In fact, however, its neutrality was already heavily qualified, for the country was being tragically abused by both the Vietnamese Communists and the Americans. The port of Kompong Som (then called Sihanoukville) was the entry point for military supplies that were transported through Cambodia to the Communists in South Vietnam. In 1969 President Nixon authorized the savage and secret B52 bombing of the sanctuaries of the Vietcong and North Vietnamese Communists just inside Cambodia's borders with South Vietnam, less than forty miles from Saigon, and the dream dissolved. Cambodia became a battleground.

In March 1970, while he was abroad, Sihanouk was overthrown in a coup d'état by his right-wing Minister of Defence, General Lon Nol. Petulantly Sihanouk allied himself with his enemies, the tiny group of Cambodian Communists known as the Khmer Rouge whom he had previously sought to destroy, and with Hanoi. Lon Nol took Cambodia into the war on the side of Saigon and the United States, and that was the beginning of disaster. Since then Cambodia has been engulfed by famine, bloody revolution and foreign occupation.

In the next five years Phnom Penh became like an armed camp, gripped by an air of never-ending siege. To the visitor during that period the feeling would first declare itself on arrival at the airport, where the hot tarmac was thick with planes. Even as one's Air Cambodia Caravelle taxied to a halt, tiny propeller-driven T28s of the Cambodian Air Force, bombs tucked under their wings, would be roaring off down the runway on another mission. Warming up behind them would be DC3s and DC4s of Cambodia's many private airlines, which thrived on flying food into the city once the main supply roads had been cut.

As American arms and ideas poured into the city its people, like those of Saigon and Bangkok, soon adopted the Coca Cola culture; they were spoilt by corruption and greed. The Khmer Rouge grew, the Americans bombed widely, and hundreds of thousands of people fled from the Cambodian countryside into the towns. The enclaves controlled by the government grew ever smaller and ever more packed with refugees from the countryside.

Malnutrition was a rapidly spreading cancer. The refugee camps and pagodas soon overflowed, and the homeless were forced to throw up shacks. On the pavements of some streets the lines of wretched hovels and the trails of bug-like children with swollen bellies and sores on their bodies grew longer by the day. Only at the Phnom, as the Hotel Royal had been renamed to conform with the fact that the former kingdom was now a republic, did the new arrival still find something of the indolent charm of pre-war Cambodia. The Americans themselves struck a discordant note. Big men in sports shirts and drip-dry trousers, pilots, ex-soldiers, businessmen, all were motivated by a common desire – to make a fast buck out of the Cambodian tragedy.

Agriculture ceased, overland transport was cut off by the Khmer Rouge and rice had to be brought up the Mekong from Saigon in convoys, running a gauntlet of heavy Communist fire from the banks. It was the world's most dangerous boat journey. In March 1974 I joined one such river convoy travelling on a freighter called *Bonanza Three*. The ambush, when it came, consisted of a rocket attack only twelve miles from Phnom Penh. The lead ship caught fire. A rocket bursting aft narrowly missed our steering column. But *Bonanza Three* survived yet another Mekong run. The end, however, was looming. After the Mekong was closed as a supply route by the Khmer Rouge in 1974 the Americans desperately airlifted rice into Phnom Penh. The runway was under a constant barrage of Khmer Rouge rockets, and I recall the heartbreaking scenes as people scrambled for the last planes out.

In April 1975 I flew across the Thai–Cambodian frontier on the last plane as the Khmer Rouge closed in on Phnom Penh. I had been in Saigon but felt compelled by some personal, emotional reason to go back to Phnom Penh the day after the Americans left to be there at the end of this dirty, inglorious war I had spent most of my twenties covering. Cambodia had become very personal to me, and I was determined not to be some mere *turista de guerra*.

It was a dramatic flight. The aircraft was a Dakota of near Second World War vintage whose American pilot was anxious to rescue his Cambodian girlfriend. He took off from Bangkok despite a faulty engine, low-levelled all the way to Phnom Penh on three engines, and landed at Pochentong airport amidst rocket fire.

The United States had abandoned Phnom Penh the day before, closing its embassy and evacuating its staff in an ignominious helicopter operation. Just four days later, on the morning of 17 April, the Khmer Rouge entered Phnom Penh and began the forced evacuation of the city. Towards the end of that morning Sydney Schanberg of the *New York Times* and I were arrested by a wild bunch of Khmer Rouge. I thought I was going to be executed: one of their officers held a pistol to my head, and there did not seem to be any reason why he would not pull the trigger.

The remains of some of the hundreds of thousands tortured and killed by the Pol Pot regime in Cambodia

But in an act of singular bravery Dith Pran, Sydney's interpreter, intervened to save our lives. Defying our captors, Pran had argued his way into an armoured personnel carrier into which we had been herded at gunpoint; he knew that only his intervention might save us. As we faced death from a squad of excited, trigger-happy teenage soldiers on the banks of the Mekong River he used all his guile to convince our captors to let us go. It was a true act of courage. But in the horrific aftermath of Phnom Penh's fall, despite our efforts to fix him up with a new identity by doctoring my second British passport and reshuffling my name, Pran was forced to leave the protection of the French Embassy. He joined the mass exodus from the city – the greatest caravan of human misery I have ever seen – and for the next four years, after we had returned to the West, endured a hell of torture, genocide and starvation. I shall never forget the moment when we were told that Pran and all the other Cambodians must leave the embassy. The agony of those days were captured well in the film *The Killing Fields*.

Eventually, we foreigners were trucked to the border. In normal times the 260-mile journey took ten hours. Once the road passed through a shimmering green landscape studded with teak houses, Buddhist pagodas and smiling, waving people; but after savage US bombing and five years of war Cambodia had become a wilderness of destruction. Whole towns and villages were in ruins, and the roads were so bad that at times we travelled at less than five miles an hour. The whole ride took the best part of three days. On the first day a newborn baby died of exposure.

I arrived at the Thai–Cambodian frontier anaesthetized with fatigue, and as I finally crossed the little bridge over the stagnant stream that marks the border I felt an incredible relief – but also desolation at leaving all my friends in Cambodia to a future which seemed already to be horrific. In the next four years almost no one could cross Cambodia's frontier from Thailand, for the country was sealed off by the Khmer Rouge. They forced the population into the fields and attempted to create a hideous new agricultural commune which began with what they called year zero.

In the year immediately after the war I was living in Thailand and often drove to the border, desperate to have a glimpse of the Cambodia I had come to love and to discover what was really happening under the Khmer Rouge. I remember walking once through Aranyaprathet to the border and looking across the bridge into Cambodia, where a couple of black-suited Khmer Rouge soldiers stood motionless in the empty streets of the town of Poipet. On another occasion, exactly one year after Phnom Penh's fall, I took a car east out of Bangkok and then we turned north up to Preah Vihear, the temple surmounting a precipice overlooking Cambodia which Prince Sihanouk had wrested from the Thais. I left the driver and walked through the woods on that blisteringly hot day. When I stepped out of the trees I saw an extraordinary sight. Below me lay the whole of the north Cambodian plain, but there were no visible signs of life. Nothing moved; not even a thread of smoke from a village fire. In normal times I would have seen buffaloes, and farmers in the fields. The emptiness was shocking.

For more than an hour I sat staring into this void, my head filled with memories. As I gazed down on the empty countryside from the heights of Preah Vihear I asked myself whether Pran was dead or whether he was somewhere beyond my vision, trapped and toiling in the giant labour camp that the new Cambodia had become. Was there any way he could have survived the vengeance of the Khmer Rouge? All the refugees I had seen along the border had told me that anyone connected with the old regime was liable to be murdered. Could Pran have possibly concealed the fact that he worked for such a capitalist newspaper as the *New York Times*?

Three years later I got the answer. A telex arrived at the *Sunday Times* offices in London from Bangkok – from Pran. Based on a Cambodian proverb, it read: 'Hi Jon. The world is round. Now I meet you again. Pran was in bad shape but the life is remained. Love Pran.' He finally limped out of Cambodia into Thailand at the end of 1979. His trek to the border took him through the Khmer Rouge execution grounds – the killing fields – which were littered with the remains of thousands of Cambodians who had been axed and clubbed to death. Pran's survival was a triumph of stoicism and endurance over an insanely brutal regime. I owe him a great debt of gratitude.

Only a few hundred Cambodians were able to escape during the period of Khmer Rouge rule; I visited them in the refugee camps on the Thai side of the frontier and tried to discover from them what was really happening under the Khmer Rouge. Their stories of wanton brutality and cruelty seemed almost unbelievable, but they were true.

Everything changed at Christmas 1978 when the Vietnamese, who had been allied to the Khmer Rouge, invaded Cambodia from the east to overthrow their former friends. After ten days of blitzkrieg their tanks stormed into Phnom Penh. The Khmer Rouge leadership fled westwards towards the Thai frontier and hid in the rugged Cardamon Mountains close to the border. Suddenly hundreds of

thousands of Cambodians liberated from the Khmer Rouge tried to cross into Thailand, free at last – or so they thought. Ten years later they are still trapped on this frontier.

The first rule of journalism is to see for yourself. The frontier is only a few hours' drive from Bangkok, and only 450 miles long. But it is a world apart from the muddled, carefree, super-urban life of that most vibrant of South-east Asian cities. At the northern extremity

Cambodian refugees fleeing to Thailand after the Vietnamese invasion

is the wild tri-border region where Cambodia, Laos and Vietnam meet. At the southern end the border runs into the blue waters of the Gulf of Thailand. Events in Cambodia have made this nervous no-man's-land a separate entity from the rest of the country; this is where the Cambodian conflict has spilled over into Thailand repeatedly since 1979. Today, there can be few international boundaries more densely packed with human problems or filled with as much international intrigue.

Almost everywhere that one roams along its length there is dramatic evidence of the Cambodian tragedy. Primitive refugee camps for Cambodians displaced by the war blight the land. Every sunbaked Thai village has its own network of crude bunkers to protect its population from random cross-border shelling. The shrubland and the dark, uninhabited forests are a frightening world, sown with hundreds of thousands of mines and spiked mantraps. Every day, people are maimed. Nothing moves here without permission.

The Thais are nothing if not merchants, and back in 1979 the border became one of the most extraordinary marketplaces in all the world. Hundreds of thousands of Cambodians coming from the east camped along it in despair and deprivation; many were in the last stages of malnutrition. From the West came traders, aid officials, CIA men, all attempting to exploit or to help the refugees.

At first the Thai military were positively unwelcoming; indeed, most countries today hate the arrival of refugees. The Thai army forced back starving people at gunpoint, often into the arms of the Khmer Rouge troops they had been trying to escape. In the most dreadful incident of all, hundreds of refugees were bussed to the mountain slopes of Preah Vihear and forced at gunpoint down the rocks into Cambodia. Scores of them perished of dehydration or were blown up by mines. The lucky ones managed to sneak back into Thailand.

But in the summer of 1979 Thailand changed its policy and began to allow refugees into the country. This was partly in response to Western pressure and partly because the Thai government had decided to rebuild the Khmer Rouge in order to fight the Vietnamese. The world's greatest mass murderers were given rest and recuperation. I remember going to the camp of Sa Keo, near Aranyaprathet, to see them being brought in from the jungles of western Cambodia. They arrived exhausted, suffering from malaria; they had their backs to the wall. But their psychological hold was still so tight that the thousands of civilians under their control had lost the will to resist or escape. I came across a group of them on the border: vacant-eyed and listless, they were leading a subterranean existence bereft of any outside contact. They were the lost souls of Cambodia whose future was as dark as the very forest they had been living in.

In Cambodia, the Vietnamese liberation became an occupation and any hope of an end to the suffering was short-lived. In the following ten years the Vietnamese fought a bloody war of containment against the Khmer Rouge and other political groups across the frontier. At least thirty thousand Vietnamese soldiers died and probably more – maybe as many as the Americans lost in Vietnam.

The way the Khmer Rouge revived into a potent fighting force is dispiriting and worth recording. The Thais, whose fear of Vietnamese expansionism was understandable, if exaggerated, used them as a buffer. The Thai army gave them refuge. The international agencies working along the border (now co-ordinated by the United Nations Border Relief Operation, or U N B R O) gave them food and medical supplies. China rearmed and bankrolled them. It had cynically pledged to refuel a war of attrition against the Soviet-backed Vietnamese in Cambodia 'down to the last Khmer'.

The United Nations continued to recognize Pol Pot and the Khmer Rouge as the legitimate representatives of Cambodia; some Western countries voted to retain the Cambodian seat in the General Assembly to ensure that Vietnam did not dominate in Cambodia. Finally, in 1982 the Khmer Rouge joined an opposition coalition led by Prince Sihanouk to fight against the Vietnamese and Phnom Penh, the third member of which was the Khmer People's National Liberation Front, or K P N L F, under Son Sann, once prime minister under Sihanouk. They called themselves the Coalition Government of Democratic Kampuchea – the name for Cambodia in the Khmer language – but the Khmer Rouge was, and still is, the dominant partner.

Over the next ten years these killers, universally condemned for their appalling human rights record, enjoyed a measure of international recognition through the diplomatic and military backing given to Sihanouk's coalition. None of the Khmer Rouge leaders, least of all Pol Pot, has paid for his heinous crimes. He is still at large even as I write a decade later; one of the great mass murderers of the twentieth century is tucked up in a secret hideout somewhere along that frontier.

My assignment to report on the frontier coincided with the withdrawal of the Vietnamese army from Cambodia after ten years' occupation; this was finally completed in September 1989. It was a poignant journey for me: I could never forget that I had looked upon this border as a symbol of freedom when I was a prisoner in Phnom Penh. Hundreds of thousands of Cambodians had also risked their lives trying to cross it, to escape the guerrilla warfare in their homeland and to reach what they believed would be the safe haven of Thailand. Thousands died making the journey. Those who sur-

Overleaf Cambodian refugees in Thailand

vived have found themselves political pawns in a conflict they do not comprehend. As I toured the border it was clear that for the three hundred thousand Cambodians in the camps the frontier was a trap, a tragic end to the nightmare that had begun in their homeland all those years before.

But while they continued to suffer, Thailand, their reluctant host, had steadily been developing into one of the richest countries in South-east Asia – despite the chaos on the other side. Somehow it has managed to retain its unique character, to survive its neighbour's troubles and maintain a proud independence. Alongside Cambodia, Thailand seems a miracle. Its generals, of course, see themselves as standing in the front line of the struggle to roll back the tide of Communism. The fact that the West has been unstinting in its support is, of course, useful and helps justify years of military build-up. Thailand, however, is not an orthodox Asian military dictatorship; it is a kingdom whose king is held in genuine affection. Before setting out for the border we filmed King Bhumibol Aduly-adej's sixty-first birthday ceremony in Bangkok. Amid the pageantry of the generals and field-marshals lining up in splendid uniforms to pay their respects it was obvious that the monarchy has provided Thailand with a thread of continuity and is unassailably strong.

History has been unkind to Asia's other crowned heads, not least of all to Sihanouk. Most of them were swept away long ago by Communist revolutions or the drive towards more democratic rule. But King Bhumibol reigns on supreme, Asia's last god-king. (It is ironic to reflect that the young King Sihanouk had once fled to Bangkok while struggling to wrest full independence from the French for Cambodia.)

To make this film I started my journey at Aranyaprathet, two hundred miles east of Bangkok, where I had crossed over in 1975. Close to Aran were the main Cambodian refugee camps I had been granted permission to visit. All the camps along the border are controlled by one of three Cambodian resistance groups united against the Vietnamese and Phnom Penh. In the north was Site B, a pro-Sihanouk camp, and Site Two, run by the K P N L F; south of Aran was Site Eight, the Khmer Rouge showcase camp. But I knew that there was also a string of hidden border camps under the control of the Khmer Rouge to which I would not be allowed to go with a film crew. The whole process of getting to the frontier is a test of one's resistance to tedium. The army issues travel permits to visiting journalists. It has created a string of spick-and-span military camps, connected by fast highways, along the frontier's entire length. The

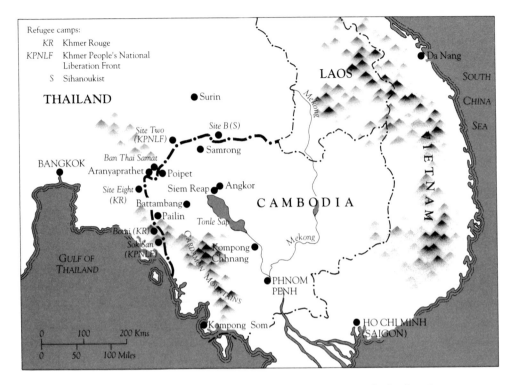

Refugee camps:
KR Khmer Rouge
KPNLF Khmer People's National Liberation Front
S Sihanoukist

papers have to be presented at every single camp and checkpoint.

After the big 1979 influx, successive Thai governments have been careful to insist on the temporary nature of the refugee camps. Their concern is understandable: if they were allowed to become too comfortable or permanent, the Cambodians would create political problems for Thailand and antagonize the dirt-poor peasants along the border. None the less, a number of camps have developed a permanent air.

These accessible camps are all United Nations-supported and are protected, in theory, by a Thai paramilitary unit, the Displaced Persons Protection Unit or DPPU, which was set up as a replacement to Task Force 80. This outfit was dismantled by an embarrassed Thai government after revelations about its brutality towards the refugees appeared in the international press. But, in reality, the camps are governed by the various guerrilla groups in the coalition fighting to win power again in Cambodia, including the Khmer Rouge.

As I approached Aranyaprathet it was clear that the little town was booming and that Westernization had arrived with a vengeance.

Over the years the international aid agencies which have made Aran the administrative centre of their aid-programme have pumped millions of dollars into the local economy. Huge lorries, marked with the U N B R O logo, hurtled through the confused streams of traffic carrying supplies. The stalls were full of Western gadgets. Some of the aid workers' houses would have seemed more in place on the shores of Lake Geneva than in this vivid green South-east Asian landscape. One ice cream parlour boasted over fifty kinds of ice cream, a dozen varieties of ground coffee, and waffles and maple syrup as good as any in the Midwest.

I could not help reflecting on the irony of the situation. In the short time I spent here I encountered many wide-eyed and dedicated Americans working with the refugees. They were almost too young to remember Vietnam; almost too innocent to comprehend the politics of their charity. Today, without realizing it, they are picking up the pieces of a tragedy that began two decades ago on the other side of the frontier, and partly as a consequence of US actions.

One resettlement team worked a short distance up the road from Aran at Ban Thai Samat, which had been one of the first camps in Thailand. I had not been here for almost ten years but I remembered every detail: a vast tented city of sick and emaciated people shattered by years of war, execution, starvation and disease. At the height of

Refugees from Site Two, desperate for resettlement, demonstrate in the hope of attracting the attention of the outside world

the exodus almost a million people had dragged their bodies across the border into Thailand. Hunger was written on every face. Rickety-limbed people moved like zombies searching for scraps of food. It was nothing to be confronted by diseased and malnourished children, fly-blown or with eyes glazed over by approaching death. The very survival of the Khmer race seemed to be in doubt. The harrowing pictures and stories of their suffering we sent back then pricked the conscience of the world and provoked a flood of aid money.

Now Ban Thai Samat has closed down and feels more like a ghost town or a film set. But every day a few refugees who claimed they might be eligible for resettlement in the West, because they had a relative in America, Australia or Canada, were bussed in from other camps along the border. The aid workers verified their identity, checked their background. The endless questions to establish who they were and where they came from was a humiliating process, reawakening painful memories, that could take weeks, sometimes years to complete. This process of cross-examining, filing and computer cross-referencing went on all day, a clinical and dispassionate bureaucratic machine sifting through their past. All this Western sophistication, I reflected, had been brought to bear on these innocent people who afterwards would be taken back to their camps to wait patiently for a verdict that would determine their future.

Every journalist and foreign aid worker stationed on the border has a favourite watering-hole, a place to go to unwind and forget; it would be inhuman not to. The Aran café was the liveliest and most interesting haunt. I could hear the pulsating rhythm of the band even before I reached it and wondered what the night had in store for me. I was carried there in a motorized cyclo, a uniquely Thai form of transport.

There was nothing elegant about the café, but it did have character. A live combo was playing fifties' rock and roll. A singer squeezed into a tight mini-skirt was crooning into a microphone. The lighting was low. I sat down and ordered a Mekong whisky. The large room was filled with tables and booths where the clients and their 'hostesses' drank and talked. The hardwood dance floor in the centre of the room surged with couples rubbing bodies and dancing. I recognized a number of off-duty Thai soldiers and aid people. But quite the most interesting character was Somporn, a Thai border-adventurer who did odd jobs for anyone prepared to pay him a buck – Thai military intelligence, smuggling syndicates, the CIA perhaps, even journalists.

Somporn was a born philanderer and raconteur. Even on the dance

27

floor he wore his Davy Crockett hat. On the sunbaked border he carried a gun and sometimes a couple of grenades slung from a belt for good measure. He was a true frontiersman. His grin was as broad as many of his stories, and as crooked.

Being a journalist in South-east Asia has made me an unwilling expert in human suffering. But on the whole I can think of few more upsetting experiences than touring the refugee camps. The most wretched one we went to was Site Eight, the largest and most accessible of those run by the Khmer Rouge. A showcase camp housing more than thirty thousand people, it is monitored by UNBRO, several other aid agencies and the Thai DPPU and is

Site Eight, the Khmer Rouge show camp

open to foreign aid workers and journalists. Site Eight nestles against the mountains between Thailand and Cambodia, two and a half miles from the border, about an hour's drive south of Aran.

First impressions were deceptive. As I passed through the gate I was met by a gaggle of children, smiling, irresistible, trying to sell me chopsticks and other handicrafts from the camp. But I soon realized that the soft and respectable image that the Khmer Rouge leadership was trying to foster here was illusory and that this secretive guerrilla organization had not changed its spots. The priority was the war against the Vietnamese in Cambodia. Now that the

Vietnamese were pulling out the incumbent government in Phnom Penh had become the enemy. Khmer Rouge officials brushed aside my questions about Pol Pot.

All the other Khmer Rouge camps along the border were closed to journalists. The UN and international aid agencies have scant access to them, if at all; all that was known was that between them they held perhaps as many as seventy-two thousand civilians under harsh discipline. Mostly the inmates of these camps survive on rations provided by China, the Khmer Rouge's main supplier of arms. The food is distributed by soldiers of Task Force 838, a hidden branch of Thai military intelligence set up to give support to the various Cambodia guerrilla armies along the border. The UN has been willing to supply only a few of these camps as no verification is possible. Several times it has cut food to a camp because the guerrillas refused to allow aid officials in to monitor the distribution. It was feared that the food aid intended for their civilian inmates would be feeding the Khmer Rouge guerrillas as well.

At Site Eight the emphasis on Khmer Rouge Communist ideology had slipped. But then it is an unashamed showpiece complete with schools, hospital and a market which the Khmer Rouge leadership hopes will demonstrate to a sceptical world that the movement has given up its destructive revolutionary ways and embraced democracy.

But even at Site Eight the Khmer Rouge makes no distinction between civilians and military. Once inside the camp I encountered men in jungle green and soft Maoist caps, uniforms I had come to identify with the horrors of Pol Pot. These soldiers hated being photographed. They had returned to Site Eight on leave from fighting inside Cambodia to see their families, and so as to keep up the façade that this was a strictly civilian camp they had left their weapons outside. Of course, the soldiers were not all hard-core Khmer Rouge. Like the majority of Cambodians trapped on the frontier they had been given no preference as to which camp they were in. Probably they had ended up in Site Eight because, when they had crossed into Thailand during the big exodus back in 1979, they had turned left into a Khmer Rouge zone instead of right into a border area controlled by the forces of Prince Sihanouk or the KPNLF.

Given a free choice, the majority of the inmates of Site Eight would move to another camp. The heartbreaking thing is that because of the stringent controls they even have great difficulty in communicating with their relatives in the other camps. One boy I talked to in Site Eight had just discovered that his mother, whom he had not seen for twelve years, was alive and in the non-Communist camp at Site Two. Officially classified as a Khmer Rouge, he could not legally join her. Now he was planning to escape by bribing the Thai border guards.

In Site Eight there is secret conscription of children younger than fifteen who are compelled to work as porters, carrying Chinese arms through the jungle to the Khmer Rouge guerrilla forces fighting inside Cambodia. No one can see the secret supply line because it operates after dark when the aid workers and journalists have left and returned to Aran for the night. But the results are there – children sick with malaria from the forests, and amputees. The border region is littered with plastic landmines – more than half a million, it is estimated. In Site Eight alone 1,600 of the 36,000 inhabitants are maimed.

I was there on the fortieth anniversary of the Universal Declaration of Human Rights, when the Khmer Rouge went so far as to put on a party. But there have been many reports of human rights abuses in their camps. Even at Site Eight Khmer Rouge killer squads hunted down and murdered two young men who had deserted the guerrilla force in the weeks before we arrived.

We drove north to Site Two, which is affiliated with the non-Communist group KPNLF, whose nominal head is Son Sann. In fact, the sprawling camp of thatched and mud-floored bamboo huts is divided among corrupt warlords who wield immense power. One key figure is General Sak Satsukhan, the KPNLF army commander. Like the Khmer Rouge he has made little distinction between civilians and the military, and has used orphans from Site Two to ferry food and ammunition through the minefields.

This refugee settlement almost astride the border holds one hundred and forty thousand people and is the world's largest Cambodian city outside of Phnom Penh; it is spread over several square miles of plain. The difference between the listless civilians in the Khmer Rouge camps and the men, women and children living in Site Two is striking. The latter thrive primarily on smuggling and the camp flourishes, with colourful trading stalls.

Site Two is an amalgamation of several other KPNLF camps. Since it was set up in 1985 it has taken on the permanence of a town, right down to an alcoholics' clinic and a special toilet for the disabled. But frustration has led to violence and weapons are easy to come by. A hand grenade costs 25p and an AK-47 assault rifle £10. Everything here is done in the name of UNBRO. Even the water has to be delivered from outside. The red tankers begin rolling into the camp early in the morning in a steady stream. There are hundreds of them grinding away, stirring up the dust. In a month they bring in enough water to fill five million buckets. It costs over £1 million a year to keep them full.

To realize that this was being done was a depressing reflection. For Cambodia, a mile away, is a country which could always feed itself. The whole culture of its people had been rooted in the land for centuries. Water was nature's gift. Each year the monsoon rains swept across the plains. The rivers rose. The waters of the Great Lake, the Tonle Sap, burst their banks and flooded the rice fields. The peasants had only to dip their hands in the water to pluck out the fish.

Now that they are refugees on the Thai side of the frontier the distribution of rice is the big event of their week. Each family has a ration card qualifying them for food – seven kilos of rice and five of fish per adult. I was conducted to watch a food distribution. The refugees sat in orderly lines for hours under the scorching sun, uncomplaining. It was hard to understand their extraordinary patience, but over the years these families have grown used to the waiting. The children born in Site Two have grown up believing that rice grows on trucks.

The resistance coalition claims to represent Democratic Kampuchea. But of course there is no democracy here, either. The people of Site Two, as in the Khmer Rouge and the Sihanoukist camps, have lacked any freedom of choice since they came to the border. Thailand will not allow them to settle permanently. They have rejected the Phnom Penh government's offer of amnesty if they return to Cambodia. Only those with relatives abroad have any chance – and then it is slim – of getting asylum in a third country.

And if all the dedication to their welfare, the food, clothes, medicine and water, have made the Cambodians the best cared for refugees in the world, it has also bred an unhealthy psychological dependence on aid. The huge relief effort still cannot make the refugees happy. 'We can feed them but we cannot give them hope,' aid workers said. If there is a reason for the waiting no one in Site Two could understand it, or tell me what it is – least of all the orphans. Their lives have been a nightmare of despair and loneliness ever since they staggered over the border into Thailand. They have never known the security of a family, and their future is bleak.

The other big camp I visited was Site B, in Surin province. It houses some fifty thousand people, the followers of Prince Sihanouk. Site B is generally considered the best-run of the camps, with vegetable gardens, plenty of water and a lovely setting among trees. But even here there are problems with domestic violence, an inevitable

Above and left
Cambodian refugees,
many of whom have
been maimed and
wounded by Khmer
Rouge mines, at Site
Two on the Thai–
Cambodian border.
This camp, run by the
right-wing KPNLF,
holds around 140,000
people and is the
largest Cambodian
'city' outside Phnom
Penh.
Overleaf Cambodian
refugees newly-
arrived in Thailand

Opposite The border crossing at Poipet, once the main crossing between Cambodia and Thailand, looking towards Cambodia. The destroyed bridge straddles a stream which marks the frontier.
Left Cambodian soldiers operating in the jungle a few miles from the border with Thailand in an area formerly occupied by the Khmer Rouge, one of whose camps, Borai, is just over the border.
Below Armoured personnel carrier of the Cambodian army at the gates of a temple at Pailin, the ruby-mining town near the Thai border which fell to the Khmer Rouge in autumn 1989.

Top Mozambiquan migrant workers recruited to work in South African gold mines waiting to be processed, having first been finger-printed.
Above Refugees at Casa Banana deep inside Mozambique, where over 12,000 destitute victims of RENAMO attacks have gathered.

Right Captured RENAMO guerrillas in jail in Mozambique. But backed by South Africa, RENAMO continues to wreak death and destruction throughout much of the country.

The high voltage electrified fence stretching along the South African–Mozambiquan border which refugees from Mozambique trying to enter South Africa illegally have to cross.

consequence of thousands of people jammed together in small huts. On the day I arrived, the body of a man was being burned in a Cambodian Buddhist ritual in a corner of the camp. He had been knifed by a vengeance-seeking neighbour in a dispute over a woman. But here, at least, is a semblance of the old Cambodia I had loved, and which the Khmer Rouge had destroyed.

I watched a festival put on for a visit by Prince Norodom Ranariddh, one of Sihanouk's sons, and his glamorous and sophisticated, French-educated wife. The girls had dressed in gold, brocaded costumes and their hands wove patterns in the air. They seemed to float as they danced to the slow rhythm of the Ram Vong and Saravan, two of Cambodia's traditional dances. With my eyes half-closed and my senses lulled by a gamelan tinkling in the background, it seemed for a moment as though I had never left Cambodia

By now I was desperate to pass through the looking-glass, as it were, to see the frontier from the Cambodian side. Each of us who lived in the shadow of the unimaginable horror of that war has memories and feelings about Cambodia which run very deep and which we will never lose. For this reason I have always been apprehensive when I return, even though during the last ten years I have been back several times.

Quite the most emotional visit was at the beginning of 1980 when I flew in by the only way possible – on a Red Cross flight from Bangkok bringing drugs and food. It was a desperate feeling to come into the still empty city of Phnom Penh from which everyone had been expelled nearly five years before. What I saw affected me profoundly. I found a wasteland of decaying and melancholy buildings, with a distraught and traumatized people desperately trying to rebuild their lives out of the carnage sown by the Khmer Rouge. In the centre not a single shop was functioning. The cavernous market was deserted, the factories at a standstill. The central bank and the great Roman Catholic cathedral had been blown up. The interior of every house had been looted. The streets were knee-deep in broken furniture and rubble and a school had been turned into an extermination camp where more than ten thousand people had been tortured to death.

The landscape too was devastated – nothing but abandoned rice fields and shattered towns and villages. The Mekong River, which gives Cambodia life, had shrunk to a ribbon of leaden water. The Khmer Rouge had done away with traditional musical instruments, abolished festivals, burned books, butchered monks and confiscated Buddhist manuscripts.

Over the next ten years I have watched the city come back to life, despite the continuing war between the Vietnamese and the Khmer Rouge. When I flew back yet again to make this film in spring 1989 it seemed that the war might finally be coming to an end. The Vietnamese were completing their process of withdrawal. Complicated negotiations between the Vietnamese, the Chinese and Prince Sihanouk, who was still in exile and leading the resistance movement against the Vietnamese (in which the Khmer Rouge were the key component), were proceeding in a typically hopeless fashion. But perhaps they would work.

My application to visit Cambodia coincided with one of the last stages of the Vietnamese military withdrawal. Ever since they had sent their troops into Cambodia to drive out the Khmer Rouge in December 1978, a large question mark had hung over the intentions of the Vietnamese. Was their objective – as Washington and Peking claimed – to turn tiny Cambodia, jammed strategically between them and their Thai rivals, into a Vietnamese satellite? Laos, the other Indo-China domino, had already fallen into their hands in 1975, and with the occupation of Cambodia and the setting up of a client government in Phnom Penh the Vietnamese appeared to have brought the whole of the Indo-Chinese peninsula into their political and military orbit.

The Vietnamese themselves have always claimed that they were not a colonial power but the first among equals of the states of Indo-China. In the early years of their presence, however, the pull was all in one direction. It was astonishing how quickly they shaped the independent and carefree Cambodians into their own Marxist mould. Official propaganda talked of eternal friendship and solidarity between the Vietnamese and the ethnically and culturally distinct Khmers. Several Phnom Penh streets were named after pro-Vietnamese Khmer resistance leaders. But gradually the old Cambodia started to reassert itself. Each time I returned I was astonished by the pace of the change. A Khmer cultural revival was taking place that flew in the face of those earlier claims that Cambodia had been turned irreversibly into a Vietnamese satellite. It was plain that the Vietnamese were no longer playing any significant role in the daily running of the country. The teams of faceless advisers who used to exercise control over ministerial decisions made by the Phnom Penh government had already gone.

At the peak of their presence there were as many as two hundred thousand Vietnamese soldiers, armed by the Soviet Union, stationed

Phnom Penh today: gradually the city has come back to life

43

in Cambodia. But even at its height, the military presence never jarred the eyes. It was common to see young conscript soldiers manning the main checkpoints on the roads out of Phnom Penh and garrisoning the provincial towns, but there was no foundation for accusations that Vietnam had an official policy of persuading its people to settle in Cambodia.

I flew to Phnom Penh with the world's press. Because of the imbecile political situation we were still obliged to travel from Bangkok via Saigon, an exhausting eight-hour detour. I arrived on a beautiful December day, almost exactly ten years to the day since the Vietnamese army had marched into Phnom Penh and driven out Pol Pot. As the Vietnamese airliner made its final approach, the sight of the Mekong looping through the countryside, the gilded roofs of the Royal Palace and the tall sugar palms dotting the landscape made the present melt away.

Cambodia's heat and landscape had not changed. Against all odds I found the country, after the harrowing past, a renascent nation. This time, all along the route from the airport into the city, smiles greeted the white Volga Sedan provided by the information department of the foreign ministry. Phnom Penh itself was now a bonanza of free enterprise. The government, under Hun Sen, the Prime Minister, had abandoned the Marxist mould of his Vietnamese sponsors. Laissez-faire capitalism was the order of the day. There were still some distressing sites: conditions in some of the hospitals were pure despair. But Phnom Penh had a lighter side, too. People were smiling at foreigners again, and shaking their hands. An elephant gave street rides. There was a marvellous government-sponsored theatre including an uproarious folk dance in which the young men blew tunes on wooden pipes while the girls played suggestively with the tassels of flowers dangling provocatively below.

The Vietnamese were holding a big ceremonial parade. Squadrons of tanks, armoured cars and Molotova trucks, carrying multiple rocket launchers or Stalin Organs, rumbled past the towering independence monument in the heart of the city. Other troops left on barges down the Mekong which slides past the edge of the city.

With their medals and well-pressed uniforms, the Vietnamese generals certainly presented a sanitized picture of their ten-year occupation. But the real truth is that the Vietnamese had finally had enough. The international, political and economic isolation imposed on them and the incumbent Phnom Penh regime since 1979 had proved too much of a burden. And behind the vain-glory and propaganda surrounding the withdrawal Vietnam is a deeply trou-

Children riding on an elephant in Phnom Penh, a popular Sunday activity

bled nation, with over a million soldiers to support, isolated politically and economically by the West because of its Cambodian
adventure, and nearly bankrupt.

Historically the Cambodians looked upon their dynamic, powerful
neighbours as the arch-enemy. These age-old hatreds meant that the
Vietnamese were never much loved while in Cambodia. But most
people are still grateful that the Vietnamese saved them from extinction by sending in their troops to drive out the Khmer Rouge back
in 1979. The truth is that in the ten years of their intervention the

Vietnamese provided Cambodia with security; with their departure the fate of Cambodia is left increasingly in the hands of its own people.

At the time I write, the Vietnamese have withdrawn. The withdrawal has forced the West, which cold-shouldered the Phnom Penh regime as a Vietnamese and Soviet satellite and embargoed all but a trickle of aid, to begin reassessing its position. However unpleasant it may be to support a regime created by Hanoi, there is no doubt that Cambodia is now being ruled reasonably humanely for the first time in many years.

There is a curious paradox in the government structure. Several members of its top leadership are themselves former Khmer Rouge who eventually disowned the destructive policies of Pol Pot and changed sides. Most notable, of course, is Hun Sen, the Prime Minister. He had been an officer in the Khmer Rouge's eastern zone abutting on Vietnam, and no evidence has ever surfaced to connect him with any crimes. Certainly he was not a member of the dreaded Khmer Rouge security apparatus which oversaw Pol Pot's murderous purges, nor was he in the upper echelons of the leadership.

Hun Sen is the most powerful and popular figure in the Phnom Penh government. By any standards he is a remarkable man. In 1971 he joined the guerrilla ranks of the Khmer Rouge, rising to command a brigade. Wounded in combat five times, he lost an eye in the final Khmer Rouge assault to take Phnom Penh and spent many months in hospital. He says he was well aware of the Khmer Rouge atrocities and realized that the revolution had gone awry. But it was difficult to oppose the Pol Pot regime at the time, so he and like-minded figures had to plot in secret. In 1977, when the Khmer Rouge mounted brutal attacks on Vietnamese border villages in which teenage guerrillas hacked to pieces hundreds of peasants, old men, women and children, and conducted a purge that wiped out a hundred thousand Khmer Rouge soldiers and civilians, he defected to Vietnam. He returned with the invading Vietnamese troops and quickly made his mark. At thirty-eight he is one of the world's youngest prime ministers. He taught himself French and lately has been taking daily English lessons in Phnom Penh. Now he is a skilled diplomatic negotiator who can clearly hold his own against Sihanouk.

In the countryside there are many sad evidences of Vietnam's fading military presence. On the edge of Kompong Chhnang, fifty miles north of Vietnam, is an overgrown Vietnamese military cem-

A memorial in Phnom Penh to the Vietnamese 'volunteers' who died in Cambodia

etery with dozens of graves of ordinary soldiers who fought and died on Cambodian soil. The road here stretches long and empty. In the paddy fields on either side where farmers moved among the rice lies the debris of bitter fighting: wrecked tanks and armoured personnel carriers with knocked-out turrets and broken tracks. In a few years this military boneyard will be cleared away or will have vanished for ever beneath layers of tropical vegetation. It is a sobering thought, but there are no victors in Indo-China – just victims. I wondered whether the garlanded Vietnamese generals fully comprehended this as they bade farewell to Phnom Penh.

In Cambodia, as in Vietnam, a car, interpreter and guide are assigned to all foreign journalists. In my case the guide was Mr Heng. He had an excellent command of English and was always keen to please. His life was typical of the sorrow of this land. He was a teenager when the Khmer Rouge marched into his village and forced his family to work as slave labourers many miles away. He survived, just, but a number of his family did not. He told me with cast-down eyes how the Khmer Rouge injected his sick aunt with muddy water one morning and she died. 'She went into convulsions,' he said. 'Her heart gave up.'

One morning there was a discreet knock on our door at the Sukhaly Hotel and Mr Heng said a helicopter was waiting at the airport to fly us somewhere close to the border. Before we left he told me to buy a large quantity of dried fish, a great Cambodian delicacy, and many cartons of cigarettes as gifts for the soldiers on the frontier. We flew north-westwards over the great Cambodian plain, passing above Angkor on the way.

The journey to the border aroused neither uncertainty nor unease. For me the Cambodian countryside has always had some special quality: the composition of water, rice fields, palm trees and misty hills was unforgettable. As we touched down at Samrong, eighteen miles from the border, it was clear that even in this remote outpost the wheels of government were turning.

Here, after a rapid military briefing and a pause for weak Chinese tea, I boarded a heavy Russian truck, escorted by a dozen soldiers shouldering an assortment of weapons. Travelling through the countryside, where life is desperately poor and revolves around the seasons, I detected a quiet confidence among the peasants on the road. It was a bone-jarring journey, and the closer we came to the border the worse it became. At times it seemed as if we would be thrown off, and only our collective faith in the driver held us to the road.

After two gruelling hours the road narrowed, then disappeared altogether, and we were walled in by jungle. Our truck lumbered to a halt in a clearing. All around were soldiers, heavily armed. Their camp, a jumble of huts, was of a spartan simplicity. Most of them have known no other life. They have been stuck out here in this remote border area for months on end, running a high risk of a particularly virulent form of cerebral malaria and of being blown up by landmines. To break the ice I shook hands; I was probably the first Westerner any of them had seen.

At last I had reached journey's end. The border was a mere hundred yards away. In a determined but vain effort to seal it and prevent guerrilla infiltration the Phnom Penh government had built a strategic fence, complete with tank ditches, barbed wire and mines, along the length of the frontier. Work on this ambitious project had been carried out by thousands of 'volunteers' despatched to the border from all parts of Cambodia. A big question mark hung over this enterprise which had been built with so much blood and sweat. How long would it take for the Khmer Rouge to fill the vacuum left by the departing Vietnamese?

Mr Heng and the soldiers accorded me every courtesy. But this was as far as it was safe to go. Tracing out the border with his foot, Mr Heng explained that I would have to hurry back to Samrong to catch the helicopter to Phnom Penh before nightfall.

What I felt then was a sense of anti-climax and anger at the sheer absurdity of it all. From a journalistic point of view there was nothing to see on this side of the frontier. But I knew that out there, beyond the perimeter fence and in the forests, were all the feuding factions of the war – Khmer Rouge guerrillas armed by the Chinese, the army of Prince Sihanouk cosseted by the West, the anti-Communist Khmer People's National Liberation Front and the enemy of all three of them – the army of the People's Republic of Kampuchea, Russian-armed and trained by the Vietnamese. All these conflicting ideologies, self-interest and superpower machinations have kept Cambodia bleeding. They are what has made this frontier a nightmare. For a moment the jungle around me was alive with sunshine and bursting with song. Once again, I was reminded how the cruelty of the last two decades has been set against a backdrop of such beauty. I hoped that peace was round the corner, but I somehow did not believe it.

The Vietnamese have gone. But the people of Cambodia still flounder between their desperate past and a dubious future. Theirs is an unwinnable war, truly a war without end.

NADINE GORDIMER

THE INGOT AND THE STICK, THE INGOT AND THE GUN

Mozambique–South Africa

*F*RONTIER WARS are supposed to be about boundaries, and civil wars are supposed to be about internal struggles for power; but the war in Mozambique is civil war in which a frontier has been the decisive factor. Without South Africa – the strongest military and economic power on the continent – as covert ally, RENAMO, the Mozambique Resistance Movement, could never have threatened the government of the People's Republic of Mozambique, which, as FRELIMO, the Front for the Liberation of Mozambique, fought for and won independence from the Portuguese in 1975.

A civil war is patricide, matricide and fratricide. My country chose to fuel and arm this destruction in Mozambique. Political jargon euphemizes the act under the term 'destabilization'; apartheid South Africa didn't want a black socialist state as neighbour in a former colonial possession with which she had close political and economic ties. So the old frontier that has had so many human consequences since the days of slave and ivory trading took on ominous meaning, yet again, for all of us who live on either side. I went on a zigzag journey to see for myself what this meaning was.

The ingot and the stick

Until the last thirty years of the nineteenth century the frontier between South Africa and Mozambique was vague, existing in the contending ambitions of Boers, British and Portuguese rather than in actual boundaries, and – as always – ignoring the sovereignties of the Africans to whom the land belonged. Old slave and ivory trade

Nadine Gordimer outside the Polana Hotel in Maputo

routes breached and blurred the supposed limits of the Transvaal Republic and Mozambique. Portugal feared powerful Britain's claims on Mozambique and so, in 1869, the Boer president was able to conclude a commercial treaty with Portugal safeguarding the Mozambique trade in slaves, ivory and guns on the Transvaal side in exchange for a definition of the Transvaal frontier. It was fixed, by implication, along the Lebombo Mountains.

But in 1881 the Transvaal Republic took in the triangle of territory between Mozambique and Swaziland, gaining ground nearer an outlet to the sea at Lourenço Marques, and extending the length of its 1869 frontier with Mozambique. The greater stretch of that frontier was to become, on the Transvaal side, the famous Kruger National Park, the buffer state of wild animals between the apartheid republic of contemporary South Africa and the black republic of Mozambique; and eventually, in the 1980s, a route of perilous exodus for Mozambiquans fleeing civil war in their country.

The years 1884–5 were the era of the most intense scramble for Africa. Europe was looking for new sources of raw materials and markets for its surplus industrial products; Africa seemed virgin land for capitalist exploitation. But whose? The conflicting demands of

Britain, Germany and Portugal mounted until these were reconciled between them by treaties in 1890 and 1891, following the Berlin Conference. They carved up the continent among themselves, with the big powers getting the larger shares. The Portuguese gained nothing, lost some territory in West Africa, but retained what they had already taken for themselves over three hundred years in East Africa.

It was common practice, in that era, for European powers to sell off to one another territories that didn't belong to them, taken by conquest from indigenous peoples. In terms of an arbitration award to Mozambique of the territory Britain had wanted, Britain had been given the right of purchase over any other nation, should Portugal decide to sell. Immediately after the award, Portugal was willing to sell Mozambique for £12,000. There were no customers; but later both the president of the Transvaal Republic and Cecil Rhodes, the British empire builder, tried to buy Lourenço Marques. Rhodes saw the port as part of his imperialist design to turn the whole of southern Africa British pink on the map.

But the discovery of gold and diamonds in South Africa brought the evidence that economic development over the frontier would mean some stimulus and advantages for the Portuguese slum of Europe's imperial possessions, and by the 1890s no part of Mozambique was up for grabs. The 640-kilometre frontier was firmly drawn as it is today.

I was born in a gold-mining town in South Africa. As a small girl in the thirties, when I went to school my path crossed those of black men, some with clay-covered locks, clothed in bright blankets and miners' boots, coming from their barracks to the row of concession stores leased by the mine to white shopkeepers. These black men were identified to me by grown-up hearsay as Shangaans. They were always referred to as 'mine boys' although they were grown men. I didn't know where they came from. They didn't look like the black people I knew as servants and street cleaners. To me they were exotic. I was taught to be afraid of them, and forbidden to cross that part of the veld where they lay about in the sun or sat on fruit boxes having their hair cut by itinerant black barbers.

Later, as a teenager learning first aid during the war, I was in a group taken by our instructor, a white male nurse employed on the gold mine close by my home, to watch him at work in his casualty station. The miners came up from underground. A mine policeman hustled them through the gate of their barracks, making them lift their work-clothes and show backs and buttocks. If they had cuts from the jagged rock underground, they were herded to a carbolic-redolent room. There the male nurse's beak-like needle dug in and out stitching together the black skin into which he had first stuffed back the gaping red flesh I stared at, horrified and fascinated. No anaesthesia of any kind was given. No whimper or wince escaped the stoic endurance in the closed black faces. This led the nurse not to remark upon their courage, but to explain that these men didn't feel pain the way 'we' – whites – did.

It was some years before I realized that I, a white child, was the exotic element in my home in Africa. Before I understood that it was one of the racist myths of my country that every black man is a potential rapist of little white girls. Before I understood that the migratory labour system is based on whites' acceptance that black men feel no pain, whether of the flesh or the spirit. One of the first stories I wrote was about the black miners at the concession stores.

I went back, now, half a century later, to an abandoned deserted barracks in the district of my childhood home. There was the enclosed quadrangle of dormitories with their concrete bunks on which the miners slept. Empty, they looked like shelves in a mortuary; they had never been fit places for the living to sleep. In the weeds of the quadrangle was the cook-house from which their food was doled out to them in the open, summer and winter. There was the arena where, on Sundays, they danced away their isolation from homes and families, performing rituals of celebration left far away across the frontier.

I went to a mineshaft where the sons and grandsons of the generation of migratory miners I met as a child were being brought up in the cage from underground. They no longer sleep on concrete shelves and eat in the open. In the 1980s, material living conditions for migratory miners have changed greatly for the better, and – under pressure from the black National Union of Mineworkers, permitted to be formed only a decade ago by the South African government – wages have begun to approach those earned by white miners. But the migratory miners, living in fine hostels surrounded by sports fields and gardens, still have to leave behind their wives and families, no matter how many years they come back and forth to labour in the mines. Over the history of the mining industry in South Africa, a very high percentage of these miners have come from over the frontier, in Mozambique.

When slavery ended in Mozambique in the nineteenth century – later than in any other southern African country – forced labour under Portuguese rule took over. In the south of the country the greater part of the workforce was soon bartered to South Africa. The

Opposite Young Mozambiquans, just arrived at the Transvaal mines, shivering with cold in their village clothes
Top Living conditions for miners
Above Gold miners working underground

trade-off of men in exchange for sea-borne traffic revenue and gold, between South Africa and the Portuguese, was formalized in 1897 in an agreement between President Kruger's Transvaal Boer Republic and Portugal. It was followed by a series of later agreements which have continued, through the defeat of the Boer Republic by the British and the formation of the Union of South Africa; through South Africa's withdrawal from the British Commonwealth and emergence as the Republic of South Africa; through the end of Portuguese rule in Mozambique in 1975, to the present.

The principle of the agreements has never changed. Gold and other mining interests in South Africa are granted large-scale labour recruiting of Mozambiquan men in return for a portion of the men's wages to be paid in gold, to Portugal during colonial times, later to independent Mozambique.

So for nearly a century Mozambique has been a labour reserve, across the frontier, for South Africa's mines.

In the first twenty years of the development of the gold mines they were almost entirely dependent on contract labour from Mozambique. Black South Africans resisted going underground, and, anyway, the fact that migrants would not be allowed to bring families with them and would return to their country after each spell of work was in accordance with South Africa's racist policy of using blacks as units of labour but having them live as far away from whites as possible.

Why did these Mozambiquans leave homes and families, crops and country to live in single-sex barracks and dig in the catacomb dark of foreign mines? Mozambique's own small mining industry offered little employment. Industry and agriculture were hopelessly undeveloped. The traditional subsistence economy did not provide for the Portuguese colonial government's taxes. Its labour laws enforced the choice between being declared 'idle' and sent to work on government projects or made to work for Portuguese settlers for pitiful wages, or signing up as contract labour for the South African mines, where the poor pay was at least better than a man could sell his labour for at home.

Since Mozambique became independent, the miners have also become counters in the political moves between Mozambique and South Africa. In the 1960s the South African Chamber of Mines had had the right to recruit one hundred thousand men a year. President Machel said bitterly of Mozambiquans' dependency on employment by South Africans, 'They made gold mines out of our ignorance.' But he could offer no alternative in the poverty-stricken, underdeveloped economy his government inherited from colonial times, and which he tried to remedy by disastrous schemes of instant collectivity. A year or two after Mozambique's independence, South Africa suspended the 'deferred pay' in bullion which was vital to Mozambique's economy. Later the gold payments were resumed as part of a new diplomacy in South Africa towards Mozambique, using an ingot-and-stick tactic in an attempt to form a 'constellation' of compliant African states in southern Africa under the domination of the power-planet, South Africa.

In the late eighties, 63,707 Mozambiquans were working in the South African mines. Thirty-five per cent of black mine workers are currently migratory, of whom the highest number are Mozambiquans. N U M, the black miners' union in South Africa, condemns the migratory labour system as a social evil and demands that the mining industry commit itself to dismantling the policy. In the meantime, the Mozambiquans still sign on, and are allowed to cross the frontier into South Africa to work in the mines for thirty-six to forty weeks at a time.

Frontiers are drawn. Flags go up. The border gates close. It's done. But frontiers never belong to the past; and the unravelling of their consequences cannot be foreseen. Human treachery breaches them, and human liens, seemingly tenuous and fragile, strangely reappear across them.

The territorial boundaries wrangled over by white settlers – Boer, Portuguese, British – were a grid laid over the homes and hunting grounds of the African tribes whose country it was. These homes and hunting grounds were mapped out quite differently in the traditional territorial accommodations arrived at through their own migrations, tribal conquests and communal needs. The white invaders' frontiers became visible to the Africans through the barriers against their free movement, the restrictions on their hunting and fishing grounds enforced by the invaders' guns, and the consequent economic necessity that forced them along the white man's slave and trade routes to hunt for him, and, soon, to provide cheap contract labour. All through the nineteenth century, in prophetic foreboding, the Africans resisted the white invaders' frontiers by ignoring them when possible, and sometimes attacking the invaders. What is now one of the world's greatest tourist attractions, the Kruger National Park, was the wilderness where much of this struggle, over ivory rather than possession of land, took place.

In pre-colonial times, the Tsonga-speaking Makuleke, one of the widespread clans of south-east Africa collectively known to whites as Shangaans, lived at the confluence of the Limpopo and Olifants

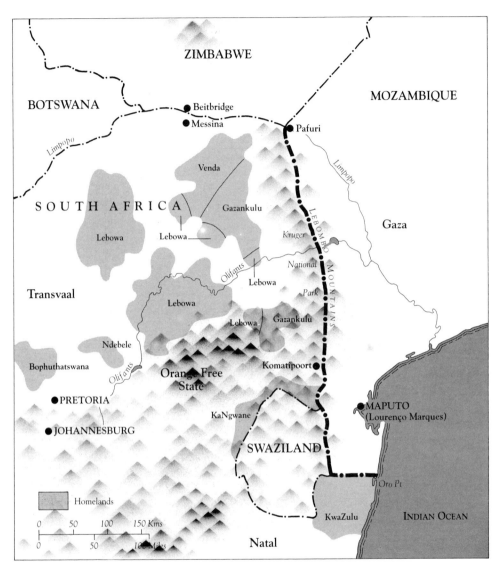

Rivers in an area that is today part of Mozambique. Early in the nineteenth century they were dislodged by the great Shangaan king, Shoshangane. They fled along an old trade route over the Lebombo Mountains and northwards into the Transvaal lowveld. There were great herds of elephant in this region and the Makuleke attempted to control the trade in ivory which was carried from there to Lourenço Marques. Where these noble elephants roamed, in the second half of the century, the situation became chaotic. The Shangaan kings were still masters of Mozambique between the Lebombo range frontier and the sea, despite the fact that white men's paper maps proclaimed it Portuguese territory. And they continued to spill their authority over the white men's frontier into what was depicted on those maps as the Transvaal Republic, where clans of their chiefdom lived.

The central conflict between invaders and the indigenous people was obscured and unconventionally pursued by adventurers of British, Portuguese and other European origins, not to mention Boers with vague titles to administration in the area, obtained from the Volksraad, the Boer parliament, in faraway Pretoria. All of them made a living by hunting for ivory which was portered down to Mozambique for export, and appeared in elegant houses in England, Europe and America as piano keys, carved ornaments, cutlery handles, and jewellery adorning wealthy white ladies. Some of the elephant hunters were slave dealing on the side; it had been outlawed internationally by 1836 but the Portuguese in Mozambique were sufficiently forgotten and neglected by Portugal to be able to carry on the second oldest profession practically unhindered. It is said that a few Boers collaborated with them.

Slave traders were the pioneers of the multinational concept of commerce; *their* commerce was established before frontiers were drawn and continued in accommodations long after. A Portuguese adventurer, João Albasini, was exporting slaves and ivory from the area as early as 1840, and as his interests developed he set himself up in the wild at various points along his trade routes. The ruin of one of his depots survives. I went to have a look at it. Recent excavation had restored some of the mud brick walls of the household he established with the Boer woman he married. Shards of the fine flowered dinner service he ate off have been dug up; they were imported, like his gin bottles, from Holland, and carried hundreds of miles by black porters from Mozambique. This was no primitive camp: under glass in a thatched shelter beside the ruin are displayed the bullets manufactured in his workshops, and photographs, blurred by heat and damp, which show him got up in braided regalia as a vice-consul of Portugal, and his wife keeping up with the fashionable decencies of high collars and jewellery. After more than a century has passed, I experienced weirdly easily the bizarre remoteness of this style of life, because its site is now part of the Kruger Park and surrounded by silent bush and wild animals, just as it was then.

In this place Albasini became a bush *caudillo* of bands of Africans set wandering by the destruction of their traditional economy on both sides of the frontier through slave trading, hunting and tax gathering. Albasini was made a tax gatherer for the Transvaal

Republic; when the Lovedu clan's Queen Modjadi the Rainmaker defied his demands for a cattle tribute, he moved his men against her people and brought back not only cattle but four hundred small children whom he trained as slave labour.

Yet Albasini, child-slaver and plunderer, is honoured in South Africa to this day as a hero frontiersman. A source of life-giving water, the huge Albasini Dam, is named for him in the eastern Transvaal, near the frontier where he plied his ugly trades.

The Makuleke extended their elephant hunting into what is now the northernmost part of the Kruger Park. They settled on an ancient trade route which passed through the area to Mozambiquan ports. There they made their home spread along the Levubu River to the Limpopo, and to the place where the frontiers of South Africa, Mozambique and Zimbabwe now meet: the Pafuri triangle.

The first permanent European presence in the region of the Pafuri triangle was established only after the Witwatersrand gold dis-coveries in the Transvaal in the late 1880s. Then labour recruiters for the miners were attracted by reports of 'caravans of blacks' who used the old trade route, crossing back and forth between Mozambique and the Transvaal Republic without regard for the white man's frontiers. Like Albasini, the recruiters were adventurers, a Victorian breed of swaggering blackguards of all European nationalities who picked up a dishonest living between the colonizers and the indigenous people, often doing the colonizers' dirty work for them. Paid so much a pair of hands, the recruiters in the Pafuri triangle sold Africans from Mozambique to the mines.

On the lonely road to the confluence of three frontiers at Pafuri I saw a giant baobab tree dominating the airy forest. With great swollen trunk and branches like amputated arms, it is an auth-oritative beacon in a landscape that seems to have no beginning and no end. From 1919 to 1927 it was the single feature that guided Mozambiquans to the point where they could sign up for the mines; they gathered there for recruitment. Near it is preserved, with a memorial plaque, a concrete trough. I walked gingerly down into it; here, until 1938, the men were dipped in disinfectant, like cattle, before they were taken hundreds of miles to the mines by cart, donkey, or on foot.

WENELA – Witwatersrand Native Labour Association – put the adventurer-recruiters, whom the mines had been happy to use for some years, out of business, and regularized recruitment. With the tens of thousands of Mozambiquan men who have been processed through this place, much of South Africa's prosperity began. Such is the power of the mining industry in South Africa that Pafuri has been a frontier post in itself, with passage only for those who come to work on the mines. Now called T E B A (The Employment Bureau of Africa), it is not functioning here for the present, because of the civil war in Mozambique, but the station has not exactly closed down. . . .

Although it is within the Kruger Park, the road leading to the T E B A site is barred, like the many roads which now lead to concealed military camps rather than viewpoints for observing the animals. Nevertheless, I got there, passing buck and warthog along deserted tracks. High up overlooking the convergence of the three frontiers was a scene out of Conrad: buried in tropical trees, low buildings where men were received, fed, medically examined, signed up and transported by better means than on foot or by donkey; a dark-browed thatched mansion surrounded by a moat of huge-leaved plants, with a magnificent wild fig tree thrust, like a tower, through the structure.

In an open shed a young ex-ranger of the Kruger Park was grinding a blade – T E B A allows him to carry out his avocation, making special knives, while acting as caretaker. He told me that the recruiting station might be used for its proper purpose again 'soon', but that in the meantime the manager's house was being put to use as a holiday lodge for high-ranking mining officials visiting the Kruger Park. There, while taking their evening drinks, they may look out, as I did, way down upon the electrified fence which now marks South Africa's frontier with Mozambique; a frontier where Mozambiquans who are not welcome labour for the mines, but refugees from the civil war, are kept out, or killed by 11,500 volts.

Long ago, for blacks, the meaning of the frontier became an enclosure within which there was little choice other than to put your thumbprint on a rogue's bit of paper and be rounded up for the mines. And in the 1930s, when the old Boer Republic had long become the Union of South Africa in the British Commonwealth, and the Pafuri area was incorporated into the Kruger Park, the Makuleke living there were cast out. Some fled across the Limpopo River to their related clans in Rhodesia and Mozambique. Other Makuleke clans resisted the South African government's ethnic social engineering right up to their final defeat in 1969. Under Dr Verwoerd's 'Grand Apartheid' plan in what was by then the Republic of South Africa, they were herded far south into a so-called 'nation unit' of Shangaan–Tsonga people which finally became the 'homeland' dubbed Gazankulu.

There, in the 1980s, they give food and shelter to the refugees from the war in Mozambique – people with whom their grandfathers

Mozambiquan refugees who have found sanctuary in Gazankulu in South Africa. Those lucky enough to reach Gazankulu are allowed to stay, as long as they do not seek work or live outside the homeland. Others fleeing to South Africa are classed as illegal immigrants and many are sent back to Mozambique.

shared a territory which had nothing to do with the white man's frontier.

In 1976 President Samora Machel closed the frontier between Mozambique and Rhodesia during the Zimbabwean war of independence and gave bases to Rhodesian Freedom Fighters against the South African-backed regime of Ian Smith. This brotherly action was to have terrible consequences for Mozambique.

The bases brought retaliatory raids on Mozambique by Smith's army, foreshadowing raids by the South African army across the frontier between South Africa and Mozambique which were to begin in 1981. A community of interest – the destabilization of Mozambique – between the Smith regime and South Africa, vengeful white Portuguese settlers and adventurers, FRELIMO deserters, and right-wing groups in Portugal, coalesced as a rebel force, RENAMO.

By the 1980s RENAMO had become a neo-colonialist army which did not hesitate to employ criminal rabble to do sickening violence on civilians. For years now, Mozambiquans have had to seek shelter in neighbouring countries. By 1988, one hundred thousand had been killed, seven million were in need of aid for survival, two million were homeless, out of a population of fourteen million. Two hundred thousand had come across the Mozambique–South Africa frontier – the ultimate irony, running from the enemy to the enemy, since South African support for RENAMO has been a major factor in bringing about the need to flee the death, hunger and wanton destruction that has wiped out their farms and villages and besieged their towns. In Gazankulu, in the middle eighties, thirty-seven thousand had sought refuge, and by the end of 1989 they were streaming in at the rate of a thousand a month.

I found Gazankulu subtropical, beautiful and poor, with a population of less than half a million living on the export of its manpower to cities outside its territory designated by whites, and on small-scale agriculture and minor mineral deposits. Yet Gazankulan families have for years taken in destitute Mozambiquans.

Mozambiquan refugees are not accorded refugee status by South Africa. They are classed as illegal immigrants and about fifteen hundred a month are deported under the Illegal Aliens Act. But a special dispensation for the refugees who manage to make their way to Gazankulu has been negotiated by the Chief Minister there, Professor Hudson Ntsanwisi. They are not deported by the South African police so long as they do not seek work or live outside Gazankulu. Supported by aid agencies who supply the minimum of food and clothing, the charity of Gazankulu keeps the Mozambiquans alive. But this is more than charity. Most of the refugees come from

Gaza province in Mozambique, where one hundred thousand people have died from starvation as a result of RENAMO's attacks on emergency relief supplies of food and medicine. These refugees were once part of Shoshangane's African kingdom. Ties of ancestry and the living bond of a common language, TshiShangaan, account in part for the deep humanity with which they have been taken in, while Gazankulans themselves have so little.

Children, children – a place of women and children. I was in the Gazankulan refugee village, Hluvukani, on the day that the Catholic Bishops' Conference, based in Pretoria but constantly challenging apartheid policies, sent a party of two archbishops and eight bishops to hold a mass in solidarity with the Mozambiquan refugees.

The local Chief gave the refugees this stretch of wooded grazing land on which to build their own village. The refugees have created it with nothing but what nature provides: branches, mud and grass. And nature, here, disguises destitution that would be appalling in a barren place. I looked in under the voluptuous shade of mahogany trees and the silvery-grey thatch of neat roofs: the one-room houses were absolutely empty of possessions. Everything these people had was left behind or lost in destruction by RENAMO. The home-made mats on which the women and children rested outside in the fierce heat, the few pots at their outdoor cooking places, were their only household goods.

Children, children, women and old men. These people had walked, some aged, some pregnant, carrying and leading children hundreds of miles down through the Kruger Park among the predators – lions, hyenas and leopards, crocodiles who lie in wait to take anyone who ventures on a river verge – and mighty herds of elephant. Only later, when I was to see such people on the other side of the frontier, would I understand how they find the desperate courage to undertake the exodus. Only then would I know the truth of the awesome statement a man made to me in this village: 'What difference, if I die on the way, if I'm going to be killed at home.'

A tall, rough, box-wood cross had been rigged up under a tree and a tarpaulin shaded an improvised altar. The archbishops and bishops, contrastingly pink-faced and coal-black, splendid in their embroidered robes and crowned with gilded mitres, suggested to me the arrival of the Magi; among all these babies, all these homeless people in this humble place.

President Samora Machel came from Gaza, like these people. (He officially abolished religion in favour of Marxism, but today freedom of worship has been restored by his successor.) He was fervently anti-Catholic, because the Catholic Church defended the slave trade and in modern times collaborated with the Portuguese in oppression of his people. But history, like the frontiers it draws, presents many contradictions. That day, the main celebrant of the mass told the Mozambiquan refugees, 'We have come here because of you. Because of your suffering, to show we have not forgotten you.'

In enormous iron pots the meat and bones of two whole oxen were stewing, and putu – maize porridge – was being stirred. People queued behind a fence so that the cooks would not be mobbed. After nearly four hours of singing, ululating, praying under the branding-iron of the sun, came the culmination of the day. It was a meagre feast for one like myself who hasn't known the ordeal of hunger. And the babies at the breast were the only ones with bar facilities.

Life in a circus tent, life in a plastic bag.

I went to another place of refuge in the same area. From a distance, I saw a circus pitch, cheerful and beckoning; a huge blue-and-white striped tent was pegged down on cleared ground. Inside, 211 people were living. They had crammed a kind of village into it. Sacking divided tiny makeshift cubicles. Calendars were tacked up. There was a dignified attempt at privacy; somehow the structures of a lost home were being recalled in there....

I spent some time with the people of the tent. Grandfather and grandmother Ngobeni had brought their grandchildren to safety after RENAMO killed their daughter. They knew exactly where to make for because old Mr Ngobeni once crossed the frontier in another capacity – as an economic refugee. He had been one of the illegal immigrants who cleared the bush for the building of the iron ore boom town near where the refugee camp now stands.

Some new refugees arrived while I was there. The Mbowani family, husband, wife, two children and baby, and two teenagers, had walked on and off for eight days through Mozambique and the Kruger Park. Starved and in total exhaustion, the teenagers looked dazed to a state of mental retardment. The camp nurse doled out a nutrient powder, instructing them to drink it mixed with water since they would not be able to digest solid food. But I saw them tear the corners of the plastic bags with their teeth and suck up the life-giving powder neat, as more fortunate children eat sherbet.

Life in a circus tent, life in a plastic bag; but these who have got away are a thousand times better off than those who have not.

Drought and floods, along with South Africa's military backing, have compounded the intentions of RENAMO to destroy normal life in Mozambique. If I had been disturbed by the plight of the survivors in camps on the South African side of the frontier, this was no preparation for what there was to be seen at a gathering place for the homeless deep inside Mozambique. Silence hung like some deadly gas over a sand waste of rotting huts; it was broken only by the incessant weak croak of coughing. In the heat, the starving were dying of pneumonia brought on by exposure.

People seemed to have lost the capacity to speak, even to call out their misery. And there were no words of my own to describe it; only those of a poet, William Plomer:

'HORROR is written on the sun.'

The place, innocently called Casa Banana, was once part of the Gorongoza Game Park; in the fifties I'd watched lions basking there. It had become one of R E N A M O's headquarters, then was captured by F R E L I M O government troops and later abandoned. Now twelve thousand destitute people were gathered there. Their presence was mangled flesh and living skeletons: beaten while kidnapped and forced to porter for R E N A M O, or starved when their crops were destroyed. There were no medical supplies and no doctor. I came from and went back to the living world by plane; there was no road transport possible because of R E N A M O ambushes, no way in or out by any other means. Food was supposed to be flown in every week, but often planes could not take off for fear of being shot down by R E N A M O. This place was only one of such, and at one period; a year later five thousand more people were starving to death under rebel attacks in another part of the country.

R E N A M O was the word written on the sun.

The ingot and the gun

From the year of Mozambiquan independence, 1975, South Africa trained commandos for her part in economic sabotage and urban raids against Mozambique. When the Smith regime fell in 1980 and Rhodesia became the black independent state of Zimbabwe, the entire R E N A M O headquarters and personnel were secretly airlifted from there to South Africa and installed in a new base close to South Africa's frontier with Mozambique.

R E N A M O was set to destroy transport routes in southern Mozambique being used by neighbouring black states. The South African Defence Force provided sabotage teams to cross the frontier and blow up the oil pipeline, power lines and railways. In 1981 its commandos crossed at night and raided Maputo, ostensibly in a seek-and-destroy attack on an African National Congress hideout, killing Mozambiquan citizens in the process. Then Maputo was bombed in 1983, in retaliation for an A N C-attributed bomb which killed South Africans in a Pretoria street. South Africa provided aircraft, submarines and parachute drops of arms, rations and equipment, extensive radio communications and supply networks, for RENAMO. She built RENAMO into an army as large as the Mozambique government's own FRELIMO. By 1984 RENAMO had made a million homeless, destroyed over a thousand medical posts, and reduced Mozambique's earnings from £163 million to £50 million.

Out of this chaotic desperation came the Nkomati Accord.

It was another trade-off between Mozambique and South Africa. South Africa undertook to stop arming and supporting RENAMO in exchange for Mozambique denying the African National Congress, the banned, principal black liberation movement of South Africa, the right to operate from Mozambique. On 16 March 1984, President Samora Machel and President P. W. Botha met at the frontier between their two countries on the bank of the river which was to give the Accord its name – Nkomati. Not being much in favour with the government of my country, I wasn't invited along with the South African and other fifteen hundred guests to the sumptuous party where the South African air force flew in twelve hundred crayfish tails and nine tons of ice to cool the champagne. But I read the speeches. President Botha said he had 'A vision of the nations of Southern Africa co-operating with each other in every field of human endeavour ... a veritable constellation of states working together for the benefit of all on the basis of mutual respect.'

President Machel said: 'We have undertaken a solemn commitment not to launch aggressive actions of any sort against one another, and we have created conditions for the establishment, with honour and dignity, of a new phase of stability and security on our common borders.'

Within two years he was dead, on the South African side of the frontier, killed in a mysterious air crash in which Mozambiquans, and many others, still believe South Africa was involved, despite a commission's finding to the contrary.

Five years later, I stood at the site on the river bank where the Accord was signed. Its only monument was a huge garbage dump.

For in the months after the Accord, RENAMO was more rampant than ever. Two years of military supplies had been delivered to RENAMO on the eve of the Accord. Over a thousand RENAMO soldiers, trained in the South African camp near the frontier, were sent into Mozambique. Trains that carried Mozambiquan miners to and from the frontier to work in South Africa were blown up, and this continued to the end of the 1980s, when the mines had to begin to transport men by air in order to have them delivered alive. In part exchange for agreeing to sign the Accord, President Machel had

Children queuing for food at a refugee camp in Mozambique

been allowed to step up the export of his country's manpower to the South African mines from forty-five thousand to eighty thousand, greatly increasing the desperately needed foreign currency the miners' earnings represent.

South Africa denied she was continuing to support RENAMO. Then in 1985 a rebel soldier's diary, found when the Mozambiquans captured a RENAMO encampment, gave details of the dates when and places where South African arms and equipment were supplied to RENAMO, both before and after the Accord was signed, and the names of the South African politicians and Defence Force officers who were advising and instructing RENAMO.

The Accord has been revived under President Machel's successor, President Joachim Chissano, again out of economic necessity and desperation to end the plundering savagery of RENAMO. And at the end of the eighties, South Africa's actions have become only more and more intricately confounding. The paradox is a deadly one for the people I saw in the camps. South Africa is pouring money into development in Mozambique; but – for example – the vast sums spent on restoring the power lines from the great Cahora Bassa hydroelectric installation I saw straddling hundreds of miles of bush down to South Africa are literally exploded in thin air, since RENAMO simply blows up the pylons again.

RENAMO continues to rampage widely. In the first half of 1989, the rebels came closer than ever to Maputo, attacking a commercial centre less than twenty miles away from the capital, and at the same time cut off supplies to fifty-two thousand people starving in the distant province of Zambezia.

Mozambique's allies are pressing President Chissano to reach a settlement with RENAMO, since support has been long and costly. Tanzania has withdrawn her troops, who were an invaluable reinforcement of the FRELIMO army, and the Soviet Union is not going to increase its military aid. South Africa, most of all, wants to see RENAMO taken into some sort of coalition with the Mozambique government, now that the monstrous protégé has done the job of terrorizing Mozambique into compliance with South Africa's economic and political domination in the region. President Chissano says he is – at last – ready to talk to RENAMO with a view to integrating them back into society under an extended amnesty, but he bluntly refuses to discuss any question of power sharing with – as he calls them – 'murderers'.

I did talk – not to one of the actual murderers – but to a man who has defected from a high position in RENAMO out of revulsion at the idea of blood on his hands, even at the distance of Lisbon.

I found him sitting in a room in a Maputo hotel empty of tourists, staring at a blank television set, listening to the music track from *Apocalypse Now*. He was white, a Portuguese born in Mozambique, heavy and tall, with the uncertain face and sorrowful eyes of a punished small boy – all pallor except for the nicotine brown on his fingers. In a voice so soft it seemed he wanted to efface himself he told how he had represented RENAMO in Europe and his headquarters had been a house in Lisbon where an elaborate radio and telecommunications system with the South African military was installed. He had believed RENAMO represented a just cause against the Leftist FRELIMO regime until he was sent on a secret mission to be the guest of South Africa and, in the company of the South African military and the R E N A M O men training in the South African camp near the frontier, at Phalaborwa, he realized that the atrocities R E N A M O was accused of were true; the subject of boasts and anecdotes among the troops, and blandly ignored by the high-ranking officers with whom he dined.

What he had to say rose in his gorge. While he talked to me, he kept swallowing. He had seen planes take off from South African military airfields at night, carrying R E N A M O troops into Mozambique; he had seen them return with Mozambiquan girl children, twelve or thirteen years old, who were, as — swallowing again — he put it, 'for the use of the R E N A M O soldiers'.

When he got back to Lisbon he gave himself up to the Mozambiquan government representatives there. His life was at risk, then, through R E N A M O's hit men. He was brought back to Mozambique to supply valuable testimony about R E N A M O, and to be produced, ever since, a strange human exhibit, for the media. I felt an awkward sympathy for him, mixed with the repulsion he seemed to feel for himself and project into the attitude of others towards him. He had crossed formidable frontiers of the mind. But he was in no-man's-land.

Before I crossed to Mozambique I had made other acquaintances among people who, like the R E N A M O defector and myself, were born white in southern Africa when the Mozambique–South Africa frontier was between two countries ruled by brotherly white minorities. The South African frontier town of Komatipoort is a place of blooming poinsettia, sandbags and security fences, these latter presumably against attacks by Freedom Fighters of the A N C, though for some years now this route seems not to have been used by them for infiltration, and such acts of violent resistance to apartheid as there have been have come from the strength of the A N C's liberation forces within the country.

The mayor of Komatipoort is a prominent supporter of the government, a farmer and local tycoon with interests ranging from a shopping mall to a mango chutney factory. After the Nkomati Accord, he went into business with Mozambique in a joint tourist enterprise to fly wealthy South Africans to fish on Inhaca Island, a safe distance off devastated Maputo, but abandoned this because the profits came in worthless Mozambique currency. He has 350 workers on his farms, many of them Mozambiquans who, he said, were recruited legally. He drove me to his private game reserve, through which sometimes refugees are found passing; he hands them over to the police.

Border post between South Africa and Mozambique at Komatipoort

His house was a place of beheadings; a decapitated hippo opened its huge mouth at me at the front door, and inside were the heads of buffalo and buck, also the stuffed corpses of a lion, leopard and crocodile. This was the fate of the animal invaders of his territory.

A neighbouring farmer supports the rival, extreme right-wing, party which opposes the South African government as selling out white supremacy in its 'reforms'. He is deeply religious and was extravagantly hospitable to me. In his fine house there was a sort of shrine to his ancestors, the Voortrekkers, and during lunch he said with passionate seriousness that he would give his life to keep South Africa white-ruled. Without the slightest awareness of any moral contradiction he compassionately described the Mozambiquan refugee he had seen who was torn to pieces by the razor wire that surrounds the electrified fence along the frontier, and went on to say that he believed South Africa ought to continue to support RENAMO militarily until the rebels share power in Mozambique, defeating 'the Communists'.

I pretended to lose my way, and so was able to blunder past a
guard-post with some plausible excuse and, out of sight, approach
the forbidden Fence. Fence! Better described as a fiendish *via dolorosa*
climbing hill and savannah in the bush, its width a thick tangle of
torture devices. Clinging to the outer diamond-mesh under a skull-
and-crossbones sign, I could look along the gleaming coils of razor
fangs, the two filaments of deadly smooth wire in there that carry
11,500 volts to kill at a touch, and the second spread of razor coils
beyond them. It was a sight for the damnations of Hieronymus
Bosch and Dante's most profound depth of Hell.

At another point, a Mozambiquan was persuaded to demonstrate
to me how the parties of refugees he brings down from Mozambique
get through the fence at those places where there are no razor
coils. He propped up the electrified wires with forked branches just
sufficiently for him to dig a shallow depression beneath them, and
then wriggled through on his belly. I held my breath for him; and
imagined what the operation would be like as it is performed in
darkness, with women and babies to be passed through like this.

The tiny plane that took me to Maputo flew low over the Fence.
From above it was no longer some terrible track of pain but a wound,
as far as the eye could see, open in the landscape.

I had not been in Maputo for twenty years, and the first time I
ever was there was in 1949, on a honeymoon. It was called Lourenço
Marques then, and I – like other South African whites – regarded it
as the height of sybaritic luxury to stay at its Polana Hotel. Hadn't
the Aga Khan brought Rita Hayworth there, on *their* honeymoon!
A character in a novel I wrote thirty-eight years later, *A Sport of
Nature*, reminisces of her sister, who would be of my generation:

> She fell in love with that wailing fado.... She fell in love
> with the sleazy dockside nightclubs, the sexuality and
> humidity, the freedom of prostitutes. That's what she kept
> going back for. To wash off the Calvinism and koshering
> of South Africa. The way people go to a spa to ease their
> joints. ... She was all our colonial bourgeois illusions rolled
> into one; she thought that was Europe. Latin. She thought
> it was European culture.

During the Portuguese regime South Africans would talk of going
to Lourenço Marques as the British talk of popping over to 'the
Continent'. Casinos were forbidden in South Africa; Lourenço
Marques was Monte Carlo. South Africa forbade sex between white
and black; in Lourenço Marques you could take your pick of flesh of
any colour.

Samora Machel sent the prostitutes to institutions of rehabilitation and closed the casinos. But the Polana Hotel survives in the crazy inappropriateness of its Hollywood architectural idiom. So I stayed there once again, now, and my fellow guests lunching on the terrace overlooking palms and pool were not tourists and honeymooners but international bankers and aid missions come to revive Mozambique's collapsed economy. Not so much as a piece of bread at the tables could be bought without foreign currency. But the three white wings of the hotel on its headland shut out the ruined city behind it and turned all gazes, behind sunglasses, to the immense blue of the Indian Ocean.

When I remarked on the poverty and wretchedness of the city I was constantly corrected: 'You should have seen it two years ago! Now there's water, there's food.' If you can afford it. I walked through displays of fish, fruit and vegetables in the huge market, but outside had to pick my way through destitute people who cannot buy anything. From the air the city has the silhouette of prosperity; in the streets it came to me as a materialization of an apocalyptic vision of urban decay. But this catastrophe has not come about by materialism and pollution; it is the result of civil war. Instead of coming into their own after gaining freedom from the Portuguese, the people of Maputo are camping out in the shell of colonialism they do not have the means to maintain. Still dispossessed, in their own capital they are like vagrants, with no choice but to squat in the structures of a style of living in which they were given no part, and that is hopelessly, uselessly, unsuited to their resources. Where the Portuguese took their aperitifs on the balconies of apartment buildings, I saw people cooking a poor meal on a tin of coal. I saw women walking up ten floors of another once-elegant apartment block with buckets of water they had queued to fetch from a tap in the street. The elevators in these blocks don't run, the cookers don't work, and there is no water in the fancy tiled bathrooms. The streets of the city are dodgem tracks, with vehicles swerving wildly round potholes; in a few places, workmen were repairing the surface, heating tar over fires burning old tyres – a fuel supply coming as a grim reminder to me of the buses and trucks blown up by RENAMO on the road from the frontier I'd seen from the plane.

Near the Polana there was one brand-new, white-and-green complex within a landscaped garden behind railings. I had thought

Right above Prostitute and client in Lourenço Marques, as Maputo was known before independence
Right below Polana's golden beaches during the Portuguese regime: then South Africa's Riviera, now deserted except for a few local people

Outdoor school in Maputo. With nearly 50 per cent of the population under fifteen, education is a vital priority for the country's economic development. But there are desperate shortages of teachers, books and buildings.

it must be an embassy; but there was no identifying flag or plaque. It was the new South African Trade Mission headquarters. South Africa has invested 48 million rands in various projects in Mozambique since 1984 and more is promised. But this is a donor with a record of giving with one hand while destabilizing with another. . . .

A Russian military helicopter was my transport for the last leg of my journey. It was hired from the Mozambique army and paid for in dollars. RENAMO had long made the road route from Maputo impassable.

The reassuringly clumsy craft whirred over the path of the fence, that ran like a river to the sea. For the frontier is lost in the Indian Ocean; it finally ends at Ponto d'Oro, a golden headland, on a splendid white beach.

As the helicopter approached the coast, I saw villas which had been deserted for years. Most hadn't belonged even to the Portuguese, let alone the Mozambiquans; they were the holiday homes of white South Africans. This was their Riviera.

In the abandoned playground of foreigners the local people are cut off from the rest of their country. Without the tourists there is no one to buy their labour or their fish. A few FRELIMO soldiers on coastguard duty (for RENAMO supplies sometimes have been smuggled in by sea) stood with their guns black and angular against the pearly sea and brilliant sky, the pure and perfect sand; the symbols of death were a blasphemy. People gathered silently round the helicopter when it was about to take off again. Many had small bundles; they were hoping it would take them away from this beautiful dead place, their isolation. As many as there was room for packed into the helicopter; sitting among them I wondered what there was ahead of them, what there was to read in their eyes.

It was hope.

'We are a continent of survivors,' Samora Machel said of Africa. The ingot and the gun have determined relations between Mozambique and South Africa for a long time on this part of the continent, but survival between the black socialist state and the capitalist apartheid state, now, means political accommodation. For this to bring peace and freedom to South Africa's black people as well as to their brothers in Mozambique is something to be hoped for. Because whether or not South Africa's investment bribes, which Mozambique cannot afford to refuse, revive the Nkomati Accord, the frontier remains to be lived with. In the end, it's not a fence or a line on a map. It's the frontier my country tried to set up in me when I was a child: distrust of white for black, the frontier between haves and have nots. And that one has to come down, on both sides.

RONALD EYRE

LONG DIVISION

Ireland

*I*BELIEVE I have outstanding qualifications to write and
present a film on the subject of the Irish border. I am less
associated with the Anglo-Irish Agreement than Garret Fitz-
gerald, less rhapsodic than Edna O'Brien, less disrespectful than
Dave Allen, less delicately placed than Cardinal O'Fiaich, less
expensive than Terry Wogan. It was a bunch of these and other
negatives that the *Frontiers* team brought to my door in October
1988. 'Are you at all interested in Ireland?' said George Carey, the
executive producer, post-pleasantries.

'Well – yes,' I replied, thinking of W.B. and Jack Yeats, O'Casey,
Jack MacGowran and Sean Kenny, Wilde, John Montague, Seamus
Heaney, Shaw, Roger Casement, Connemara marble, the Dubliners,
Dana and Barry McGuigan. 'And – no.' When holidays came round
I had never gone to Ireland, knew Galway Bay, Killarney and the
Mountains of Mourne only from old songs and, I suppose, preferred
holidays in a place where I wouldn't be disliked. As dislike of the
English – as boozers, fans, bigots – has spread more generally round
the world, Ireland starts to look more attractive. I agreed to work
on the film.

'Ignorance,' said Lady Bracknell, that great Irish creation, 'is like
a delicate, exotic fruit; touch it and the bloom is gone.' A few weeks
into the project and the bloom went: I resigned. It was not simply
the size of the reading list that deterred me; nor the impregnable
sub-text beneath even the lightest Anglo-Irish exchanges; nor the
discovery that the most interesting stuff – like what Edward Heath
really said to Brian Faulkner about internment on 7 August 1971 –

Ronald Eyre beside the pre-Christian, Janus-head figure in Caldragh Cemetery on Boa Island

was stashed away for a hundred years in a vault marked 'Secret'. No; it was the slow realization that, just as surely as every Frenchman carries a marshal's baton in his knapsack, every Englishman carries an Irish skeleton in his cupboard.

That long chain of serfs I call my family tree, sweltering in the ditches, mines and steel mills of South Yorkshire, never, as far as I know, expropriated any Irish land or put any Irish to the sword, but how far do I know? There could have been an Eyre with Oliver Cromwell for the massacre at Drogheda. At least, I cannot prove that there wasn't. And some Irish observer observing me being an English observer may feel in his bones that there was. Then what becomes of objectivity, fairness, balance, describing what's there and rising above it? To agree to be English and to cast the long shadow that anyone English casts in Ireland and then to give your shadow the slip is, I would suggest, a more exacting contortion than merely going for objectivity. This, perhaps, is the true Anglo-Irish yoga: it takes time to learn, and practitioners can expect constant bone-ache. Objectivity on any grand scale abandoned, I withdrew the resignation and never looked back.

The precise birth date of the Irish border is hard to establish. This is odd when the date of the Battle of the Boyne is unforgettable. As soon as governments in Westminster came to accept, in the early years of the twentieth century, that some form of Home Rule for Ireland was inevitable, powerful forces set about working out how to remodel it from the inside. If power were to be devolved to Catholic Dublin, Protestant Belfast would go its own way in a form of apartheid – separate development for the north-east of Ireland in a union with Britain. The question for Unionists was, literally, where to draw the line. A tight fortress of four north-eastern counties would be Protestant all right, but could it stand up on its own? A nine-county unit would resurrect the ancient boundaries of Ulster, but would it be loyal? The six-county solution seemed the least bad compromise.

The new Dublin administration, set up in 1920, had a civil war on its hands and paid scant attention to developments in the North, regarding Unionist manoeuvres as a skirmish before Ireland settled down to its destiny. They even collaborated on a three-man Boundary Commission set up by the 1920 Act to iron out border creases. A leak to the press of the eventual report in 1925 so enraged Nationalists by its mild recommendations that it was suppressed, and the three startled governments – Dublin, Belfast and London – shook hands on the straight six-county solution. On that day, the Dublin government did not speak for all the people of the Free State and the seeds of Republican agitation were sown; the Belfast government did not speak for all the people of Northern Ireland, and Catholic discontent was left to fester; the British government, in getting itself off one hook, unwittingly impaled itself on another.

So, what is the precise date of the Irish border? The Government of Ireland Act is dated 23 December 1920. The tripartite agreement for Dublin, Belfast and London was ratified on 3 December 1925. But the real date of the establishment of the Irish border has to be the date at which any individual accepts that it is there. For a Fermanagh Protestant landlord, compiling his submission to the Boundary Commission in the early twenties, the border was already in place. For Paddy Short, proprietor of Short's Bar in Crossmaglen, south Armagh, in 1989, it has not happened yet, nor – if he has any say – will it. All the time I was doggedly pursuing a geographical line called the Irish border, I had to learn that the real border is between two religions, histories, sets of perceptions and is carried in the bloodstream and the head.

Filming began on the morning of 24 April 1989. We were at the northerly end of the border near Muff on Lough Foyle. I was required to stand on a bridge near the Southern customs hut unfolding a map. The idea was that I would need help to get my bearings and the customs officers would supply it. As we were filming, two officers of the Northern Ireland Department of the Environment happened to drive up in a van to take some measurements. Instead of starting at the bridge we had all agreed to be the beginning of the border, they walked thirty yards or so into the Republic to a further bridge and began measuring. The ensuing gentle row between Northern DoE and Southern customs gave a lift to the spirits. Here was a border incident of low-key farce – without guns – on the first day of the journey.

The Irish border runs for 303 miles in a loop from Lough Foyle in the north to the Carlingford Lough in the east. It is crossed by an estimated 290 roads of which 80 have been blown up or blocked, and 20 are designated 'approved crossings'. Seventeen of these 20 have customs checkpoints. The remaining 190 are designated unapproved roads, which has tended recently to mean open, but eyed with suspicion. That said, what is a road? A leap over a ditch is a road if a smuggler and a few head of cattle can make it. A sudden swerve into a ploughed field is a road if, by doing it, a car can bypass a concrete army road-block. Once in County Fermanagh I emerged from a border trek in the company of a farmer. The bog had almost topped our boots. The way forward was by leaping from tussock to tussock of marsh grass. We emerged in a farmyard, washed off our boots in a tub, walked to the car parked alongside. 'Been rustlin'?' shouted the farmer's wife by way of greeting. Down which 'road' did she imagine we had been rustlin'? I couldn't see a road.

Here is a classic Irish smuggling story. A carter once confided to a customs officer that the following day he would be bringing contraband across the border in his cart. If the officer agreed to let him pass uninspected, he could share the profits. The following day, when the carter arrived, a different customs officer was on duty and

Overleaf British army checkpoint on the south Armagh border

Garda checkpoint on the Donegal Road near the border with the North

drew the man into the inspection bay.

'I hear you're bringing in contraband,' smirked the officer.

'Ah, no, your honour,' replied the carter. 'That was yesterday.'

Once or twice during filming we were likewise poised to make a catch. Once we were even promised a ride across the border and past a customs post with a cargo purporting to be contraband and with cameras blazing; but the rendezvous was never quite finalized and our contact was never near his telephone at quite the right moment. In any case, we were nagged by the thought that Customs and Excise might have set him up as an *agent provocateur* so that a BBC film crew would be caught red-handed and clapped in irons.

Colm Tóibín's book *Walking Along the Border*, published in 1987, speaks of a popular building manual by Jack Fitzsimons called *Bungalow Bliss*, which lays out a range of dream houses from the retirement chalet to the Spanish-style hacienda, inspired by sunshine and high sierra, destined to go streaky in the Irish rain. All the piggy-banks in Ireland lined up tail to snout could not have paid for some of them. Yet they have sprung up here and there in border areas, alongside no factories, no mines, no wealthy pasture. They may all be just rewards for honest toil. I raise the question, though, whether one or two perhaps could have been subsidized by smuggling, but do not expect an answer.

For fifty years, smuggling and the Irish border have grown together like dock leaves and nettles. The priest who bothered to chastise smugglers would be chastising many of his congregation and possibly himself, and who would want to be such a spoilsport? Smuggling – like the blissful bungalow – has come in many sizes: at one extreme, the Saturday shopper fattened out by a ten-shilling dress-length wound round her on her way from a cross-border market; at the other, the multi-millionaire using underground marshalling yards to hitch and unhitch cabins, number-plates and trailers and operate a wide-berth, cross-border Colditz story.

At the height of imparity between the produce and currencies of North and South, the border has acted as a sluice-gate: the greater the imparity, the greater the pressure on the gate and the more impassioned and ingenious the attempts to breach it. During the Second World War the South had booze and butter, the North had tea. More recently prices in the North, especially of petrol and electrical goods, have undercut those in the South and a generation of ungazetted petrol and refrigerator barons has risen to cream off the difference. While there was a subsidy to be had on either side of the border, the same cattle have been shunted back and forth, their ears tagged and untagged, their meat and milk less valuable than their mileage. The lifting of the EC tariff barriers in 1992 will cause some spectacular redundancies.

Johnny Doherty lives in Donegal, a few yards from the border and three and a half miles from the city of Derry. He rents his house from the Northern Ireland DoE and keeps an eye on their nearby reservoir. His daughter has married a customs officer. Whatever his fortune is – and there is speculation about the size of it – it has come in large part from fifty years of zestful smuggling. He has outrun, outsmarted and outraged generations of customs officers and police-men. He has even discussed himself with one of their number who was lying in a hedgerow waiting for him to pass. He is his own chronicler and has shaped his stories into a smuggling saga. In all of them, as with Brer Rabbit and Brer Fox, the characters are true to type. The policeman plods and scratches his head; the customs man investigates the front room while a mountain of contraband butter is removed from the back; the British army is festooned in compasses and webbing and is lost; the smuggler alone is fleet-footed, protean, nocturnal and ahead of the game. Once, in 1971, the army turned the tables. They scooped him up in a helicopter for five weeks of interrogation in Belfast. He remembers enjoying the food. If the army's experience of him was like mine *he* would have extorted a full confession from *them* long before five weeks.

'Tell me,' I asked him, 'as a stranger in these parts, I know I will always meet politeness, but do you think I'll ever get a straight answer?'

He gave me a straight answer. 'No. I wouldn't say you'd ever get a straight answer. No.'

Have you ever been in a place where you knew immediately that passing through was not enough? You needed either to embed yourself and wait and see, or skip it entirely. It was with a strong sense of wanting to stay that I was dragged to and from St Anthony's Retreat Centre at Dundrean on the Donegal border, three miles or so outside Derry. And, now, to write about it on the run is exactly what it does not deserve and cannot take. St Anthony's is the latest initiative of a priest and twenty-two ecumenically-minded Catholics who form the Columba Community. It is a place without a telephone. The terminal for the telephone is at Columba House, 11 Queen Street, Derry. Fr Neal Carlin comes to Derry when he wants to do battle publicly. When he wants to do battle where it really makes a difference, he retreats to his cell at St Anthony's and faces his own blank walls.

It was inside the blank and sometimes shitty walls of Magilligan and Long Kesh prisons that Neal Carlin preached reconciliation during the desperate seventies and into the eighties. It was while saying his prayers with a fellow priest and a Presbyterian minister and his wife that the thought of a town community house arose. No. 11 Queen Street had been blasted by an I R A bomb in 1970. In 1980 means were found to buy and restore it as Columba House. It now works as a drop-in centre for those in need of advice, companionship, a cup of coffee, somewhere to sit quietly. The Columba Community comprises men and women, clerical and lay, and (in future, they pray) Protestant and Catholic, divested of centuries of institutional crud and hosed down as basic Christians.

St Anthony's springs from the gift of a farm in Donegal in 1985. The community seized the chance of an isolated place to provide work, retreat and silence. To help St Anthony's was no part of the British army's plan when they blocked the road with a double layer of slabs of concrete, but the effect has been to turn what was a country thoroughfare into a useful cul-de-sac. The farmer a hundred yards away over the border in the North squinnies suspiciously across at the developments down at St Anthony's. The road-blocks nearest to his farm have been painted a warning red, white and blue. In

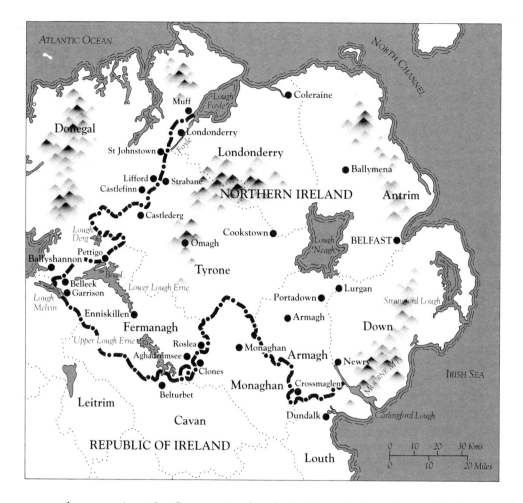

the meantime the Community has built four simple cells – called Matthew, Mark, Luke and John. A signpost has been erected in the hope that, one day, it will point the way to a conference centre and more cells. The soil from various excavations has made a mound which carries a striking, brightly painted wooden rainbow. Neal Carlin? Sweeten the internecine complexities of religious bigotry, sour politics and tribal loyalty in Ireland? He's got a hope. A real hope.

I suddenly know why I do not want to dip into and skirt past St Anthony's and the Columba Community. Here is a man, a priest, with the physique of a Gaelic football player (which he was), winner in 1989 of the Derry diocesan golf trophy, firm-faced, raw-handed, a candidate for Hollywood stardom if Sam Spiegel in a persuasive mood had passed that way, and for marriage and parenthood if he had not opted for celibacy; above all, you would think, an action man. Yet he chooses to play second fiddle to the Holy Spirit. He waits. It is enough to stop anyone in their tracks.

The border scoops Derry into Northern Ireland and, about four miles south of the city, moves eastwards to join the River Foyle, flowing south to Strabane. Along the Northern (that is, the eastern) bank of the Foyle, the clean-cut A5 connects Derry and Strabane. On the Southern (that is, western) bank a variety of more ambling roads connect Derry with Strabane's other half, Lifford. For covering the distance in the shortest time, the A5 is preferable. For variety, views and charm, go through the Republic.

Either side of the river, the drive is through flat, rich, spacious farmland, set about with neat farmhouses. To speak tribally, about 75 per cent of this land is owned by Protestants whose claim to it is based on a grant by an English government for English political purposes, and three hundred years of fruitful occupancy. In St Columb's (Church of Ireland) Cathedral, Derry, there is a crumbling monument to 'John Elvin sometime mayor of this city who came over on the first plantation thereof and departed this life the 29th day of December in the year of our Lord 1676 and the 102nd of his age'. John Elvin, then, was forty-six when the Pilgrim Fathers set sail for America. In other words, the first English and Scottish settlements in Ireland predate the white invasion of North America. If the whites have a right to the hills of Texas and Nebraska, the plains of Indiana or the jam-packed pavements of Manhattan, Protestants have a right to their bits of Ireland. The technical difference between the settlement of America and the settlement of Ireland is that the American settlers took care to exterminate the indigenous population or, at least, so reduce it that it lost heart; whereas the Scots–English settlers in Ireland achieved no such thing, though there may be evidence that from time to time they tried. Lord knows, this observation is not made to stir animosity, but to discourage simplistic diagnoses of the 'Irish Problem' from whatever side.

There is a magnificent address to the 1890 Jubilee Assembly of the Presbyterian Church of Ireland, held in Belfast. It was the work of the Revd R. J. Lynd, father of Robert Lynd, the essayist, and gives elevated expression to two great myths that still have power among the descendants of the settlers. The first is the notion of a divine intention; the second is a view of their Catholic Irish neighbours.

When a people then are providentially sent to occupy a country or a section of a country by the world's and the Church's King, it is an assured sign that they have there specific work to do which can be better done by them than by others. . . . We rejoice in the rich gifts with which our fellow countrymen are endowed; their genius, their poetic fervour, their native refinement, warm-heartedness, fidelity and hospitality evoke our admiration; but it is a simple fact that they have long lacked the industrial discipline and patient, plodding laboriousness which secures success in the struggle of life.

Dr Lynd does not push his argument on to suggest that, if Presbyterians could be less prim and corseted and Catholics less whimsical and feckless, they could fertilize each other in a great Irish stew. Some such possibility may have been in the mind of Captain O'Neill, Prime Minister of Northern Ireland, when in 1969 he arranged to meet Sean Lemass, Taoiseach of the Irish Republic, and described the meeting as a lovers' tryst between a sweet colleen and a gallant swain over a fence. This flight of fancy – plus, no doubt, the whiff of sex – so enraged the Revd Ian Paisley and extreme Loyalist opinion that Captain O'Neill, seeing perhaps what he was up against, stood down.

St Johnstown is a formerly elegant settlement on the banks of the Foyle, just in the Republic about six miles from Lifford. Its most conspicuous buildings are a fine Presbyterian church founded in 1726 and an Orange Hall of 1825, conspicuous for no architectural merit but for being painted bright blue. All but a few of St Johnstown's inhabitants are now Catholic. Seeing the camera playing over the Orange Hall and me talking to Mr Robert Fleming, a local Unionist and retired businessman, a woman left her house to answer questions I was not asking. No one was investing in St Johnstown, she said; there was no work for the men; for a job in a shirt factory a woman had to go eighteen miles to Buncrana; money and business had moved to the North; if there were some way to have this said on film, she would be grateful. Mr Fleming, whose family landed from Scotland in 1665, also regretted the decline of St Johnstown. He pointed to a row of twelve fine houses in the main street with only one occupied and that by a single old lady. If, he said, the Boundary Commission set up in 1920 and ignored in 1925 had been given real teeth, St Johnstown and its environs would now be in the North. Better – if Ireland North or South had studied its best interests generally it would never have severed the British connection and

Orange Hall in County Tyrone

floated off alone in the first place. As we spoke in the street outside the Orange Hall, some who would not agree with Mr Fleming, whatever he said, had climbed into their cars and were revving past us at full throttle. It was like being buzzed by MIGs.

Knowing at least one Irish Catholic who would vote for a United Ireland within the United Kingdom and one Irish Protestant who would vote for a United Ireland under Dublin, I hesitate to call all Catholics Nationalists leaning South and all Protestants Unionists leaning across the sea to Westminster. Yet it was on the assumption that this was probably so that the border was first drawn up. In a pouch at the back of the 1969 publication of the *Report of the Irish Boundary Commission 1925* are two maps. One is of the small adjustments that the Commission proposed to the Six-County Northern Irish solution. The other shows what it calls 'complexion by religion', based on the 1911 census and coloured pink for Protestant and green for Catholic. A great arc stretching north and south from Belfast is pink. The centre of the Six Counties between Lough Neagh and Strabane is largely green. The western border is a jigsaw of green and pink. The southern border is so green that it is hard to imagine how the British Government of the day saw fit to claim south Fermanagh and south Armagh for the North.

Even to this day, hitting the solid Catholic pocket of the central-eastern province makes the ears pop. On a ride from Belfast to Derry on a hot Sunday I had spent a dozy hour listening to Beethoven from the Barbican on the car radio and passing through neat, familiar farmland. Gradually the road rose, the farms dropped away and, suddenly, the hills opened up to a magnificent panorama of gorse, rock and bogland. (There is a wry Catholic joke about the redistribution of the land in the seventeenth century: 'They got the land; we got the views.') At that precise moment the radio signal from London was displaced by a stronger signal from, presumably, Dublin: a priest and congregation were saying their prayers in Gaelic. I had the same feeling thirty years ago at a party in London which thinned out to a group that wanted to stay into the night and hear Jack MacGowran sing Irish songs. In the early hours I looked round at the crooning assembly. 'My God,' I gawped, 'they're all Irish!'

Castlederg is a border town in the jigsaw, pink/green, bogland/pastureland stretch that runs south from Strabane through western Tyrone to Lower Lough Erne. It belongs, with Strabane, to an area with the highest rate of unemployment in western Europe; 32 per cent of the male population overall, 70 per cent and more on the housing estates. The centre of the town is impeded with barriers for security reasons. I went there first with Alison Hilliard, our researcher. The week before, an R U C (Royal Ulster Constabulary) man had been shot. As we parked the car and strolled towards the nearest café for tea and a scone, I noticed I was carrying a road map. Without telling my companion, I covered the R A C logo with my thumb in case someone misread it.

The saddest tale I heard in Castlederg was of a seventeen-year-old boy, apprentice of the year in a youth employment scheme and a Catholic. He had died trying to fix a bomb under the car of his workmate, a Protestant plumber and part-time policeman. In the wake of such a sickening event limp a whole leper colony of sour,

Republican graffiti in south Armagh

Northern Irish one-liners: that tolerance means tolerating those who share your point of view; that good community relations mean one side having such a majority that the other does not count. It was the legendary Mrs Partington who took up her broom to sweep the Atlantic out of her back door, and I was reminded of her when meeting some of the people in and around Castlederg who are taking up their brooms against similar odds in a furious determination that despair shall not prevail and that theirs is a hopeful place for investment, industry and, eventually, prosperity. After all, if the tide had turned at the right time, even Mrs Partington might have won.

In the spring of 1989 the hot issue for cross-border, cross-community (that is, Catholic and Protestant together) action groups around Castlederg was the threat to a road. As long ago as the early seventies the British army had scored great impassable ditches across the mountain road from Castlederg due west into the Republic at Cairn Hill. Their stated aim was to hamper terrorism. Now, in the run-up to the dissolution of the EC customs borders in 1992, the Southern customs appeared about to close their checkpoint on the Kilclean road going north from Castlederg to Castlefinn in the Republic. Small in itself, that closure might have been the first in a line of dominoes that could have ended with a large explosion and a crater where the road once was. All along the western border of Tyrone and the southern border of Fermanagh, roads have been terminated, forcing the population on either side to turn back from their near neighbours as seaside towns turn back from the sea. Looking in opposite directions, they settle for separate identities. This the Committee to Keep Kilclean Road Open were determined to prevent, at least this time.

Their agitation began with a public meeting in April 1989. A campaign of press advertisements and lobbying accelerated through May. A protest rally was to take place at the Border Inn near the Southern customs hut on the endangered road. It so happened that on the day that it was convenient to hold the meeting, it was also convenient for us to film it. On the same day, the tide turned. John Doherty (not the smuggler), the committee chairman, read out a letter from the customs headquarters in Dublin. On second thoughts their hut would stay. Smiles, warm applause, handshakes. The brooms had won.

The story goes that, on the night of the storming of the Winter Palace in Petrograd in 1917, Eisenstein had a ticket for the theatre and, when revolution struck, he was mainly annoyed that it might be wasted. While Eisenstein was stuck in a tram, Miss Emily Bridges of Boyle, County Roscommon, may have been thinking that, at twenty-six, she should be making a move. In November 1919 she arrived from Boyle to take up a teaching post on Boa Island in Lower Lough Erne. Though she had written her application to Canon Stack at Muckross Rectory, she had not prepared herself for a real island as she, her case and her bicycle were handed into a small boat. In Caldragh graveyard on Boa Island there are two extraordinary ancient stone carvings of powerful wide-eyed beings from the tenth century, compulsory viewing for anyone driving across the new bridge to Boa Island today. Miss Bridges never went to see them. The appetite for antiquity must have been different for a busy schoolteacher in 1919. She does, though, remember Miss Chettick who played the organ for the choir and with whom she stayed until her marriage; after which she joined and now outlives her husband, Robert, and his two brothers in a mill-house in the village of Pettigo. There they farmed, traded, produced the first local supply of electricity and lived in peace.

Overleaf The British Army's presence in Northern Ireland constantly intrudes on the daily life of the people there

But Pettigo in its day has been a flashpoint in border politics. The River Termon that flows by Mrs Shaw's mill-house is the border between Donegal and Fermanagh. In January 1922, the treaty which brought the Irish Free State into existence was ratified. In January 1922, Mrs Shaw gave birth to her daughter, Ruby. Troop movements at the time – Brits out, Irish in – were such that Mr Shaw had difficulty catching the attention of a doctor or a nurse to help with the birth. In May 1922, the I R A occupied Pettigo and a triangle of territory extending to the neighbouring village of Belleek. In June 1922, Winston Churchill obtained Cabinet authority to send two companies of troops with howitzers to recapture the two villages. In the centre of Pettigo there is a war memorial, English on one side, Irish on the other: 'In proud memory of Patrick Flood, Bernard McCanny, William Kearney who died fighting against the British forces in Pettigo 4–6–22 and of William Deasley who died of wounds 6–6–22.' Doing her daily shopping, Mrs Shaw, a pillar of civil obedience, has had to walk past a memorial to men who are both rebels and heroes.

During and after the Second World War Pettigo achieved another sort of notoriety – as a boom town. In *Border Foray*, published in 1959, Richard Hayward writes:

> About half the people of Pettigo live in Northern Ireland and half in the Republic, and in the days of great disparity in commodity prices this was a town indeed. In those days you had only to cross the street to get cigarettes and whiskey at half the price you would pay if you didn't make that move, and even today many things are much cheaper on the Republican side of the highway. The circumstance is reflected in the fact that there are six pubs in Republican Pettigo and only one in the Northern Ireland part of the town. Pettigo enjoys its two-world character and has not been slow to take full advantage of it as a tourist attraction, for the average human being never fails to be fascinated by the idea of smuggling, and here you can indulge in that activity by merely strolling across a roadway.

Since those days the customs advantage has tended to favour the North and, if Mrs Shaw had wanted to indulge in a little light smuggling, she could have flung a guide-rope from her back yard across the river and swung contraband ashore. Her demeanour suggests that she never did.

Pettigo has suffered less than other border towns in the troubles of the last twenty years, but the Northern customs hut across the river was blown up by a car bomb. The bomber tried to telephone a warning from Kilkenny, but could not get through until too late. No one was hurt, and by now Mrs Shaw has forgotten the incident.

Her mill-house is on the pilgrim trail from Pettigo to Lough Derg four miles away – the site of St Patrick's Purgatory. Here, says the tradition, in an island cave St Patrick kept vigil and was granted a glimpse of Purgatory. Since the twelfth century, even in penal times, pilgrims have braved bad weather, dangerous roads, highway robbery, to follow in the footsteps of St Patrick. Today, in easier times, about thirty thousand pilgrims gather annually between early June and mid-August to circumambulate the holy place on their knees and spend the night with their bellies empty. For nearly seventy years Mrs Shaw, a Church of Ireland Protestant, has watched Catholic crowds pass her door summer after summer. She must at least have felt outnumbered. Had it ever been a problem for her to be Protestant in Pettigo?

'Never. I never heard the words "Protestant" or "Roman Catholic", and I was brought up among them. And now nobody ever mentions anything like that to me and they all come in, all classes of children.' As, indeed, they do.

The night before we arrived to film Mrs Shaw, a relative had told her not to forget herself in front of the cameras. He could have saved his breath. Mrs Shaw knew exactly how far she was prepared to go. Needle-sharp when she chose to be, otherwise charmingly amnesiac, she withdrew her attention from anything that could waste her energy and let it rest on what pleased her. In that may lie one of the secrets of living to be almost a hundred.

'A very Protestant car they've given us,' observed Derek Bailey, the director of the film, at the Avis desk at Belfast Airport. It was a noticeably British make rather than the universal Ford that would have slid unremarked round the watery landscape of south Fermanagh on my first and his umpteenth border foray. When the Boundary Commissioners had toured the same area in the early twenties, they had been less self-effacing. According to the *Irish Times* of 19 December 1924: 'The car in which Mr Justice Feetham usually travels is a high-powered Crossley.' Dr O'Neill, the Dublin Commissioner, accompanied him in a 'great yellow touring car'. More modestly transported, we also cut less of a dash on our feet. 'The Chairman of the Commission,' said an eye-witness, 'is quite an adept mountain-climber and negotiated ditches and jumped dykes and bogholes with surprising ability.' Had he returned seventy-five years later he would have had, in addition, to negotiate cratered roads, bombed hotels, blocked windows, military scrutiny and twenty-five-mile detours to reach villages six miles away. Yet, left to flourish, the Fermanagh lakeland offers incomparable fishing, sailing, trekking or simply breathing in and out. Imagine the frustration of a tourist board that knows it has one of the richest assets in western Europe and yet cannot, hand on heart, swear that no one will try to spoil it.

In the meantime visits to Belleek, Garrison and Enniskillen are highly recommended. How else is anyone to grasp the anomaly that it is possible for borderers to be in an exposed situation, to bear the scars of twenty and more years of troubles and, at the same time, like spiders on broken webs, to return with little evident rancour to repair the gaps.

Rooney's Bar in Belleek serves an excellent cup of coffee. True, there are bullet marks in the wall outside and one through the window frame and up into the plaster. True, the old battery across the river in County Donegal has been a favourite perch of IRA gunmen looking for someone to pick off. When last I was there a group of British soldiers were coming down the main street in their usual formation, front man scanning roads and windows ahead, back man backing, middle men guarding the flanks. The corporal in charge, once past his unenthusiasm at seeing a film camera, told us that his lads called the right-angled bend in the road ahead 'Splat Corner', marking the spot where one of his company was 'splatted' from the battery. The detachment moved off by darting in scattered formation across the road and up an alleyway. At the same time, but on some different timescale, the gift shop sells fine photographs of Belleek Fair from the end of last century: crowded streets, livestock, farm produce, sideshows; and a committee has been set up to revive it again to catch summer visitors.

Alongside, there is new management at the Belleek Pottery, a magnificent mid-nineteenth-century palazzo of a place facing the river that separates North from South. As plans ripen, there will be a new visitors' complex – restaurant, showrooms, eye-catching displays of those flowery baskets, thatched cottages, shamrock fruit-bowls, winsome pottery pets and rustic swains that perpetuate an Irish never-never-land in the display cabinets of the world-wide Irish diaspora.

Jim Flanagan, born in Belleek, employed at the factory for thirty-six years, offers a less fond vision of local history. Belleek, he explained, has pre-Christian burial grounds. The Danes wintered there. The first battle of the Nine Years' War to save Ulster from anglicization was fought here on 14 October 1593. Long before Oliver

Cromwell, the Flanagan ancestors had worked the waterfront of Lough Melvin and Lough Erne around Garrison and Belleek. Cornered with a question about the border and his hopes for the future, his answer went: 'I'd rather see us all together, you know ... but I wouldn't take up a gun to bring it about. I guess it has to be a unity of hearts and minds because there's no square inch of territory worth anybody's life. That's my estimation.'

Half of Fermanagh is lakeland: Lower and Upper Lough Erne are navigable for fifty miles from Belleek in the west to near Belturbet in the east. Shortly after the lough narrows into a river and becomes the border between Fermanagh and County Cavan, its course is obstructed by a demolished bridge. Alongside it at Aghalane, near Derrylin, is a thatched farm, the home of Joan and Story Bullock.

The Bullocks are a well-respected Fermanagh family. A second cousin, Shan F. Bullock, wrote an extensive library of Fermanagh tales and novels including *The Loughsiders* (1924), which the Bullocks of Aghalane indeed are. When in the early 1970s Story Bullock found that his farmland was a salient in the I R A campaign against Loyalist forces in the North, he could not have been blamed for selling up. As a non-political, non-confrontational figure, he chose to stay. His wife had been a theatre sister at Belfast's Royal Victoria Hospital. She came to Aghalane when she married twenty-one years ago. Here she rusticated without rusting. As well as the farm work, she practises photography; notes and conserves animal and plant life; holds open house for musical relatives in County Monaghan who bring their instruments and play; and has shared with a local Catholic priest and a group of co-workers a Shell Award for planting a neglected crossroads not with Scottish Protestants but with grass and flowers. When film director John Huston was asked which faculty he would like to keep till last as he got older, he answered: 'My curiosity.' He and Joan Bullock both.

Until the early seventies the Bullocks could cross by bridge from their farm in Fermanagh to the rest of their land on the South side in County Cavan. The town of Belturbet was $2\frac{1}{2}$ miles further on. In 1972 the bridge was blown up, possibly by the army though the demolition crew were all shapes and sizes. A bailey bridge was thrown across the river as a stopgap, but that too exploded in the night, sending hot metal too close to the thatch for comfort. Now the journey by road to Belturbet is twelve miles. Two small boats are moored at the bottom of the garden for river crossings. An amorous Fermanagh bull, if the cows are in County Cavan, has to swim.

The Bullocks are not rapacious farmers. Story has been known to scythe round rather than through a clump of rare plants; and a walk with Joan along the riverbank is a botanical treasure hunt. In early May, the golden saxifrage covered the riverside. There were cuckooflowers, primroses and an uncommon buttercup, the goldilocks. The wood anemones had just finished and early purple orchids were starting to appear. A badger had left a barrow-load of earthworks on the path. On midsummer evenings, the woods attract the rare purple hairstreak butterfly.

A few hundred yards away, past the willows and the Scotch pine is the former house of Bullock cousins Thomas and Emily. On 21 September 1973, Joan and Emily had been shopping. As they stepped from the car, Emily noticed that they were being watched by men in another car. 'They'll know me the next time they see me,' Emily remarked and she and Joan went their separate ways. At about six o'clock that evening, the men called at the house. It appears that Emily tried to shield Tommy. They were both shot. Tommy had been a member of the Ulster Defence Regiment.

The Story Bullocks have bought the house but have not yet had the resources to restore it. 'I'm optimistic,' said Joan Bullock. 'There's really very few who are responsible for the trouble here. Most of the people are fine.' And with that we threaded our way through the thicket and the marsh-grass, the orchids and the buttercups, back to the farm. At the end of the filming, when all who had been working together (a ragbag of Catholics, Protestants and Don't Knows) were asked which person in the whole trip had impressed them most, the vote went to Joan Bullock.

Aghadrumsee church, about two miles from the border near Roslea in Fermanagh, sits on a hilltop next to an Orange Hall. Edwy Kille, originally from Minehead, has been rector for fifteen years. Skirting the gravel path round to the church door are the graves of his parishioners killed for being Protestant, or for owning the land, or for being members of the Royal Ulster Constabulary or the Ulster Defence Regiment, or out of sheer meanness of spirit during the worst of the troubles of the seventies. Though there was at least a remission in the violence during the early eighties, some interior clock stopped when those murders were committed and, though life goes on and often with good humour, no amount of winding, tapping and shaking seems able to get it started again. Inside the church is a lectern presented by the children of John McVitty, an RUC reservist shot on his tractor as recently as July 1986. His twelve-year-old son was seated alongside him and lives to remember.

At our first meetings with the rector and some of his parishioners,

The grave of John McVitty at Aghadrumsee Church in County Fermanagh

we were met with something like hostility. Mr Kille gave us our time slot and, at the end of half an hour, the interview was over. We had grown accustomed to (even overfaced by) tea and cake and wheaten bread in neat kitchens with the little red bulbs flicking away under Sacred Heart pictures and photographs of Padre Pio tucked behind the clock. But there was no tea at Sunshine Rectory on that first visit. However hard we signalled that we were individuals – a director, a researcher, a presenter – assembled to do a specific job, we were seen as 'the media'; and 'the media' had been responsible for ignoring and misrepresenting the plight of border Protestants in south Fermanagh. The rector hesitated to use the word 'genocide' to describe the IRA campaign to pick off the only sons of Protestant farmers, but he was enraged that, in its fervour for what it wrongly perceived as the underdog, the BBC in particular should duck its responsibilities.

In took three visits to convince the rector of Aghadrumsee that we were willing to listen, and three visits for us to start to appreciate the courage, warm-heartedness and radical piety of the man we were listening to. He was not in his preacher mode as he proposed Jesus Christ as the only force that could transfigure the politics of the border (and start stopped clocks). He was just saying something he would die for.

Down the hill from the church live two of Edwy Kille's parishioners – Ernie and May Madill. Ernie is a retired R U C officer who risked his life pulling a tanked-up passer-by (a Catholic, as it happens) from the site of a suspected car bomb. The bomb exploded: the passer-by had a shattered ankle; Ernie lost half a leg. In 1975 he received the Queen's Gallantry Medal. He has now pulled back on selfless exploits and concentrates on protecting his bungalow and his wife and family. *Glasnost* is not so far advanced in south Fermanagh that Ernie Madill will own up to the precautions he takes, but they certainly include a gun at the ready.

'It sounds a bit like a Western,' I chanced.

'Well,' he volunteered, 'the country is a sort of Western now.... Take for instance, down in Belfast.... It's worse than the Wild West was. In Wild West times you had to do something before a man shot you. Now you have to do nothing.'

So why doesn't he sell up and leave?

'If I was going to leave I'd leave when I like, but I'm not going to let anyone drive me out.' How far, I asked May Madill, would they have to move away from the border to feel safe?

Her reply: 'I just couldn't give you an answer. There are some all-Protestant towns, but the I R A go in there with bombs and shoot people. Actually, you're not safe any place.'

And the reason?

'Because you can't mind-read.'

To the Madills, the border separates two traditions, two separate identities. Where I might have wished, for their sakes, that the red, white and blue markings on the kerbstone down by the main road would weather away, the Madill impulse would be to give them a lick of paint and wait to see how chicken-hearted the security forces would be in defending them. The Madills' is a defiant stance. Not for them ecumenical initiatives, cross-cultural interplay. 'The Republic is the Republic; we are us. You can't mix oil and water.' And as the border is perceived as moving northwards, appropriate action is to do what Noah did and build an Ark.

Douglas Deering did not build an Ark. He ran a business in Roslea, five miles down the road from the Madills' bungalow. He was a Plymouth Brother, an apolitical figure, but he was shot through the head in his shop in 1977. With him died the last Protestant business in Roslea. His widow sold their two-storey house to the church. It is now Sunshine Rectory and Edwy Kille lives in it.

After this catalogue of outrage, I was scared to go into Roslea. Eyes flicking up and down the street, I all but backed into the pub and found a corner from which to watch the clients. The landlady seemed relaxed and friendly. The coffee and sandwiches were fresh and generous. Bit by bit I withdrew the ghastly projections I had thrown over everything and blinked my way back into the daylight. A dog was eating a dead cat in the road. The keeper of a motor accessory shop talked about working in England. A sixteen-year-old boy on a bicycle said the British army sometimes hassled him. Two women helping each other across the road directed me to the next place I needed to be. The murders are real; the fear is real; the dog is real. Roslea is an awful place; Roslea is a perfectly ordinary border village. Roslea may not be a problem to itself, but to me, wanting the picture to settle, it is a splitting headache.

For light relief I found myself fantasizing solutions to the Anglo-Irish problem in general. It is too late for Prince Charles to marry the Spanish Infanta. What about the making of F A T – the Federation of Atlantic Tribes – with Scotia run from Glasgow, Mercia from Sheffield, Anglia from Hemel Hempstead, Gallia from Aberystwyth, Hibernia from Dublin, Nova Scotia II from Belfast; cultural exchanges, profits shared equally, foreign policy and coinage in common? Then, when the words 'Fatties go home' appear scrawled on the walls of Marbella, all of us, Scots, English, Irish, Welsh can gather at the duty-free (except that after 1992 there won't be any) and rubbish the Spaniards.

There is a linearity about the Irish *Frontiers* film, symbolized by the little silver Vauxhall Astra which bumps over 'sleeping policemen', stops for the British army or the Irish customs, and connects farmland, bogland, lake, mountain on a single thread. Only once in the forward planning did we envisage stopping and seriously taking stock. The site would be Hilton Park, a generous border mansion in the South near Clones in County Monaghan, where Johnny and Lucy Madden live. One of Johnny's forbears bought the house in 1743. He and Lucy farm, garden, cook, take in discriminating guests. The income just about keeps the heart of the house alive and, if it increased, could spread to the inevitable dilapidations at the extremes. Lucy came to Hilton Park from England eighteen years ago. I can see that on the narrowest interpretation of what it is to be Irish (that is, utterly Catholic, Gaelic, aboriginal, unmixed with Dane, Norman, Anglo-Saxon, Scot) not just Johnny Madden but a large proportion of his fellow countrymen would have to hand back their passports. But, over the millennia, Ireland has absorbed old marauders, old overloads, old guest-workers, old immigrants, old refugees and felt the benefit. Johnny Madden, you sense, is poised between these two perceptions of being Irish – one narrow, one generous – and is throwing his weight whole-heartedly, fingers crossed, towards the second.

At Hilton Park we planned an in-house version of *Any Questions*. There would be a dinner party that would spill over into a filmed discussion. The Maddens would be hosts. I would be resident alien. Variegated guests would throw light on the border through either living on it or otherwise knowing about it.

Any Questions, as it turned out, boiled down to just one question and it was not about the border. It was about Irishness. Who truly are the Irish? When I tried, in pursuit of the film, to ask questions about the border, no particular emotions were stirred; though I learned about the follies, annoyances and irrelevance of the border, as seen from the South. When we opted to forget we were making a film and let the discussion shape up as it wanted to, feelings started to rise, hurts to show, and the evening circulated round the thorny question of nationality like a dog pawing at a hedgehog.

The bad news for Johnny Madden was that, though the proud bearer of an Irish passport, an Irish name and an Irish history, he could pass for an Englishman in England and a European in Europe, and that single fact seemed to make him, in some eyes, less than Irish. He was outraged. The bad news for one or two of his guests was he could be outraged at what they saw as self-evident. They were crestfallen. The bad news for me was that I, by proxy, was somehow at the root of the problem: it was, according to one of the guests, English colonial ambitions that had caused the Irish to resort to guerrilla wars, sometimes with bomb and bullet, sometimes with words at a dinner table. I should have been crestfallen too. The reverse happened. 'At last,' I thought, 'they're dropping the charm, the geniality, the roguishness and saying what they really think.'

To travel on the tip of an Irish boot is a prime way to reach south Armagh and the end of the border. It is an area dominated by British army watchtowers in a neo-Norman attempt to keep an eye on the activities of the local population. The mythology of the towers – quite apart from what they actually achieve – is extensive and gothic. From them the British are credited with being able to tell in which pocket a man carries his keys and what lovers say in bed. Rays from the towers are thought to cause deformities in livestock and debilitating sicknesses in human beings. Only cattle bred to withstand the close attentions of helicopters can be guaranteed not to panic and maim themselves. In a bugged room conspirators have been known to run a bath to scramble the surveillance system. Over a whole landscape, no one can reach the tap; and to judge by the

Above The border crossing in the divided village of Pettigo, looking towards the South of Ireland
Below A familiar sight on country roads near the border – concrete blocks and rusty iron bars
Overleaf Army lookout post on the south Armagh border

Crossmaglen in
County Armagh, the
southernmost town
in Northern Ireland.
In this strongly
Republican area the
British army is much
resented.

Like Ireland, Cyprus is a divided island, split in two by national and religious rivalries.

Right Turkish Cypriots celebrate the establishment of separate republic in the north of the island in November 1983.

Below The Greek flag flies over a Greek Cypriot guard post overlooking the UN buffer zone in Nicosia.

Top Greek Cypriots outside a bar in Limassol, the second town in Cyprus and the main port, on the southern coast of the island.

Above The Turkish quarter in Nicosia. Both Greek and Turkish Cypriots have their capital in the divided city.

fearless local criticism of the British army presence in a vastly Republican area, no one seems to want to. The British, in the meantime, are in a 'heads you win, tails I lose' bind. If they throw the watchtowers open to guided tours and allow choc ices to melt over the technology to prove how feeble it really is, they forfeit their propaganda advantage. If they maintain the mystique of the watchtowers, they fuel a hostility that hinders what they are there to do.

Most of the English who reach south Armagh these days are soldiers. English civilians ordering a pint at Paddy's Bar in Cross-maglen have to prove that they are not military in mufti before they are served. Torn between fellow feeling and a wish for the army not to have to be there, I did what everybody else had to do: waited at checkpoints, crawled past armed cars, tried to hit on the right body language to reassure someone a third my age who is pointing a gun at me. Not once over six months of meeting them on the border was a British soldier anything but friendly. But then, I am not eighteen, my name is not Seamus, I do not have a slept-in leather jacket, Irish mother and an Irish accent.

Crossmaglen is not in itself the end of the border, but it is another sort of terminus. It is the southernmost town in the southernmost part of Northern Ireland. The border sags south like a sling and, if the sling is to have a stone, Crossmaglen qualifies. It is assembled round a fine market square that dates from the thirty years either side of 1800, except that the army have transformed the RUC barracks on one side into a fortress with a helicopter pad. After the report of a lightning flight to Crossmaglen by Mrs Thatcher, a Fleet Street reporter telephoned Paddy's Bar and, knowing that Paddy Short, proprietor since 1947, is a local oracle, asked him for a reaction.

'She hasn't been in Paddy's Bar,' he replied. 'So she hasn't been.'

Crossmaglen sits in poor farming land and never excited the envy of great landlords. Usefully neglected, it developed a strain of independence and has never learnt to tug its forelock. The independence has been omnidirectional. It shocked Eamon de Valera in 1918 when he campaigned in Crossmaglen on behalf of Sinn Fein and was all but assassinated for his pains. It inspired local men to enrol on the British side in the First World War in such numbers that (according to Cardinal O'Fiaich in a television interview) Crossmaglen in those days was not considered to be an Irish town at all. Now it turns against what it sees as a British army of occupation. That, in a nutshell, is a version of the Paddy Short view of Cross-maglen and its history. The other view – the one presumably held by Merlyn Rees when he dubbed south Armagh 'bandit country' – is not much heard in Paddy's Bar.

It was about this point in the journey, when Newry came into view and the easterly end of the border on the Carlingford Lough, that I proposed a novel ending to the film. Instead of lamely driving to the sea and parking, wasn't there some way of using the frustration, anger, sadness, disbelief, puzzlement, shame and fatigue that had accumulated over six months to fuel an entirely spontaneous lift-off from a high hill? Something like the end of the Prophet Elijah but minus the divine chariot and plus the splintering sound of an English observer cracking up. How does a chameleon feel when it wanders over a viciously flowery tablecloth? Does it try to do justice to all the shapes and colours? Does it switch to black and white? Does it explode? Who would be so rash as to gaze at an appendectomy scar and try to work out from that small length of flesh and cross-stitch the history, destiny, state of health, job prospects, psychological quirks of the rest of the organism? To look at the border, you have to stand away, away, and ask big questions. What are the problems of being an island that is a highway to the Atlantic and to nowhere else? What are the problems of having an Ice Age that could have produced coal but produced bog and peat instead? What are the problems of being Hibernia, the eldest unmarried daughter of a tyrannical, colonizing father who needs her, neglects her, will not let her go, cannot keep her, even when she shouts into his deaf ear: 'But I'm not even your daughter.' Murders have been committed for less.

In the upshot the lift-off idea was abandoned and I did as I was told – drove dutifully to the last customs hut on the Carlingford Lough and, in the fading light, said my bit into the camera:

> It's odd to think that, as an English stranger, I may in a sense have more to do with the Irish border than an Irish resident. It was a Westminster government in the early twenties that put a cordon round the Six Counties and called them Northern Ireland. It was an English initiative three and a half centuries earlier that, like the house that Jack built, made the claim, that settled the land, that caused the grief, that split the folk, that led to the call for a border.
>
> Short of wearing sandwich boards to tell passers-by that, though English, I am a well-wisher, I cannot think how to duck my English heritage. Even then, I'm still from England. When, on my side of the water, viewers, listeners and readers block out, switch off, the news from Northern

Ireland – which they surely do – it is a sign not of indifference but of raw, puzzled, helpless involvement. Family
involvement. Plus the fact that the news from the border
is always about the troubles and never about the lack of
troubles. And, in that respect, I suppose part of the trouble
is the likes of me.

It happens that I have enjoyed myself in Ireland and
should like to come back. But what brought me here in
the first place was the border – this (what would you call
it?) this oddity, this alarm system, farce, eyesore, red-
white-and-blue tide-mark. Now, duty done, border
described, film written, perhaps my pennyworth towards
the ending of the troubles would be to imagine how we all
look from central Europe or South America or the hole in
the ozone layer. Two offshore islands, in the same weather
system, surrounded by the same polluted sea, under the
same greenhouse if the poison gases go on rising and the
same fall-out if a reactor explodes. But still, at our worst,
as blind and tribal as our ancestors chipping flint. What
a waste.

CHRISTOPHER HITCHENS

THE ISLAND STRANDED IN TIME

Cyprus

I HAVE BEEN as a journalist to Panmunjom in Korea where the parallel divides north and south. I have been across Checkpoint Charlie and back. I have been to the Allenby Bridge on the River Jordan, and to Derry. But the 'green line' as it runs through Nicosia still strikes me as the rawest wound inflicted by a century of partition. Unlike Panmunjom, it runs through houses and streets in an arbitrary and violent manner. Unlike Checkpoint Charlie (I began writing this in the days of 'The Wall'), it cannot be crossed by citizens of the country it divides.

In years of visiting the island, I had never succeeded in securing the three permissions – Greek, Turkish and UN – necessary to visit the 'buffer zone'. I had seen what any journalist and diplomat can see, which is the one checkpoint in Cyprus at which the line may be crossed. It is called the Ledra, after the lovely Ledra Palace Hotel which used to magnetize correspondents from all over the Levant and at the bar of which much journalistic lore had been woven. Now, slightly pitted with bullet holes, it serves as the barracks for the UN and sits astride a stretch of heavily guarded roadway. To either side of this runs a sort of moat, which follows the outline of the city's old Venetian walls and is now fringed with a modern litter of sandbags, oildrums and barbed wire. At regular intervals firing emplacements and lookout posts punctuate this rather forbidding scene.

But until we filmed there, I had not appreciated the depth and extent of the 'dead zone', as the Greek side calls it. Whole streets, with empty houses and shuttered shops, are enclosed within this no-man's-land. The Olympus Hotel, once the jewel of the red light

Christopher Hitchens with UN soldiers in the buffer zone in the centre of Nicosia

district, stands lifeless and forlorn. A huge underground car park and showroom, once owned by prosperous Armenians, is still crammed with 1974 model vehicles, canopied in dust. A sad café, its windows broken, still has the tables and chairs standing as they were left, but now serving only a family of cats. Schools, gardens, public lavatories, fine old balconies, new offices, discreet restaurants – all given over to nothingness. Only the U N can walk along the streets, but every few yards they come across either a Greek or a Turkish Cypriot guard post, and at some points these are close enough for the opposing soldiers to see each other's faces. Irregular shooting and shouting incidents have, after fifteen years, persuaded the U N that these posts should be further apart. In June 1989 some of them were 'de-manned', which means that the flags still fly but the guns do not bristle and that the risk of an accidental conflagration is slightly reduced. This is the only adjustment the petrified line has undergone since 1974. East and west of the capital, from end to end of the island, guard posts sit baking in the heat, flying flags at one another exactly as before.

Cyprus is the third largest island in the Mediterranean after Sicily and Sardinia, and is located at the eastern end of it, north of Egypt and within a few miles of the Syrian/Israeli/Lebanese coast. This geographical position has made it a focus of interest for stronger powers throughout its history. Settled by Achaean and Mycenaean Greeks two thousand years before Christ, the island led an existence quite separate from the Greek mainland, coming under Egyptian, Assyrian, Persian and Roman rule. It was later governed by the Lusignans during the Crusader period, became part of the Venetian Empire and was then wrested from Venice by the Turks in the late sixteenth century. The Turkish Cypriot minority dates from the three hundred years of Turkish imperial government.

In the later stages of Ottoman domination, the Greek-speaking majority (which also kept the Greek Orthodox faith) began to rebel. Its leaders were generally bishops, two of whom were hanged by the Turks for showing sympathy with the 1821 Greek revolution that brought independence to the mainland. In 1878 the island was ceded by Turkey to Britain, as part of an agreement by which Disraeli allied with the Sultan of Turkey against imperial Russia. It took its place in the chain of British possessions that stretched along the route through Suez to India.

In the 1930s the Greek majority again raised the demand that they be allowed to join the island politically to Greece. British troops had to put down one serious revolt, and different constitutional arrangements were mooted, all of which fell short of this maximal claim. After the Second World War, the logic of decolonization was not applied to the island because of its crucial position as British strategic headquarters for the Middle East. A guerrilla war began, demanding *enosis* or union with Greece, and was bitterly fought between 1955 and 1960. In the course of this conflict, Turkey made it unmistakably plain that she would never allow the island to become part of Greece. The demand for the return of Cyprus to Turkey was made, and a Turkish guerrilla force was set up to prosecute this claim.

Faced with the dissolution of their authority, the British convened three-party talks on a compromise, and in 1960 the island was granted limited independence and self-government. The religious leader of the nationalist revolt, Archbishop Makarios, became the first Greek-speaking head of government in the island since antiquity, in return for his renunciation of the once-holy idea of *enosis*. The Turkish minority were awarded a permanent vice-presidency and various entrenched clauses in the constitution as well as numerous vetoes over legislation. The British were given land to use as bases, and Greece and Turkey were allowed to station contingents there.

Four years after independence, political differences between the Greek and Turkish Cypriots erupted into armed conflict. The Greeks demanded amendments to the constitution to remove the Turkish minority veto, and the Turks called for a fifty-fifty partition of the island between the two communities. The British government convened several unsuccessful meetings between the two sides, and eventually President Makarios invited the United Nations to station peace-keeping forces in Cyprus, which have been present since 1964. An uneasy truce descended, punctuated by occasional inter-communal blood-letting.

The situation became more grave in 1967, when an extremist group of officers seized power in Greece itself. Committed to a highly nationalist ideology, they sought to add Cyprus to their dominion and campaigned unceasingly against Makarios for his abandonment of the goal of *enosis*. This in turn put the Turks and Turkish Cypriots into a mood of intransigence. Meanwhile American foreign policy, which had replaced that of Britain as the dominant one in the region, evolved in favour of splitting the island between Greece and Turkey – a proposal which was anathema to the Greek majority.

After seven years of extreme tension during which the international aspect of the problem outweighed the internal one, a major crisis erupted in July 1974. Using its influence over the Greek Cypriot national guard, the Greek junta instigated a coup against the Makarios government; it failed to kill Makarios himself, but drove him into exile and installed in his place Nicos Sampson, a notorious Greek Cypriot extremist and former gunman. This coup was the signal for a major Turkish landing on the north coast of Cyprus, which took place after the British government had turned down a Turkish offer to intervene jointly under the terms of the 1960 Treaty.

Frantic negotiations at Geneva and Vienna were cut short by a second Turkish incursion, which pushed southwards and occupied almost one third of the island, driving tens of thousands of Greek Cypriots before it. The junta in Athens had by then collapsed under the pressure of events, taking its Cypriot partner along with it, and Makarios returned to the divided island to resume the presidency.

The Turkish authorities demanded that all Turkish Cypriots be moved to the north, where they still held many Greek Cypriots under occupation. In the course of 1975, a reluctant 'exchange of populations' was completed.

Since then there has been a political stalemate, with protracted United Nations mediation having so far failed to make any progress towards reunification or federation. Increasingly the Turkish Cypriot leadership has gone its own way, proclaiming a separate state in the north in 1983 and conducting business under the protection of a large Turkish mainland garrison. The new state in the north is recognized only by Turkey and has so far met with no success in its quest for international recognition.

President Makarios died in 1977 and was replaced by his deputy Spyros Kyprianou. In 1988 Kyprianou was defeated at the polls by George Vassiliou, who pledged to reopen negotiations for a federal solution that would place Cyprus under one government, with territorial and constitutional guarantees for the minority and the withdrawal of all foreign troops. The long-standing Turkish Cypriot leader, Mr Rauf Denktash, continues at the time of writing to attend the negotiations but holds firmly to the view that the Turkish Cypriots must be treated as equals on a fifty-fifty basis, and not as a minority. The gap between the two positions remains extremely wide, and has imposed a great coolness on relations between Greece and Turkey proper.

While many frontiers represent a single instance of a multiple phenomenon, the line that runs through the island of Cyprus is a sort of multiple example of a familiar problem. It is a line of separation between the Greek and Turkish Cypriot communities, who represent respectively about 80 and 20 per cent of the population. It is a line of demarcation between both Greece and Turkey, who each maintain forces on the island in a state of readiness, and is thus the only frontier 'within' NATO. Armies of the same alliance are pointing weapons at each other here, and in 1974 actually employed them to a deadly effect. Moreover, as Cyprus moves closer to full membership of the EC, and as the Turkish application is considered more closely, the possibility arises that the Cypriot 'green line' (originally named for the green crayon with which a British officer sketched a rough demarcation on a hastily requisitioned map) will become an anomaly within the political economy as well as within the military balance of western Europe. Everywhere else, the borders and barriers are coming down, and the movement of people and goods is unrestrained. In Cyprus, the barriers are hardening. Many Greek Cypriots made a point of telling us with bitterness that their passports would soon enable them to live and work and settle anywhere in western Europe except in the towns and villages where they were born, and where they are not even allowed a visit.

Right above The heavily-shelled Presidential Palace after the coup which ousted Makarios in July 1974

Right below Makarios on his return from exile in December 1974

At the eastern end of the island, the frontier joins another frontier; the one that marks the outer limit of the British sovereign base at Dhekelia. One hundred square miles of Cyprus actually belong to the United Kingdom, not as part of a lease or agreement but in the same sense as the Isle of Wight belongs to it. Since Britain gained this military concession as part of the price of conceding independence in 1960, many Cypriots feel that the territory was extorted from them at a time of their maximum weakness. Here you can see roads called

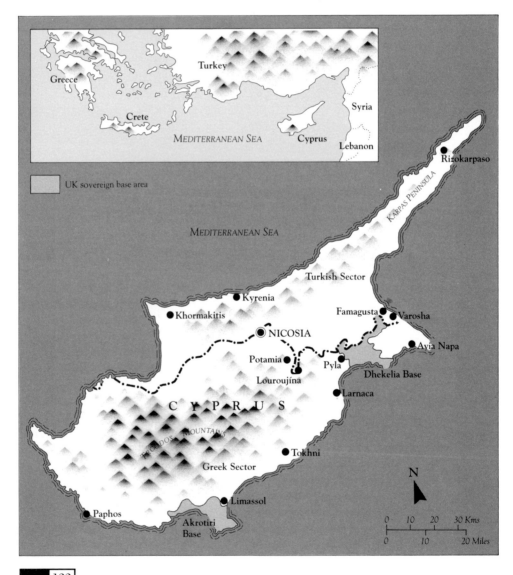

Nelson Way and Waterloo Drive, and fall victim to British traffic laws if you transgress. Cyprus in this sense marks the last 'frontier', apart from Hong Kong, between the former British Empire and its former subjects.

In case you think that's enough frontiers, you have also to consider the geopolitical position of Cyprus as a whole. Since the collapse of Beirut as an open society, and the waning of the Western presence in Lebanon, Cyprus has become 'the front line state' between the West and the Middle East. Most of the press corps has moved here from Beirut to take advantage of the excellent communications offered in the Republic, and a large number of heavily staffed embassies testify to the importance of the island as a listening post and point of contact. The same point is made in different ways by the large number of Lebanese refugees who have moved here; by the small but active Maronite Christian minority that has been here for centuries; by the fact that Cyprus is the only member of the non-aligned movement to maintain full diplomatic relations with Israel and the PLO; and by the existence of the old walled city of Famagusta, scene of *Othello*, which for many years was maintained by the Crusaders in some splendour as the nearest Christian city to the Holy Land. (Today, Famagusta has a different distinction. The new city, named Varosha by the Greeks, is the only empty town in Europe. It has been a ghost city since 1974 and stands, with its vacant hotels and housing projects and streets, as the most striking reminder of the terrific force with which the island was torn in two in 1974.)

Finally, there is the invisible partition – the one that runs through the mind. No visitor to the island can fail to be struck at the role played by memory and history here. Greeks and Turks speak of the events of 1963 or 1974 as if they were yesterday, and keep up a lively and intense combat of rival interpretations. Although there is a Cypriot consciousness to be found on both sides of the line, the tendency to speak generically of how 'the Greeks did this' or 'the Turks did that' is also very pronounced. The two communities celebrate different national holidays, teach different histories, honour different national flags – mainland Greek and Turkish as well as local Cypriot – and, though they are secular in temper, profess different faiths. (Yet another frontier here is between Christianity and Islam, as well as between the inheritance of Byzantium and the inheritance of the Ottomans.)

In this context of multi-faceted division, the term 'United Nations' strikes a rather hollow chord. Yet the Republic of Cyprus was in effect created by the UN in 1960, as a compromise between the idea of *enosis* and *taksim* (partition, with the northern sector going to

Turkey). The plus side of the agreement on an independent republic was that Britain, Greece and Turkey all bound themselves by treaty to uphold the territorial integrity and the constitution of the new state. The minus aspect was that all three – at Turkish stipulation – also reserved themselves the right to intervene unilaterally. The Treaty of Guarantee in effect licensed the war of 1974. Since 1964 the UN has maintained a large policing force on the island, with its main contingents drawn from 'neutral' countries such as Canada and Austria. After Namibia and Palestine, the issue of Cyprus is the oldest unresolved problem on the official international agenda.

The UN occupies a physical position which perfectly illustrates both the consistencies and the anomalies of the partition line. Its headquarters are just outside Nicosia, and include the vast tract of the old international airport, now a cameraman's dream with its echoing, empty terminal and its huge, lonely expanse of runway. This is where the fighting stopped in August 1974, and the moment is frozen in time with a bullet-riddled Cyprus Airways plane parked forlornly on the runway.

Life of a sort goes on within this dreary landscape of the buffer zone around the line. Some of it is a symptom of eternal human nature – the Canadian soldiers told us that Greek and Turkish guards, bored in the blistering heat, covertly exchange drugs for pornography. Some of it is even sadder: we met another Canadian whose job it was to go out and shoot the rabid wild dogs which live on the uncollected and unsupervised garbage. Some of it is reminiscent of those who grow vines on the slopes of Etna or Vesuvius. At the village of Louroujina, a Turkish enclave situated within a kink in the line, the villagers still cultivate their fields under the eyes of watching soldiers, and pursue laborious compensation claims through soldiers of three countries under the UN flag. When we visited the village it wore an air of torpor and abandonment. The young people, we were told, like so many Turkish Cypriots, had chosen the option of emigration. There is something about the buffer zone and its dead ground that blights the areas that touch it.

As you get further away, it is possible to forget the division for as much as an hour at a time. Cyprus is rich in beaches and resorts, and every year receives more tourists than it has citizens. The Greeks have an entrepreneurial edge here, and more experience in the holiday business (the 'green line' is also a border between modern, soph-isticated salesmanship and more backward and impoverished con-ditions). But the Turks are catching up despite the fact that their airport is not internationally recognized and the fact that most of

UN peace-keeping force patrolling the 'green line' in Nicosia in 1964

their hotels were confiscated from Greeks and are on a Cyprus
government boycott list; this case has been pressed as far as the
House of Lords in an effort to limit tourist use of 'stolen' Greek-
owned property. But sit for any length of time in a café and you will
find, if you talk to Cypriots, that the border is never far away. One
person in three, for one thing, is a displaced person and no longer
lives in, or is permitted even to see, the town where he or she was
born.

Sense of place is not something peculiar to Cyprus of course, but

125

it is felt here to an extraordinarily refined degree. Time and again while we were filming we faced the difficulty of conveying to a British audience the attachment felt by Cypriots to ancestral villages, lands, farms, orchards and homes. The nearest short encapsulation I can come up with is from the writing of G. B. Pusey, an English wanderer who came to Cyprus more or less by accident in the 1920s and stayed for good, founding a newspaper in the process. He referred to 'the pull of the Cyprus earth'. We illustrated this pull by convening a meeting of Greeks who had not seen their home town of Zodhia for fifteen years. They met us at their club, the Zodhia Club, in Nicosia, and brought maps, photographs and memories. Every one of them felt uprooted and almost foreign, even though they were living among their fellow countrymen a few miles away from the original village. After protracted negotiations, we received permission from the Turks to cross the line and film Zodhia as it is today. When we returned to the club with our video and some Polaroid and still shots, there was unfeigned and prolonged excitement, often expressed in terms of woe and outrage. The new inhabitants, said the Zodhia folk, did not love and care for the place as they had. Look at the lovely church, its cross knocked off the spire, converted into a mosque. Look at the buildings which needed a lick of paint. Look at the lifeless streets and the fact that no new building had been done. There was a positive growl from the company when we showed them the old Greek high school with its Doric façade, and a huge bust of Kemal Atatürk placed in front of it. It was a wound right in the heart. No propaganda could possibly counterfeit this demonstration of feeling.

The Turkish Cypriots also long for their lost homes and mosques, but their emphasis is different. In many cases, their memory of the old days is one of fear, and is less encumbered therefore with nostalgia. At the village of Tashkent in the Turkish-occupied area, we found dozens of Turkish Cypriot women who said that they were surviving widows of the village of Tokhni, in the south. In 1974, they said, all their able-bodied menfolk had been rounded up by Greek Cypriot extremists and marched away, never to be seen again.

Visiting Tokhni for ourselves, we found Greek villagers who confirmed this. They were ashamed, they said, of this blot on their history. The deed had been done by the ultra-rightist supporters of General Grivas, who were at the time in revolt against the constitutional government of Archbishop Makarios and who had killed Greeks as well. (The military junta then ruling Greece was arming and training an underground group, known as E O K A–B in order to suggest its descent from the original E O K A which fought against the British. Its commander was the same in both cases – General George Grivas, a Cypriot-born ultra-nationalist and rightist. It was an open letter from President Makarios to the Greek mainland government, denouncing their sponsorship of EOKA–B and its attempts on his own life, that precipitated the Greek-sponsored coup against him in July 1974.) I shall not easily forget the moment when a black Mercedes pulled up outside the coffee shop in Tokhni, and the owner told us quite casually that its driver was one of the men suspected of carrying out the massacre. The camera was fortunately loaded, but it was awkward to step out into the sunshine and ask the man if he would mind answering a few questions. He came straight to the point, however, telling us loudly that the Turkish Cypriots were not really human and that Cyprus should be united with Greece. In his car, as our brave Greek Cypriot researcher and translator pointed out swiftly, was a medallion bearing the face of General Grivas. (We were extremely fortunate, in several weeks of filming very sensitive scenes, to have on our team a woman from each Cypriot community neither of whom flinched from asking awkward questions of their 'own' side.) We were able to get a debate going in the Tokhni coffee shop over the village's deadly secret, and to show photographs of a place that had become hateful to them to the villagers of Tashkent. This was more than mere 'balance'. It showed the intense, localized reality of the Cyprus problem through the voices and narratives of its inhabitants.

To set against the stories of revenge and dispossession, we also found numerous instances of co-operation and even solidarity. Yannis Kleanthou, the former keeper of Kyrenia Castle, told us of a period of terrifying imprisonment after the Turkish invasion, but also made a point of saying that he and others had been saved from the firing squad by the intervention of a Turkish Cypriot. He boldly told the camera that he would go back to Kyrenia and live under a Turkish administration as long as it was made up of Cypriots and not of invaders from the mainland. Mr Savvas Prastitis, a jovial Nicosia clothier, told us that he still sends clients to his old friend Mr Osman, a Turkish tailor on the other side. In the nature of things, these recommendations can now only be made to diplomats and UN officers (and to me, who commissioned a very fine Greek-Turkish suit in this fashion), but the connection still holds and when Mr Osman's granddaughter was so ill that she was given permission by the Greek Cypriot authorities to cross under UN auspices to be treated at the better-equipped hospital on the Greek side, Mr Prastitis was on hand to help.

These kinds of tales, naturally enough, are only told by the older generation. The teenagers of Cyprus today have never met a member of the other community unless it is (as it quite often is) in London, where there is a friendly symbiosis. We even met young conscripts in the National Guard who would testify to that, some of them in impeccable North London accents. But generally, the Greek Cypriot accusation of an 'apartheid' system is not much exaggerated. The segregation by community is nearly complete, and though it is justified by the Turks in the name of 'security' one is forced to wonder if it is not laying up trouble for the future.

Where there is still co-habitation, there is not much by way of co-existence. In the panhandle of the island's north-eastern peninsula, in the town of Rizokarpaso, some hundreds of Greek Cypriots still live. They were bypassed by the fighting of 1974 owing to their geographical position, and although the rest of the Karpas peninsula was rapidly cleared of Greeks after the fighting had stopped, the United Nations was able to stop the Turks from evicting all the original inhabitants. Every week, convoys go from UN headquarters to the town, taking food and mail and medical supplies, and one day we went with them. We spoke to the Greek schoolteacher, who was torn between four different courses of action and who perfectly illustrated the Cyprus tragedy at its personal level. First, she said, this was the village of her ancestors who had cared for its land and passed it on through generations. But second, it was now under strict Turkish occupation and she no longer felt safe or wanted. Third, she had four children and the Turks had broken their promise to allow secondary schooling in the town, so they had to leave for the south at the age of eleven and a half or give up their chances of an education. Fourth, she was one of only two teachers and if she exercised the option of leaving to join her own children she would be abandoning the other little ones in her care. It seemed an unbearable dilemma, made no easier by the unfriendly questioning to which she was subjected by the Turkish police for having talked to us. What was clear, and melancholy, was that no matter what she decided the Greek population of Rizokarpaso would soon die out. This would mean that the whole northern swathe of the island, which bears the imprint of Hellenic civilization since at least two millennia before Christ, would cease to hear Greek spoken. This cultural aspect of the problem is what troubles many Greeks the most, and is also what troubles international bodies like UNESCO who have expressed repeated concern about the looting and neglect of the Greek and Byzantine heritage in the north. We saw numerous examples of fine churches left open to the elements, or standing in disrepair, or turned

UN-manned border post at Rizokarpaso on the Karpas peninsula

into mosques, or even in extreme cases into pens for animals.

A Turkish Cypriot wishing to return to his home is faced in theory with no opposition from the Greek authorities. The law allows him or her to reclaim any abandoned property and to hold a passport from the Republic of Cyprus with all the rights of citizenship. Not many Turks have exercised this option, but we did speak to some who had returned and found that their circumstances were often far from ideal. One had had quite a tussle to get his home back (admittedly, it had been occupied by Greek refugees at a time of acute housing shortage) but also told us that the police paid him too much attention and that he could not get permission to make a civil marriage with an Englishwoman. None the less, he was able to display his Turkish name proudly on the front of his butcher's shop, which occupied a prime site on the Limassol corniche. He could at least put the authorities to the test of their word – an opportunity for which Greek Cypriots would be grateful, if Mr Denktash's word was not the repeated statement that Greeks and Turks can no longer live side by side.

In the two remaining villages where they *do* live side by side, quite different traditions are at work, both of them strong in Cyprus. One is the leftist and the other is the commercial. Cyprus has an extremely strong Communist Party, which stands for inter-communal co-operation at any rate on paper, and a smaller but very activist Socialist Party. In the village of Potamia, not far from Nicosia, the radical tradition has been durable enough to keep a community of Turkish Cypriots in place; relics of a time when there was bi-communal party and union membership.

Further away, on the verge of the buffer zone at Dhekelia, stands the anomalous village of Pyla, with Greek and Turkish coffee shops facing each other guardedly across a hot square that is invigilated by Swedish policemen of the U N. The business of Pyla is business – it is a smuggling zone where customs duty can be easily evaded, and where allegedly 'designer' goods and cartons of cigarettes can be bought cheaply. Lately, the Greek Cypriot police have been 'discouraging' visits to the village; but life there has a way of going on, and even as we were interviewing the Greek head-man of the place a Turk came up to him and asked in fluent Greek for help in acquiring a passport so that he could go abroad and bring back an imported car. Certain Levantine transactions take more than a mere civil conflict to stop.

Finally, on a building site near the resort town of Ayia Napa, we found a foreman who employed hundreds of Turkish Cypriots in the booming and labour-hungry construction business. The Turks crossed through the British bases every morning and returned every evening, having made twice the wage they would make in the Turkish-occupied area. We talked discreetly to the workforce, which was fifty-fifty Greek and Turkish, and found that they were members of the same union, were paid the same, conversed either in Greek or in English (the *lingua franca* of the island) and had never had a quarrel or an incident amongst them. This wasn't typical enough to be encouraging, and we were urged not to identify any of the Turks since on the last occasion this had occurred the workers concerned had gone home one night and not shown up again the next morning.

Microcosms are hard to create in Cyprus in any event, because both communities consider themselves to be the minority. The Turks are the minority on the island, although they have made spirited attempts to alter this situation since the invasion of 1974 by importing perhaps fifty thousand settlers from mainland Anatolia and some thirty thousand soldiers as a garrison. (These figures may be on the high side, but the repeated 'no comment' on settlers from the Turkish authorities is designed to encourage speculation, and leading Turkish Cypriot opposition politicians have spoken of the native inhabitants being 'swamped' by colonists.)

By taking these two steps – the military and the settler invasions –

Turkish troops in the ancient walled town of Kyrenia in northern Cyprus

the Turks have confirmed the Greeks in the view that *they* are the real minority, situated on a small, vulnerable island under the shadow of Anatolia. Since the island was part of the Turkish empire until 1878, it has always been difficult for the Greeks to see the Turks as just a numerical minority. They tend to regard them instead as the wedge used by Turkey to regain its old position as the master of Cyprus. Students of Northern Ireland, Israel–Palestine or Sri Lanka will already know how toxic and bedevilling a confrontation of the 'double minority' sort can be, and how psychologically acute is the mutual conviction that each community is faced with extinction or

131

elimination. This is all you need to know in order to understand the repeated failure of the U N to bring about anything even approaching a rapprochement, despite the current examples of successful meditation in such stubborn cases as Angola, Afghanistan and Central America.

Mainland Turkey's deliberate effort to alter the demographic composition of the island has led to more than a vast increase in the ancestral fears of the Greeks, and to more than bad blood between Cypriot Turks and mainland Turks. (In his newspaper *Halkin Sesi*, the prominent Turkish Cypriot leader Dr Fazil Kutchuk published a series of articles saying that the new arrivals were bringing crime and drugs and political extremism to the island; these are the very complaints one hears from the average Turkish Cypriot, who considers the island to be culturally more advanced than the mainland.) It raises the question of whether there can really be two independent states on one island with a total population of less than one million, and it raises the spectre of another round of military confrontation. The worst-case prospectus reads like this.

The majority of Greek Cypriots have evolved away from the simplistic and romantic idea of *enosis*, and have in fact created an economy far more prosperous and modern than that of Greece. They are prepared in the main to concede that the past cannot be undone, and that the Turkish Cypriots wish to run their own show. This acceptance is grudging but real. It stops at the point when the Turks wish to annex some part of Cyprus in perpetuity. A Turkish canton, under mainland Turkish protection, could be sold to the Greek Cypriot electorate. Over time, its border might erode under the human pressure of trade, cultural exchange, tourism and other informal influences. It would also stop short of an outright declaration that Cyprus had been partitioned. But the proclamation of a separate *state*, as made by Mr Denktash in 1983, is another matter. This state uses mainland Turkish money, has mainland Turkish soldiers, breathes with the same economic and political lungs as Ankara and is, as Turkish Prime Minister Turgut Ozal incautiously said on a recent visit, in every way 'like a province of Turkey'. This enormously adds to the Greek fear, put to us with urgency by the acting President, Dr Vassos Lyssarides, that Turkey wishes in the long term to bring the whole island into its orbit. This in turn may lead in the future to a revival of *enosis*-type nationalism – the very thing that Turkey ostensibly intervened to prevent. Given that Greece has stated, repeatedly, that it would regard a further incursion in Cyprus as a *casus belli*, and given the humiliation that Greeks and Greek Cypriots feel at the crushing defeat they endured in 1974, the situation is potentially much more combustible than it looks from the languorous beaches and mountains on any one of the succession of impossibly hot and beautiful days that the island supplies to its guests.

That, at any rate, is a summary of the forebodings that an enquiring visitor may uncover. Certainly, Turkey has reiterated that it, too, would regard any move to *enosis* as a *casus belli*. The paradox, then, is that the apparent common sense of a two-state solution (one each, what could be more reasonable?) has enfolded within itself some highly destabilizing potentialities.

These things are hard to capture on film, as is the general atmosphere of military preparedness that prevails on the island. Few of us had ever been to such a camera-shy place. At any distance from anything remotely describable as a military or security zone, there is a rash of 'No photography' signs. At different times, we were detained or obstructed from filming by the Greek Cypriot National Guard, the Turkish police, a Danish UN post, an Austrian UN officer and a Canadian UN contingent, as well as by the British military police in the sovereign base areas – which, incidentally, were the only parts of the island in which we were forbidden to film at all. In each and every case, all we desired to film was a straight representation of the status quo, in a country which is subjected to more aerial reconnaissance and satellite photography than almost any other. The business of securing multiple and interlocking permissions for the simplest activities, in what is claimed to be an open society, gave us a slight insight into the desperate intransigence and repetition which have befallen more complicated Cypriot negotiations.

The fact that this is a very small and intimate society, which is the reason why almost everybody knows everybody else by their first name, which in turn is the reason why complex permits can always be negotiated or cajoled in the end, is also what lends Cyprus some of its dramatic tone. I have already mentioned that people have long memories and a strong attachment to place, and it is also true that they tend to have extended families. It is very difficult to find someone, therefore, who is not at least related to someone else who is an illustration of the island's conflicts. Nowhere is this more true than in the case of one of the great emotional subjects – the missing persons.

In the summer of 1974, a large number of Greek Cypriots disappeared. There was a great deal of violence and confusion at the time, and it is not possible to say with certainty what happened to many of them (the number is just under two thousand) in the context of a civil war between Greeks and an invasion from Turkey. However, a number were positively identified by photographs and by solid independent testimony as having been in Turkish military custody when last seen. By analogy or extension, this is presumed of many more whose fate is unguessed-at.

Accusations have been made that the Greek side keeps the issue alive for the purpose of propaganda; and it is said, further, that the Turks also have missing people. The first accusation would not, I think, easily survive a visit to the refugee village of Ayios Athanasius, just above Limassol on the south coast, where a number of survivors and relatives of the missing are concentrated in the same place. One can become hardened to stories of grief and bereavement, and think that one has learned to detect the false note, but the interview we conducted there was nothing if not genuine and unfeigned. A woman who has lost four male relatives, and who last saw her husband alive but as a prisoner, does not readily abandon hope or tire of telling the story. Artifice and propaganda are beside the point. The widows of Tokhni, gathered in the village of Tashkent, likewise need no prompting. Reporters and cameramen know when they are being 'got at'. At one point, we wanted to object when a Turkish man proposed to speak of a mass grave (he being the sole survivor) in front of his children. He looked at us surprised: the little ones, he said, had heard the story many times already.

We did not find that this sort of thing had any cheapening effect. It comes naturally to Cypriots to stick together, to keep things in the family and to take the past seriously. There was a classical edge to some of the stories, as if justice itself could not be served or even contemplated until these rites had been completed. Yet every now and then, one could see a slight embarrassment on the faces of the professional press officers employed by either side. And I believe we all stiffened a bit when told by Dr Kenan Atakol, foreign affairs spokesman for the Turkish Cypriots, that two dozen 'missing' Greek Cypriot prisoners had in fact been shot 'while trying to escape'.

It was not just a desire to vary the diet of rival Greek and Turkish claims that led us to the flourishing miniature world of the Cypriot minorities. Their story, too, is part of the fabric of the island's society, and they were able to tell us a good deal about the consequences of its bisection.

In a curve of the 'green line' just by the Ledra Palace checkpoint lies a cluster of churches and sites which helps to alleviate the simplistic picture. We called first on the Roman Catholic church, which boasts an American priest who has also in his time doubled as Papal ambassador on the island. Attached to the Franciscan Order in the Holy Land, he has served more than one tour of duty in Cyprus and was offering mass in 1974 when bullets began to chip away at his church. He showed us the pock-marks that still bore witness, adding with some aplomb that the windows in his church were safely high up in the walls and that the service had gone on. His quarters were surrounded on three sides by the Turks, which meant that he could not open one of his main doors – it had been used once by a worshipper to cross between north and south with her baby. But he still received parishioners by the main entrance, which was guarded by stolid soldiers of the Canadian U N contingent.

Further along the same road one reaches the Maronite quarter, which features a large church and a couple of clubs adorned with the cedar of Lebanon and portraits of the Lebanese Christian political leadership. The Maronite Archbishop of Cyprus, a humorous and shrewd man, is named Gemayel and is a member of the famous Lebanese Christian political clan of the same name. He proudly showed us his collection of icons, and talked of the many centuries during which the Maronite community had prospered in the island. They came to Cyprus from Lebanon in the twelfth century, in the first instance to avoid persecution, and adopted the Greek language while keeping their own distinct ritual. Unhappily, he reported, the congregation has now been divided. Most had joined the exodus to the south during the 1974 hostilities, and those who remained in the Turkish sector were finding it difficult to hold on to their land and property in the face of age and other kinds of attrition. He himself was able to journey north to offer the sacrament, but of his flock only those with relatives on the other side were permitted to make the journey. As with the Greeks of Rizokarpaso, the enemy was time, as the traditional village populations declined and were not replenished.

We were able to confirm this for ourselves when visiting the ancient Maronite village of Khormakitis, on the north-western tip of the island, a few days later. All those to whom we spoke mentioned the decline in population, and most of those we saw were well advanced in years. Khormakitis is distinguished by being an area with Aramaic words in its local dialect (which is principally Greek). This, say the believers, is the very language in which Jesus of Nazareth preached. Archbishop Gemayel was able to recite for us a few staves of the

Overleaf Demonstration by Women Walk Home in March 1989 crossing the 'green line' into Turkish territory. The movement is working for the withdrawal of Turkish troops and settlers, and for equal rights for all in a federated, reunited island. A few months later, on the anniversary of the Turkish invasion, a more militant break-away group of Greek Cypriot women, some carrying Greek flags, entered the buffer zone in Nicosia.

mass in Aramaic, and to show us a service book written in the same tongue. It will be sad if his population of some five to six thousand people is allowed to do this only in one half of the island.

The same point is registered in a different way by the Anglicans, who lead a relatively untroubled life in both halves. Long used to being laughed at as 'The Ancient Brits' for their decorous retirement homes on the Kyrenia coast, many English residents endured a good deal during the fighting of 1974, and their attention to their neighbours did not disgrace the British reputation for fortitude under bombardment. (It was perhaps to win them over that the Turkish Cypriot authorities recently took the rather bizarre decision to issue a special commemorative stamp for the wedding of Prince Andrew and Sarah Ferguson – a philatelic curiosity which has adorned many a letter or card home to the United Kingdom.) English retirees living in the north before the division are allowed to cross the border and avail themselves of the better-provisioned and more efficient Greek Republic, even to the extent of flying in and out of Larnaca airport. But they complain humorously about having to change their number plates at the Ledra Palace checkpoint in order to do so; about having to give friends overseas a mainland Turkish address in order to receive mail and circumvent the unrecognized Turkish Cypriot postal system; and about the hazardous fact that Turkish cars have steering wheels on the left while Cyprus traffic still drives on the left – making overtaking a near-impossibility. (This anomaly, like so many others, is about to be solved in the north by the adoption of Turkish law and custom and of right-hand drive.)

The difficulties faced by these minority groups, who are mostly composed of well-established citizens with the capacity to support one another, paled a little by comparison with one unrepresentative fellow whom we met. He was a Kurd from Turkey, drawn to Cyprus by promises of a better life. A hairdresser by trade, he had found that the streets of Turkish Nicosia were not by any means paved with gold. He had been evicted from one lodging, and had suffered from the general dislike and suspicion which the mainland settlers have aroused among the native Cypriot Turks. He had decided to move into one of the fine but dilapidated old houses that abut the 'green line' and have been going to waste these many years. With no encouragement or help from the authorities he had set about the work of refurbishment, even though his garden door opened on to the buffer zone and he was forbidden to use it as an exit, or as an entrance, or as an access for his children to play. Moreover, he told us, the title deed of the property was held by an Armenian (most of the Cypriot Armenians were pushed on to the Greek side, or fled

there, during the vicious inter-communal fighting in 1963) and thus
if there was a settlement he would be asked to move again. On the
other hand, he wanted a settlement because he saw no point in
continued friction between the two main communities, or indeed
within them. To be a Kurdish refugee living in an abandoned Armenian house on the border between Greek and Turkish Cypriots is to
have experienced a little of the twentieth century.

A familiar cliché about countries riven by civil war, and a cliché to
which reporters have frequent resort, is the contrast between natural
and human beauty and the consequences of violence. This is often
remarked in such places as Lebanon, Palestine and South Africa. I
had been coming to Cyprus for nearly a decade and a half, while for
most of our team the experience was a new one, so I had the chance
to see it again, as it were, through their eyes. They fell for the same
things that I had – the exquisite tradition of courtesy and hospitality
to strangers, expressed often in what English people find to be
embarrassing generosity on the part of those with limited means; the
extremely democratic and informal manners of the place. Then the
extraordinary scenery: the Crusader castles of the Pentadactylos
range; the arresting splendour of the abbey at Bellapais; the cool
magnificence of the Gothic cathedrals – long since adorned by min-
arets and turned into mosques – in Nicosia and Famagusta. Something about the pace and the texture of life seemed to be, for want
of a better word, civilized. Yet so often in the rear of a club or a
coffee shop were the rows of photographs on the wall, showing the
'martyrs' of this or that village or community. And it took only a
polite enquiry to unburden an encyclopaedia of ancient grievances,
enhanced if anything by the small and intricate scale to which the
island's society is used. Not everything miniature is attractive, and
the mentality of the village feud can be very ugly when it sees it has
attracted the attention of the world.

Yet it would be arrogant for outsiders to tell the Cypriots to let
bygones be bygones. At every step of our filming and questioning
we came upon the influence of outside powers, many of whom had
employed the passions of the village feud for their own purposes.
Even though there is no animosity against British people, we found
we were often blamed for using 'divide and rule' tactics during the
guerrilla wars of the 1950s (The British had, for example, made a
point of using Turkish policemen against the Greek revolt, and
had encouraged the mainland Turkish government to step in as a
counterweight to Greek majority demands.) The influence of the
fallen Greek junta was everywhere to be seen even at this late date,

with faded slogans and emblems still painted on church walls, calling for *enosis* and a holy struggle against the Turks. A Turkish Cypriot officer told us that above a certain rank in the armed forces of the north, every senior officer is a mainland Turk, and certainly the hand of Ankara is not difficult to detect as one goes about the Turkish sector. Osker Ozgur, the main Turkish Cypriot opposition leader, told us plainly that he fears the annexation of the north of Cyprus by Turkey and said that the Turkish Cypriot community is being 'dissolved like sugar in water'. An observant film crew a few years before us had filmed United States U-2 flights taking off from the British sovereign base airfields. To ask the Cypriots to accept all responsibility for the grievous state of their island seemed patronizing, even if the hardest thing to record on film is the discreet influence of foreign powers on a strategically positioned bit of real estate.

In the course of our last few days in Cyprus, there occurred the fifteenth anniversary of the 1974 invasion. Nothing could better illustrate the depth and extent of the division than the way that the two communities chose to mark the occasion. On the Turkish side there was a large military parade, with exhibition parachute drops and columns of tanks. The slogan of the day was *Sukran*, the Turkish word for gratitude and an offering of thanks to the delivering Turkish army. Though the crowds were small, they were single-minded.

On the Greek side there were a series of solemn commemorations, all mourning the loss of northern Cyprus and all stressing the right of Greek Cypriots to return to their homes. On the evening before 20 July, the day when the Turkish army set its first boot on the Kyrenia coast, a large posse of unarmed Greek and Greek Cypriot women pushed their way across the 'green line' in Nicosia and penetrated the buffer zone. Several of them were arrested by the Turks and taken to prison, which led to an increase in the intensity of the demonstration. At the checkpoint a large crowd of Turkish Cypriots gathered, waving Turkish flags and banners denouncing the women as 'stooges'. Within hours, that sector of the buffer zone had become a microcosm of the inter-communal confrontation, with Greek loudspeakers playing the music of Theodorakis and Turkish equipment blasting martial airs. The Greek women waved not only the olive branch and the flag of Cyprus (which has the olive branch as its central motif), but the flag of mainland Greece. A double line of United Nations soldiers, Canadian and British, faced both ways along the barbed wire and there was life in the shuttered, empty, bullet-pitted streets that we had filmed in all their desolation a few days before.

Chatting to civilians, one found nothing even remotely resembling a meeting of minds. The Greek women had slogans in Greek and English but made no appeal in Turkish. They also displayed icons and emblems stressing the primacy of the Orthodox Church, and were led in the first instance by two Greek Orthodox priests who managed to get themselves arrested also. They looked very brave and determined as they faced the troops of the UN and, behind them, a phalanx of Turkish policemen and commandos. But to the Turkish Cypriot in the street they seemed a threat; a reminder that the Greeks do not accept the legitimacy of the Turkish 'state'. One could find no trace of sympathy for them or their tactics; only a repetition of ancient wrongs suffered by the minority.

The deepest and widest line of division, as I wrote earlier, is the one that runs through the mind. For Greeks of all parties and persuasions, and for the non-Turkish minorities on the island, it makes no sense to have two state systems on an island this size. Nor will it ever seem anything less than outrageous and humiliating that a third of the Greek population has been evicted from a third of the territory of Cyprus. The innumerable difficulties and anomalies of crossing the line, even with a British passport, a press card, an escort and all the other amenities, give one a third-hand sense of how bitter that might feel. For the Turkish Cypriots, or at least for the strategic majority of them, everything is resolved by the one word 'security' and the need to have a defined and protected area of their own. There are Greeks who are willing to concede that this mentality is understandable, but not if it means the alienation in perpetuity of a third of Cyprus and its gradual absorption by Turkey.

How does the future look? For the generation that remembers the fighting of 1963 and 1974, experience has been a rough teacher. On both sides, it is accepted with some reluctance that reality does not permit maximalist demands and that compromise on the ground is mandated. For the generation now growing to adulthood, that has no memory either of inter-communal strife or of inter-communal co-existence, things can often be made to look simpler. The appearance of a permanent divide to the contrary, then, it is a safe bet that the Cyprus problem will stay on the international agenda for a considerable time, and that it will continue to be a source of friction and recrimination as well as of political and military insecurity.

NIGEL HAMILTON

THE PRICE OF INDEPENDENCE

Finland–USSR

*U*NDER A CLOUDLESS SKY, a small, dark green patrol boat skates across the placid water. Describing a great arc, it surges past a series of yellow, pencil-like buoys lolling at different angles. We are at Virolahti in the Gulf of Finland. On the shore, the greenness of the land is bewitching, dense forest blanketing the horizon in spiky jade. We seem to be making for a white triangle, borne by a tripod of old telegraph poles. It is nine o'clock. Apart from the calling of the seabirds over the marshes there is, once the lieutenant cuts the engine, no sound. A few granite boulders show above the reeds, like pink birthmarks.

The lieutenant, his blond hair cropped short and wearing cotton camouflage fatigues, points to the right.

'Over there,' he says without emotion, 'is the Soviet Union.'

He swings his arm to the left.

'To the west is Finland.'

At first I can see no difference. But as we disembark and make our way across the marshy ground to the white triangle, two coloured posts come into view, each about eight feet high, like giant liquorice sticks. The one is painted in wedges of white and blue, the other in dark green and red, with a copper disc near the top, bearing, in relief, a hammer, sickle and the letters C C P.

These posts stand fifteen feet apart. Between them, beneath the great tripod, is a small white stone bearing the numeral 1 over 1. The lieutenant explains. This is post number one, of section number one, of a border which runs north between these strange liquorice sticks for nearly a thousand miles, from the Gulf of Finland to the

RAJAVYÖHYKE
PÄÄSY ILMAN LUPAA KIELLETTY

GRÄNSZON
TILLTRÄDE UTAN TILLSTÅND FÖRBJUDET

GRENZEZONE
EINTRITT OHNE ERLAUBNIS VERBOTEN

FRONTIER ZONE
NO ENTRY WITHOUT SPECIAL PERMIT

ZONE FRONTIÈRE
ENTRÉE INTERDITE SANS AUTORISATION

Nigel Hamilton at the border at Virtaniemi in northern Finland

north of Lapland, just short of the Arctic Ocean.

I had somehow expected to see a high fence of electrified wire. Instead there is simply a narrow chasm in the forest with walls of pine and fir trees on either side, perhaps a hundred feet tall. The ground, carpeted in rough grass, berry leaves and bracken, is soft and still wet with dew, for the sun has yet to penetrate this strange arbour separating two nations, two worlds. The silence is eerie. Focusing my camera, I am aware I am the first civilian authorized to take this photograph in fifty years.

Why? What is so secret about this border that it has been hidden from the eyes of the world for so long?

On the horizon, in the cleft between opposing forests, I see heads bobbing suddenly. The figures, well camouflaged against the green of the foliage, seem to dance around two further liquorice sticks in the distance, then move, five abreast, towards us. As they get closer

I can see slight differences in their clothes. Three are dressed in fatigues like the young lieutenant beside me, their tunics unbelted and some sort of winged insignia above the right breast-pocket. The other two uniforms are paler, more pastel green. They have leather belts around the waist and across the shoulder, also their forage caps are flatter, and have earflaps folded over the top. On their open collars are baize-green tabs, each tab bearing a small bronze badge with the Soviet hammer and sickle.

The sight of the two Russian officers amid the group of Finnish soldiers causes a certain *frisson*, yet in themselves the Russians do not look frightening. Whereas the Finnish major stands well over six feet tall, with a weather-beaten, rectangular face and jutting nose – a Viking face, with firm, blue eyes – the two Russians are short, rotund, rather overweight in fact, with small, round faces. The Russian captain has a drooping, insignificant sort of moustache and a protruding lower lip; his colleague – a major – is clean-shaven, the exposed soft flesh of his open-necked field blouse giving him a slightly babyish look.

The Finnish major seems pleased; he is thirsty and looking forward to a cool drink now that the main work is done. And the work? By agreement, he explains, delegates from both sides must carry out an inspection once a year to see that the eight-hundred-mile border is 'properly maintained'. They have now completed the first, southern-most section.

I am fascinated by this. How can a small Western, democratic country like Finland, with only four million inhabitants, 'properly maintain' a land frontier of such inordinate length with a Communist neighbour like the Soviet Union, whose population exceeds 286 million? How have two such different systems existed side by side since 1918 – and how do they co-exist today?

The major, thinking of imminent refreshment, briefly recounts the terms of the 1948 treaty between the two nations, signed after the Second World War and regularly extended. He then explains the sort of maintenance he means: the clearing of any obstructions – trees, branches, shrubs, debris or whatever – that might interrupt a clear demarcation of the border from the Gulf of Finland to the north of Lapland, or impede the proper policing of the same.

In single file we then leave the liquorice sticks and follow a path through the forest, till we reach the table at which the two parties will sign the certificate of annual inspection. Both table and benches are made of massive pine logs, sliced clean through the middle, the yellow wood-grain punctuated by an occasional polished knot. Beside this stands a tiny hut, the size of a kennel, in which fish are smoked,

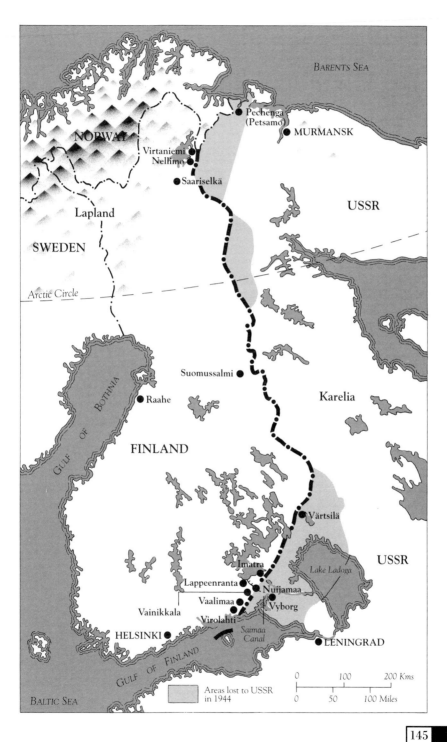

BARENTS SEA

NORWAY

Pechenga
(Petsamo)

MURMANSK

Virtaniemi
Nellimo

Saariselkä

USSR

Lapland

SWEDEN

Arctic Circle

Suomussalmi

Karelia

Raahe

FINLAND

Värtsilä

USSR

Imatra

Lake Ladoga

Lappeenranta

Nuijamaa

Vaalimaa

Vyborg

Vainikkala

Virolahti

HELSINKI

Saimaa
Canal

LENINGRAD

GULF OF FINLAND

GULF OF BOTHNIA

Areas lost to USSR
in 1944

BALTIC SEA

0   100   200 Kms

0   50   100 Miles

and a nearby cabin where they will have a sauna. The conversation is very jolly. The only thing that disturbs the friendly image of this, the Frontier of Peace as the Finns call it, is a hundred-foot-high steel watchtower rising ominously above us, with massive steel restraining cables cemented into the rock.

Although my wife is Finnish and we have a summer home in eastern Finland, the actual frontier between Finland and the Soviet Union was a revelation to me. After months of parleying between Helsinki and Moscow, permission had been given for me not only to visit but to film the border – for the first time since the Second World War. *Glasnost*, the new openness, had extended to Russia's very border with the West. How much they would really reveal remained to be seen.

The first great revelation came on the Finnish side of the border, however: for although I have spent the summer in Finland for the past thirteen years, I had never suspected the existence of what is called the Finnish frontier zone – a 2–$2\frac{1}{2}$-mile-deep buffer zone running the entire length of the border from the Baltic Sea to the northern tip of Lapland, ruled by the Finnish frontier guard and in which there are a series of special, indeed unique, laws which visitors and residents alike must obey.

Residents? Again, despite the many years I had been holidaying in Finland, I had not suspected the existence of a population that must live in a special Finnish zone, subject to special laws that must be unique in Europe, if not the world. I had of course heard the word 'Finlandization' – meaning the puppetization of a neighbouring state without needing to occupy it – but had always considered it to be a misleading description of a country that not only enjoys one of the highest standards of living in the world, but is in many ways a model of democracy and freedom. Only when I visited the border and got to know its long-kept secrets did I begin to acknowledge the truth of the term.

The Finnish frontier zone had not appeared on any motoring map I had ever seen. To meet some of its residents I had first to obtain a permit from the Finnish security police in Helsinki: this is the rule for any foreigner who wishes to enter the area, anywhere along its 1289-kilometre length. Even a Finn has to obtain written permission to enter, from the local police station; and this is the source of much unpublicized ill-will in Finland, as I found once I talked to residents in the Värtsilä region.

The Finnish frontier guard warrant officer who accompanied me was genial enough, but even he was embarrassed when I asked him

Finnish border guard

to recite the laws and regulations which operate in the zone. A huge yellow sign by the roadside warned us that we were entering a forbidden area in which civilians may not light a match, shine a torch, throw away a newspaper, use binoculars, take a photograph or *even raise their voices*! The warrant officer shrugged when I asked him why – and blushed when I asked him whether this was still sovereign Finnish territory – for these rules are clearly designed to placate Big Brother next door, across the border.

   In this Finnish no-man's-land, the 'maintenance of peaceful conditions and irreproachable order' is the imperative: an absolute injunction against doing anything that might upset or merit the reproaches of the mighty neighbour, under whose dreaded shadow Finland has had to live for over a thousand years – first as a colony of Sweden, then as a subject people of the Tsar, and finally, from 1918 to the present day, as an independent state. The penalty for transgression is either a fine or 'imprisonment for a maximum of two years'.

Two years in jail for shining a torch, or raising your voice – in your own country! I asked Pekka Kunnas, a young farmer whose house stands on a hill only four hundred yards from the frontier, what it was like to live under such a strange system, with the armed border guard of his own nation watching him night and day to see that he never infringed these strange regulations, so unknown to most people like myself in the West. He smiled. For his father, from whom he had inherited the farm, it had been a different matter. For him, it was a fact of life with which he had grown up. The most irksome aspect, he said, was that he was not allowed to use his rifle or his shotgun on his own property to kill vermin or animals eating his crops. I asked what sort of animals.

We were in Pekka's *tupa* or living room: the traditional kitchen-cum-dining and sitting room of old Finnish houses. He pointed to the glass cabinet lining the wall. Inside, a huge Russian bear stared back at us!

'I shot it three years ago,' Pekka recounted, smoothing his lank blond hair, his clear blue eyes alight with pride. 'It used to come across the border each night, eat its fill, then go back. As long as it stayed in the Finnish frontier zone I couldn't do anything – I couldn't even shout at it! One day it went too far – into Finland proper. I was ready.'

He patted the trophy affectionately. The nuisance of the zone, with its long list of don'ts, is something he's learned to live with.

Pekka's wife is less assenting. The Finnish summer is short and idyllic, but the police will not allow her brothers to stay with her on the farm with their wives and families, for the wives are Norwegian. Since Norway's own border with the Soviet Union takes over in northern Lapland, where the Finnish border ends, this seems incredible. But so it is.

Just across the lake from Pekka Kunnas's farm live the Löytyonens, an elderly couple whose small farm was bisected by the new frontier which Stalin dictated at the end of the Second World War. Stalin's advisers told him that the Värtsilä steelworks would be very useful to the Russians; when drawing the line of the new border on the peace treaty map, the story goes, Stalin left his thumb over the town of Värtsilä – forcing the line to swing around it. Eero Löytyonen's house was left on the eastern side of the new border, and he had to watch the Russians burn it, as well as razing the church and churchyard where his parents are buried.

To Eero and his wife the Finnish frontier zone is a scandal. 'This is *Finnish* soil!' he states emphatically. '*My* soil! Why do I need a permit to live here? And can you imagine what it is like when even the taxi driver needs a permit to collect us? Or in winter the oil tank runs out – and they cannot deliver more heating oil till the driver gets a permit to enter the zone. Why, even the doctor would have to get a permit to come here!'

'It's like being in prison!' his wife chimes in.

I asked if they blamed the Russians for this.

'Not the Russians!' they protest. 'It is the Finnish government that has made this zone!'

And this seems to be the case: that in order to make sure no one on the Finnish side of the frontier in any way irritates the Russian bear – which might become angry – it was decided to create this two-and-a-half-mile-deep buffer zone, with its host of restrictions on ordinary human liberties.

Although the Löytyonens blame the Finnish government and frontier guards for their prisoner-like status, the guards I met cannot be reproached. Without exception they seem friendly and well-disposed – indeed it was largely their efforts that secured Soviet agreement to this first-ever filming of the border, including the strange way in which the two sides still communicate with each other in the late twentieth century.

This time-honoured protocol I found puzzling. It was demonstrated for us at Nuijama, one of the two main road crossings on the border: a sort of Checkpoint Charlie for the hundreds of lorries, buses, trucks and private cars that go over each day.

To communicate with one another, the two sides do not use a telephone or radio. Instead they employ flags: a blue flag for the Finns, a red flag for the Russians. Raised on a short pole on one side, it will in due course be answered by the raising of a flag on the other. This indicates that the originating side has a written message from one border delegate to his opposite number on the other. It was in this way that our proposal to film the border had been conveyed and answered.

It seemed very antiquated – frighteningly so if one thinks of emergencies such as Chernobyl. But the senior Finnish officer assured us they clung to such methods deliberately. Slowing down communication can also slow down Big Brother's demands.

This may well be so. But what sort of demands does Big Brother make, apart from insisting the Finns keep 'irreproachable order' on their side of the border?

Major Bak, the Russian border delegate for the Vyborg area, had a Korean-looking face and a row of medals. His khaki uniform looked tailor-made and his broad, flat officer's cap with its dark green band gave him an imposing dignity not matched by the Finnish forage caps and grey-blue battledress uniforms. Major Bak and his interpreter accompanied us everywhere along the border to see that we observed the special agreement reached over our filming. He would smile, chat, smoke and watch as we were shown Finnish patrols at work in boats across the lakes, sniffer dogs working along the border trail, or the big railway crossing at Vainikkala; but neither he nor the Finns would divulge the true secret of this border for the past forty years, since Finland made peace with Russia in 1944: the real reason no one is allowed to film or photograph the border.

At the top of a Finnish watchtower at Nuijama I finally put the question that had been nagging me as I conversed with the armed patrols or listened to the Finnish sergeant explaining to me the tracker skills of his Alsatian, Serro – a dog that can walk twenty-five miles on patrol, but is only 'useful' for just over six, since his ability to smell 'anything out of the ordinary' then deserts him. Major Autio, the chief of staff to the commander-in-chief of the Finnish frontier guard, had looked very dapper in his English tweed jacket in Helsinki. Here, at the top of the forbidding watchtower, he looked younger than his years: more ill-at-ease. Gingerly, I started by asking him the purpose of such a watchtower.

'This kind of watchtower, it's one way of controlling this border area. It's one way of fulfilling our tasks at the border, the tasks of the Finnish frontier guard.'

I asked him how he saw those tasks.

'I think our tasks are very important for the Finnish government, and to take care of our politics too.'

'What do you mean by that? Are you trying to stop people from crossing the border?'

Major Autio looked very uncomfortable. It was very hot – almost 30° Celsius – and he had a plane to catch back to Helsinki.

'We want to maintain a good peace at the border,' he answered, 'and in this way to help our politics by keeping the Finnish zone calm, and stop any interferences.'

One by one we catalogued the restrictions that operate in the zone.

'The idea is that you don't want to irritate this big neighbour with its huge manpower and armies?'

'Yes.'

'Is that the idea?'

'I think so. This bilateral agreement we made after the war was

specially made to limit the possibilities for these kinds of interferences, to make them as small as possible.'

'What happens if you catch somebody actually crossing the
border?'

The major smiled. We had come to the heart of the matter.

'We catch him first and we examine him, who he is, where he is
coming from and where is the exact place the border was crossed.
And after that – '

'What do you do then?'

'We deliver him to the Finnish police.'

'You give him to the police? You don't send him immediately
back over the border?'

'No, no,' Major Autio protested.

'Never?'

'Never!'

'And roughly how many would you catch trying to cross the border
in a year?'

Major Autio stammered. 'Er-the-the number is very small, very
small.'

'Is that because you are very efficient in guarding the border?' I
asked. 'Or because your neighbour is very efficient?'

He laughed. 'I think *we* are very efficient and *they* are very efficient.
But the most important thing is that not very many people even try
to cross the border illegally. We have many crossing points where
you can go legally across the border. It's no more any problem to
anybody.'

Problem or not, the purpose of the Finnish frontier guard, with
its patrols and dogs, was clearly to prevent illegal crossings, was it
not?

'Of course,' Major Autio responded. 'It's our main task. To control
the border in order to stop this kind of illegal crossing – and catch
people who have done it.'

For a moment I felt like a Red Cross official visiting the com-
mandant of a working concentration camp – only, in this case, the
Finnish officer seemed to be doing the Russians' job for them. It
reminded me of a joke I'd heard about a US senator visiting the
Finnish–Soviet border, and asking the Finnish officer if it was a
difficult job to guard such a long border – Russia's longest with the
West. 'No,' said the Finn with surprising honesty. 'We are both
facing the same way!'

The major had to rush to catch his plane, but the film crew and I
remained in the nearby town of Lappeenranta, and it was there a

few days later, through Amnesty International, that I met Georgi Ivanov – a Russian defector who had managed to cross the border illegally some years before. Ironically, he had crossed beneath the very tower where I had interviewed Major Autio, as I discovered when Georgi showed me the spot where he remembered coming over. It was the first time he had ever been back, and he was clearly nervous as we stumbled through the forest undergrowth.

'I came from over there,' he said, pointing to the east, across the border. 'I crossed the little pond and went towards this house. I kept very low to the ground because I was afraid they might see me ... then I crossed that field and went behind the houses on to the big road in the direction of Lappeenranta – but very carefully so as not to be seen either from the tower or by the guards on the road.'

I asked how difficult it had been to get through the Russian border zone.

'In this area it is some twelve miles wide,' he explained. It starts at Vyborg, and then goes all the way to the Finnish border. There are three large fences, electrified, and there are ploughed strips, and many Russian guards with dogs patrolling them. It's a very difficult border to cross. One has to be lucky to cross it without being seen. I was simply lucky.'

Georgi's luck, which enabled him to escape from Russia, soon ran out, however – in the so-called free and independent, democratic Western state of Finland.

'Just after I crossed the border I found myself on the main road. After all the hardship I'd suffered in the Soviet Union – for I'd tried to escape once before – after all that lack of freedom, I finally felt like a human being. It was a very good feeling.'

Having walked the few miles to Lauritsala, a nearby town, he tried to take the train to Helsinki and his destination: the American embassy. At the sight of his roubles the booking clerk at the railway station rang the police – and Georgi was taken by car to the capital. Not to the American embassy, however, but to the Security Police headquarters, where he was interrogated for a week, without access to a lawyer or even to a telephone, and was ultimately taken back to the Finnish frontier guard near Lappeenranta – who, after a similar flag-heralded parley with the Soviet border officials to the one we had witnessed, handed him back.

Georgi was sent to a Soviet psychiatric hospital and sentenced to a number of years' detention in a forced labour camp. Five years after his release he succeeded in crossing the border again, not far from his original crossing point. This time he had Western currency with him, and was careful not to speak to any Finns on the journey to Helsinki where, at the American embassy, he was granted political asylum.

How many Georgis cross the border each year is difficult to say, since the Finns, understandably, are ashamed of this Faustian pact – and keep everything to do with extradition secret.

I asked Georgi if he felt bitter. His arms were folded across his chest. Occasionally he would scratch the skin beneath the short sleeves of his summer shirt. For a while he didn't answer.

'I was a young man,' he said eventually. 'I had dreamed of coming to the West. I knew nothing of Finland's special agreement with the Soviet Union – I thought Finland was a free country. It was a terrible disappointment.'

I was shocked and saddened by Georgi's story. But there were other disappointments as I got to know the border better: revelations that cloud the usually smug Finnish self-image which they would like the world to credit.

I knew, for instance, that Finland does a great deal of business with the Russians – about a fifth of its foreign trade, in fact. What I didn't know is that Russia never actually pays Finland for the Western goods it buys. For political reasons the volume of trade must remain at around 20 per cent, in the interests of 'good relations'; but Russia reserves its hard currency for more important trading partners such as Britain, West Germany and the USA, forcing Finland always to take an equal amount of Russian goods – whether or not the Finns really want them, and delivered at the discretion of the Russians, not the Finns.

Nowhere is this lopsided trade agreement more conspicuous than in the Saimaa Canal – the Suez Canal of the north. The canal was built in the nineteenth century to link the great lakes of central Finland with the Baltic. After the Second World War half of the Saimaa Canal was seized by the Russians, when Stalin moved the border between the two countries westward. The Russians refused to rebuild their end of the canal – and only permitted the Finns to do so providing they paid every penny of its reconstruction costs, as well as an annual rent for the area now inside the Soviet Union – a rent that would exceed the tolls charged on Russian vessels using the canal. In effect, the Russians got the Finns to rebuild the canal at Finnish expense, while allowing Russian ships to use the canal free of charge.

To add insult to injury, these Russian ships carry Russian wood through the canal *into* Finland – a country which is already 65 per cent forested! This carrying of coals to Newcastle is the strangest sight – but, since the Russians will not pay for Finnish high-tech (from ice-breakers to paper-making machines) in hard currency, and since the volume of trade must be kept around the 20 per cent mark, Finland takes Russian wood *faute de mieux* – never knowing in advance when the next contingent will arrive, since the Russians do not seem to know themselves.

The Finnish lock-keeper whom I met was disgusted by the arrangement – but he spoke by radio-telephone to the Finnish pilot aboard the MS *Pelomorsky*, a Russian wood freighter steaming up the canal from Vyborg. Once it was inside the lock I was permitted to board it.

The silver-haired captain spoke English – having in his youth sailed the Seven Seas. Now he plied between Leningrad and Imatra, carrying birch logs to the great paper mill at Kaukopää. He would not discuss the economic morality of his cargo, but was otherwise quite friendly. I asked him what he would buy in Finland, while waiting for his ship to be unloaded. A gift, perhaps, for his wife or children?

Captain Kuljoshok looked hesitant.

Some modern Finnish jewellery, perhaps – or Finnish clothes, glassware, fabrics, electrical goods?

A sort of smile played on his sunburned face.

'A car.'

'A car? A Western car?'

He shook his head.

'Russian car.' And to my consternation he explained how in the Soviet Union he would have to wait four years to get a Russian car; whereas in Finland, with the hard currency in which the Finnish shipping company must pay him, he can get one immediately, second-hand.

It seemed ironic and somehow appropriate, having pressured the Finns to import sub-standard Russian cars in order to bulk up the barter trade between the two countries, that Russia should get at least a few of them back!

Of course there is, as across every border in the world, an inevitable traffic in illegal goods. The customs officers at Vainikkala railway station, through which about a quarter of a million passengers travel by train to and from the Soviet Union each year, as well as those at Vaalima, which funnels half a million travellers by road, claim there is no smuggling apart from occasional bottles of vodka. But from my relatives in Finland I got a very different picture.

The first contact I was given proved to be pure farce, for Risto

Lahnala is a Finnish eccentric who drives his white, unmarked van as close as possible to the Soviet border and then sends bibles illegally across the frontier – by red balloon!

I met him in a forest clearing just off the main Helsinki-Leningrad road. Before my eyes a small rubber balloon no bigger than a badminton racket swelled to the height of the van itself, inflated from a hydrogen cylinder in the back. Mr Lahnala tied the nozzle with thick thread, then attached a plastic bag filled with bibles and religious literature printed in Russian. In this age of *perestroika* and *glasnost* it seems a dying trade, but in better days he used to release as many as forty balloons a day, he boasts – dedicated to 'Russian girls'.

The second contact I was given was less eccentric. Ari Pitkanen is

Timber on its way down the Saimaa Canal to the Baltic Sea

twenty-four, a coach driver who was unlucky enough to get caught
smuggling icons and old paintings from Leningrad in his tourist bus.
With a boyish grin he told me his story, sitting in the very tourist
coach in which he was arrested. It was owned by his father, who had
a tour company, and Ari was *expected* to smuggle as his main wage
for the trips he'd make to Leningrad.

The smuggling was apparently organized by a West German and
'fixed' in Helsinki. The German gave Ari the name of a Russian
contact in Leningrad and a rendezvous was arranged. The concealed
compartment on Ari's bus was perfectly constructed, welded behind a
sub-floor storage area. Ari made many such trips, each time bringing
seventeenth-century paintings and old icons rolled up in tubes, before
being stopped as the result of a tip-off;

When the Russian customs and border guard ordered all the
passengers to leave the bus, Ari knew he was in trouble. A second
bus was being searched alongside his; it too was carrying smuggled
goods. After five fruitless hours the Russians began to rip the other
bus apart – ceiling fittings, wall panels.... Ari's nerve broke – he
had no wish to see his father's new bus, worth perhaps a million
Finnmarks (£150,000), wrecked for the sake of a rolled up tube
smuggled for £300 a trip for a West German. He voluntarily revealed
the hiding place.

Taken to Vyborg and then to Leningrad, Ari was questioned by
the K G B and Russian police for several weeks. So desperate are the
Russians for foreign currency that he was told he could meanwhile
stay, if he consented to pay in Finnmarks, at the Finnish-built Hotel
Leningrad rather than in a police cell!

Ari's story ended in repatriation, fines and personal debts of over
200,000 Finnmarks (nearly £30,000) – as well as the end of his bus
driver's visa to Russia. He had played the innocent 'beginner' to the
Russians, but, he claims, it was his twenty-sixth smuggling trip, and
almost every bus driver travelling to Russia is involved in smuggling
of one kind or another: silver, gold, antique jewellery, paintings and
icons.

Most worrying, however, is the illegal trade in anabolic steroids.
These drugs, taken by athletes to improve their performance, can
kill or maim.

To find out more about the steroid drug trade I drove to the
Helsinki railway station, where, behind the smart Pullman cars of
the Helsinki–Leningrad express, in a quiet siding, I spoke to two
young drug smugglers. They would not consent to their faces being
filmed, but otherwise spoke quite openly about their trade.

Each ampoule costs less than a rouble in Russia, but fetches over

200 Finnmarks (almost £30) in Finland. On a good trip the young men will bring five hundred to a thousand ampoules, often concealed in the lining of a thick jacket specially tailored for the purpose. Russian customs officials don't care about the export of steroids, while Finnish customs officials – the young men claim – never search one's person.

Netting themselves between 100,000 and 200,000 Finnmarks, (£15,000 to £30,000) per successful trip, the pair alternate their mode of travel – car, bus, train, ship or air – to avoid detection. One of the young men hands me an ampoule. It is a simple glass capsule, filled with yellowish liquid, with an elongated narrow end.

'And this isn't obtainable in Finland?'

The smuggler shakes his head.

'But in Russian you can buy them openly?'

'At any chemist.'

'It seems incredible!'

'If you don't believe me, why don't you go to Leningrad? I've got a friend there – he'll show you.'

And so, improbably, I went to Leningrad to check out the smuggler's tale. I had no visa – the Russians were still trying to make up their minds, after four months, whether to permit filming on their side of the border. But a ferry boat sails from Helsinki every few days, and as long as the passengers stay with specially chartered bus tours they may visit Leningrad for a day without a visa.

Bidding farewell to the B B C film crew I settled into luxury cruise life – a welcome rest after two weeks of border filming. The B B C had loaned me a small video camera to film my adventure and I fell asleep that night hoping the promised friend would show up at the harbour. . . .

The next morning, as the ship docked, I scanned the pier. Three Russian soldiers in familiar loose green shirts and K G B hats were certainly there, waiting with a portable desk containing index cards and a telephone, its wire snaking ominously across the quayside. An hour went by before we were disgorged, but to my relief I caught sight of my contact: Osko Manninen, a legendary Finnish tour operator who has personally conducted eight hundred bus trips from Finland to Leningrad over the years. Captured in the Second World War, he had to learn Russian in the P O W camp in order to survive – a skill which stood him in good stead when the border was reopened to Finnish tourists in 1954. He stands well over six feet tall, silver-haired and still handsome, an excellent singer and accordion player. Felled by a Finnish drunk a few years ago, he had since retired, but was spending a few weeks in Leningrad, where he is still treated like royalty.

Just how royal I was to find out. Skipping the official bus tour in the city centre, I met Osko at the Hotel Pribaltsk, as agreed. Osko led me up to the entrance canopy, beneath which stood a huge black limousine – 'Gorbachev's car,' Osko called it. With its doors open, its curtains screening the luxurious passenger 'compartment' and gleaming in the summer sunshine, it looked very much the favoured transport of Politburo members. . . .

'Please,' said Osko, pointing to the rear of the limousine. 'Take your seat!'

The limousine was booked to fetch diplomats later that day from the airport. For the moment, however, as one of only four such *tschaikas*, or official VIP cars, it could earn Boris, its driver, some useful pocket money – in Finnmarks.

'Where to?' Osko asked, sinking into the plush back seat with Misha, his faithful Russian interpreter and factotum, as well as Esa, a little man resembling a forest dwarf who hailed from central Finland.

Through the majestic empty Sunday streets of Leningrad we drove. Restored to its former pristine glory after destruction in the Second World War, this Venice of the north – founded on the drained marshes between Lake Ladoga and the Baltic Sea by Peter the Great – is one of the most beautiful cities in Europe. Thanks to the current heatwave, half of its five million inhabitants seemed to be crowded on the shore of the River Neva in various stages of undress, while we, in our 'Gorbachev Machine', paid a visit first to the Palace of Marriage. Beneath chandeliers and gold-lacquered mouldings Osko explained how, for a certain sum of money, a Finn wishing to keep a second wife in Russia can get the necessary forged stamp and bride of his choice. Conversely, a Russian girl needing a foreign husband in order to leave the Soviet Union can, by knowing the right person (and paying perhaps 30,000 Finnmarks – £4,500), be found a Finnish spouse – a man like little Esa perhaps, in his sixties but a bachelor still. . . . Osko smiles wickedly.

That Russian girls could only see the West by paying £4,500 to marry an elderly foreigner seemed sad. Excellence in sport, however, is another way of achieving the same end. International excellence is, of course, almost unattainable without the use of steroids, freely available in the Soviet Union. But can I *really* walk into any chemist's and buy steroids over the counter? I asked Osko.

Because it was Sunday most of the shops were closed, but the main chemist on Nevsky Prospekt (the Champs Elysées of Leningrad) is always open. We walked straight in and asked for the steroids. For 1.85 roubles, paid at the cashier's desk, we were given a little piece of paper that entitled us to a box of three ampoules, complete with a metal file for removing the tips ready for injection. I even filmed the sequence with my video camera in order to prove the ease with which such drugs can be obtained in the Soviet Union.

For Osko Manninen, ex-prisoner of war, corruption in Leningrad was the inevitable result of a ridiculous system. We subsequently drove to the famous Peter and Paul Fortress – where Dostoevsky was imprisoned before his mock execution in 1836 – and, passing a few Finnmarks to the doorman, made our way into a private dining room reserved for party members. Here we had a magnificent lunch, culminating in a series of heartfelt toasts to Finnish, Russian and English friendship. And why should we not be friends, after all?

The paranoia with which Russia guards her borders seemed as incredible to us as to Misha, the Russian interpreter. But in order to understand it, Osko insisted we must visit the Piskaryovskoye Memorial Cemetery, twelve miles north of the city centre, where the dead are buried in three layers, covering forty acres: the graves of half a million people killed or starved to death during the siege of Leningrad.

It was a chastening experience. From concealed loudspeakers came the strains of eerie, classical music as ordinary Russians, in their Sunday best, walked past the mass graves, leaving flowers by the Eternal Flame or the bronze statue of liberty.

Was Stalin right in 1939 to fear foreign invasion and thus insist on moving the Finnish frontier further west, claiming that Leningrad was within artillery range of the border? On 29 November 1939, having seen the ease with which Germany had over-run Poland, Stalin attacked Finland – and met determined resistance.

How Finland managed, in the Winter War of 1939, to halt an invasion by a Russian army eventually totalling a million men, is one of the legendary feats of military history, on a par with the Battle of Britain. 'The few', in Finland's case, were young men, boys in their late teens or twenties, who were given rifles, submachine guns and skis, and told to halt whole Russian armoured divisions. Driving to Suomussalmi, nearly four hundred miles north of Leningrad, I came across the road down which the Russian tanks invaded, hoping to cut Finland in two, and which has been preserved as a Finnish national monument: the Raate Road. Still untarred, it winds its way through the forests and around the lakes of north Karelia – lakes that had frozen solid in December 1939.

Five veterans from Suomussalmi village came to meet me on the

Raate Road. They show me the trenches and forest dugouts from which they fought on the west bank of the River Puras. Were they daunted by the disparity between their forces – estimated to be *thirty to one*?

'Of course I was afraid!' Pekka Heikkinen remembers. 'It was snowing and quite cold. I didn't hate the Russians. I just felt angry they were invading my country.'

'I'd never seen a dead man before,' Toivo Heikkinen recalls. 'Once we'd surrounded them I went forward, with a colleague to take prisoners. It was terrible – one man was still sitting with his hand to his mouth, smoking a cigarette, frozen to death in that exact position.'

'They were brave,' concedes Arvo Hiltunen. 'Only a few ran away. The rest fought – and froze – to the death. We were used to the forest – they weren't.'

But at the village cemetery, where some three hundred Finnish soldiers lie buried, each with a granite cross bearing his name and dates, Hannes Heikkinen remembers his brother, who was one of the first boys from the village to die.

Standing bolt upright by the grave, fifty years on, Hannes recalls Paavo as he was then, aged twenty – his favourite brother who had only worn uniform for a few days, having mustered with the other youths of the village in front of the fire station. 'When the news came through that he'd been killed ... I knew I was going to make them pay for this,' Hannes says quietly.

He did. Though the Russians have still not officially counted their losses, it is estimated that, on the Finnish front alone, over a million Russian troops were killed in the Second World War – many of them dying because of poor or non-existent medical facilities.

By contrast Finnish medical services were exemplary, and still are, as I found when I paid a visit to the War Veterans' Hospital at Kauniala. The hospital houses 267 patients, cared for in surroundings more like a forest retreat than a hospital. One, Veikko Raisanan, has been at Kauniala since it was opened after the war, having lost both his legs when a Russian shell exploded near him. Looking back, was it worth it?

When he speaks, the lids of his eyes close – yet his voice does not waver. 'Yes – and I would do it again.'

'What were you fighting for?'

He pauses. 'To keep Finland free.'

'Do you feel you succeeded?'

He nods emphatically.

'Even though Russia later moved the border by force?'

The Eternal Flame at the Piskaryovskoye Memorial Cemetery in Leningrad

He nods again. 'We are still independent.'

'Will the day ever come when Finland gets back the territory the Russians took by force in eastern and southern Karelia?'

Veikko smiles, shaking his head. 'Who knows? I doubt it. The Soviet Union is a very big country!'

The hospital matron, Marja Koskelainen, is clearly devoted to her patients but her own emotion displays itself in shining eyes and nervous movements of her head. She herself was one of the half million Finns who had to evacuate their homes and homeland in Karelia when Finland finally sued for peace and the border was moved where Stalin dictated. One-tenth of Finland had to be handed over to the Russians – the Finns also having to pay crippling war

Left Russian dead in the Winter War of 1939–40
Above Russian troops occupying the Finnish peninsula of Hangö, leased to Russia for thirty years, in March 1940

reparations for the 'crime' of having defended their own country from Soviet predation in 1939–40, and then having sought to get their territory back from 1941 to 1944, with German help.

Her eyes fix mine. She swallows and then looks away. What trials Finland underwent during the war, and what it meant to surrender so much of Finland, is something that still rankles – all the more so since Russia makes no use of this 'stolen' territory. West of a line from Vyborg to Murmansk it is kept almost entirely as an uninhabited border zone, requiring a special permit for a Russian to enter. The official reason for this is the fear of western invasion; but the trip wires and K G B border guards – part of a K G B army some three hundred thousand strong – have but one *real* purpose, like that of the Finnish border guard: to stop ordinary Russians from reaching the West.

Finnish veterans of the Second World War remain convinced that Finland's price was worth paying. Looking around, they see a completely Western country, as prosperous and capitalist as any other, yet small enough to operate enviable social and medical services for all. The standard of living is now one of the highest in Europe, and the quality of life, with almost every other Finn owning a summer cottage in addition to his own permanent home, is surprising. Small is truly beautiful here: the Finnish landscape as yet unspoiled by industrialization, yet the country able to hold its own within the world, thriving in competition with great nations enjoying far greater economies of scale and home markets. *Finland Survived* was the title of a recent account of Finnish post-war history. In retrospect it seems miraculous – a balancing act performed on the very frontier of the Soviet Union with great skill and patience. My only qualms are that Finland has paid a hidden price for a hidden border: it has gone, and continues to go, to almost any lengths to appease its neighbour and avoid her wrath.

An example of this attitude is the way a recent Finnish film was held up for a whole year before being passed for distribution in Finland. Entitled *Born American*, it was the dreamchild of two young Finnish film-makers in their early twenties, René Harlin and Marcus Selin. They wanted to make an action movie in Finland that would be entertaining and popular, in the manner of Bond or Rambo. Using the simplistic story of three American boys spending a high-spirited autumn holiday in Finland, it followed their adventures across the Russian border, north of the Arctic Circle.

'It was completely harmless stuff,' Selin recalls. 'We needed a plot that could be based in Finland, but which would interest Western moviegoers. The Finnish–Soviet frontier was an ideal hinge for the story. We mocked it up, after careful research. We even spoke to defectors, who drew diagrams of the Russian trip wires and so on.'

The snow-covered landscapes in the film are ravishing, but the Finnish censor was not amused. Responding to political pressure in Helsinki, he refused to grant the film a certificate.

'We couldn't believe it!' Selin remembers. 'It was so goddam innocent! And here it was, held up in Helsinki, creating tremendous controversy in the newspapers and behind the scenes, all on account of it possibly upsetting the Russians! In the end we had to hold the premiere in Norway, near *their* border with Russia! It was shown in all Western countries – but not Finland!'

Eventually, after a year of waiting, the film was granted a Finnish certificate – but only after some four minutes had been cut.

Meanwhile, the hypocrisy of Finland's negative policy towards

Russian refugees, when hundreds of thousands of Finns cross freely into Sweden to find work, does not escape Selin or other thinking Finns. That the Finnish frontier guard is, in effect, acting for the Russian K G B border army is something all Finns know – but which few will admit. What was once vital self-censorship in order that Finland did not arouse Russian wrath and go the way of Poland, East Germany, Czechoslovakia, Romania or Hungary in the 1940s has now become an established fact of Finnish life, has in fact eaten its way into the very fabric of Finnish education and culture. Neither the border zone nor relations with Russia are ever discussed in any meaningful way; censorship and self-censorship have led even university-educated Finns into 'an uncritical approach and an awe for authority', as the late Donald Fields – himself married to a Finn – declared in *Index on Censorship*.

Over dinner in Saariselkä, Finland's cross-country skiing centre in Lapland overlooking the Russian border, the tall, young, tousle-haired head of the Finnish Tourist Board defended the Finnish agreement on returning defectors, and Finnish submission to Russian interests always. In his eyes, the sacrifices made by the older generation of Finns were in vain – for Stalin's wishes had to be met.

'You mean, Might is Right?'

'If you like to put it so,' he acknowledged, his sunburned face flushing. 'I am a realist. I believe in peace. We have a very good life here in Finland. Why should we rock the boat?'

Why indeed?

For the four thousand genuine Lapps who live in this part of Finland, north of the Arctic Circle, such matters are academic – for their challenge is not the preservation of Finnish independence, democracy and the freedom of speech, but the preservation of their Lappish culture against the predations of modern capitalist life – since the lure of bright city lights and jobs is proving too strong for many of their children. Though they have centrally heated, modern farmhouses and snowmobiles – arctic motorbikes – to help herd the reindeer and to reach their fishing holes far out on the lakes, it is a harsh, long winter lasting almost nine months of the year. You need to be physically and mentally tough to survive – as I became aware when I returned in February to find the whole of Lapland under four feet of snow.

There are compensations, though. Reindeer are notoriously diffi-cult to train, but from their herds the Lapps pick out the best for racing: perhaps the most extraordinary form of four-legged racing I have ever seen. A circuit is prepared on the frozen lake, five or six reindeer are dragged or coaxed to a starting line and, at the command

The Orthodox church at Nellimo in Lapland

'*Aja!*', stampede forward, towing 'drivers' on skis. Often the reindeer collide, or show *their* independence by leaving the track and leaping off over the snow-covered ice. But the Lapps revel in the sport – and by tradition the race meetings provide an opportunity for Lapp families to meet in order that parents can cast an eye over potential suitors for their daughters – and vice versa.

Traditionally, the Lapps have been left free by Scandinavian governments to take their reindeer without hindrance across the Nordic borders. They are, in their way, the Bedouins of the north, and they include among their tribes the Kolts, a small Lapland tribe which once lived, fished and kept reindeer in the Petsamo area, in the days when Finland's border stretched to the Arctic Ocean. Stalin's invasion of 1939 put paid to their ancestral lands. Their houses were plundered and their churches razed and only after great sufferings were the survivors able to rebuild their community at Nellimo, the last village on the Finnish–Soviet border.

One of the village elders, Katrina Jefremov, greeted me in traditional Koltish costume, her quaint head-dress almost medieval in appearance. This tiny, bird-like woman is translating the Bible into Kolt; she is an embodiment of the will to survive. Proudly she led the way through the snow-clad forest (the trees smaller, sparser than in southern Finland, owing to the paucity of the sun) and up a little hill upon which they had constructed their own, log-built Orthodox church. Father Henry, the Orthodox priest whose 'parish' includes the whole of Lapland, explained how it was modelled on the old Kolt monastery church in Petsamo – now beyond the border. 'They can never go back,' he said, tugging at his beard. 'It is a Russian military area. But this church is their reminder.'

From Nellimo a Finnish border guard helicopter whisked us the final eighteen miles or so to the end of Finland's border with the Soviet Union – for there is no human habitation beyond Nellimo, and no road. We landed on a frozen lake and were met by a Finnish snowmobile patrol which took us to a nearby forest camp-fire. Here the Finnish captain introduced me to the Russian colonel in charge of the Murmansk area of the border. He had a chubby, not unfriendly, well-shaven face, wore a grey astrakhan hat and camouflage anorak, and was accompanied by a handsome young interpreter with mischievous blue eyes. The colonel told me his Russian ski patrol was waiting in the woods nearby, by the 'Corner of the Three Nations', where the frontiers of Norway, Finland and the USSR meet.

I donned a special Arctic snowsuit and we skied through the silent, snowbound forest – the Russian officers towed in state on sleds pulled by the Finnish snowmobiles – until we reached the brow of the hill, where a swathe had been cut through the forest, like a surgical scar: the Finnish–Norwegian border. We skied along the edge, until the captain stopped and pointed. There in the virgin snow stood a mound of stones, on top of which were engraved the names of the three converging countries: Finland, Russia and Norway.

I had reached the end of the Soviet border with Finland 1289 kilometres from where it began, by the marshes of the Baltic Sea. I undid my ski bindings and, watched by officers and soldiers of the Finnish and Russian border guards, clambered through the deep snow to the mound of black stones. It was four o'clock on 23 February 1989. The sun was already slipping below the western horizon, and the forest would soon be dark.

A nation of four million Finns bordering the Soviet Union for almost a thousand miles. I took my hat off to the Finns for their courage in the Second World War and the manner in which they have kept their independence since then – unlike so many central European countries from Poland to Hungary. But looking behind me at the watching faces of those Finnish and Russian frontier guards, I thought too of the price of collusion. I knew in my heart that, were I a Russian refugee, it would only be now, in sight of Norway, that I could finally say I'd reached true freedom. Perhaps *glasnost* will alter things. But, at least I knew now why the border has been kept secret for so many years.

JOHN WELLS

THE STAKE THROUGH THE VAMPIRE'S HEART

East–West Germany

*V*ILSHOFEN, 150 miles south-east of Munich, is a romantic old fortified city, with primrose-yellow walls and slender onion spires reflected in a still green stretch of the Danube. The Red Cross refugee camp there in the first days of the great exodus in September 1989 could have been a car boot sale: off a main street in the modern outskirts of the town, on the site of the weekly market.

Behind the snub-fronted, shabby East German cars there were tents, notice-boards offering jobs, a big hand-painted sign saying East or West they were all Germans, and mounds of old clothes being distributed to the young refugees. I realized I was inadequately dressed to present a BBC programme on the subject when a kindly old man came up, took my right hand in both of his, and welcomed me to the Free World.

The refugees all gave different reasons for leaving home. There was a girl who was tired of being treated as 'a second-class human being' in other Socialist countries: 'You say you're German, they're all over you. East German, they don't want to know.' One man had spent two years collecting the materials for a house and then been refused permission to build it. There was a fourteen-year waiting list for a new car. Hard work wasn't rewarded, you might just as well idle along like everybody else. One told the story of his brother who'd done his national service as a border guard: the pay was better, but he lived in terror of being put in prison if anyone escaped to the West through his sector of the fence.

In some cases they'd been on holiday in Hungary, heard on the

John Wells outside the ruined church of Völkershausen in the DDR which the
East German government claimed collapsed because of underground explosions set
off by West German engineers just over the frontier

car radio that the frontier was open and come across on impulse. All
of them were near to tears at the relief of being out, most of them
well aware that life in West Germany wasn't going to be easy;
crooked insurance salesmen had already been in the camp that
morning, offering them insurance they didn't need. Most of them
had abandoned families or friends, and were already homesick.

In making the programme we travelled the whole length of what

Above Red Cross camp for East German refugees at Vilshofen, September 1989
Opposite East Germans arriving by train at Hof, in Bavaria, on 5 October 1989

is locally called the German–German frontier, trying to establish what the frontier meant to those who lived on either side of it.

Swaying and clanking out to sea to the north of Travemünde is a line of yellow buoys, a hundred yards apart, each perhaps twice the height of a man above the water, with the word *Grenze* painted on the side in black. This is the northernmost end of the frontier, 860 miles long, cutting down from the Baltic coast just east of Hamburg through farmland and forests, severing old roads, villages and deserted railway lines as far south as Czechoslovakia.

There is something slightly ridiculous about a frontier drawn in water: like the air, the sea is always moving. Waves constantly slap against the yellow marker buoys and surge on by, forever flattening and sliding, indefinable, currents carrying volumes of warmer or colder water through below the surface. Fish must swim through it all the time, just as birds cross and recross the border further south: but this was still a man-made barrier between two political systems, and hundreds had been killed trying to cross it.

Mike Liesche had tried swimming across it in the spring of 1989: he started at night unobserved by border guards on the beach, and was thirty-six hours in the water. Half drowned in the undertow of a ferry that ran him down in the dark and almost carried back through the demarcation line by the tide, he managed to cling to one of the buoys, undetected by the grey patrol boats from the East, and was eventually rescued by a West German diplomat returning from a yachting trip to Poland.

Mike was due to meet us at the office of the harbour mistress in Travemünde. There was Wimbledon live on the television, and outside the window a hot wind rattled the rigging of the millionaires' yachts that floated in their own reflections in the marina. The harbour mistress told us she was a war widow. She was in her sixties, handsome and well-groomed, a fine example of old-fashioned Hamburg respectability. She held forth with great amusement about the ghastliness of New Zealand, where she had once had to go to visit a married daughter. She described the way they balanced their cups and saucers on the abnormally wide arms of their sofas, and were always pestering one to take more cake. It had been 'too terrible'.

Mike, in his early twenties, came and went, bringing cakes and coffee from a little kitchen on the other side of the front door. From her criticisms when he was out of the room, an East German upbringing might not be so bad as coming from New Zealand, but it left a lot to be desired. Before she'd taken him on he'd looked a dreadful mess, he had never cleaned his shoes, never brushed his hair, and had no table manners at all; he had no idea about work, and was shockingly unpunctual. Under her influence he had clearly improved: his shoes were polished, his fingernails were clean, he was studying, had a part-time job to support himself, and was well on his way to becoming a solid West German citizen.

Afterwards he showed the harbour mistress and me some colour photographs. He had, improbably, within weeks of his escape, risked going back to Prague to meet his girlfriend and their baby. The colour photographs were of his visit. His girlfriend and the baby in a park in Prague, his girlfriend sitting on the grass with her T-shirt off. 'Ach! Oben ohne!' – 'Really! Topless!' The harbour mistress did not wish to see that one, and put it on the bottom of the pile.

'Oben ohne' recurred oddly enough in conversation ten miles to the east when I was having lunch in a workers' holiday home on the Island of Poel, in the German Democratic Republic, the DDR. The warden had asked me where I'd like to sit in the dining room. I said I didn't mind, but as we were making a film it would probably be better if I joined a table rather than sitting on my own. I was taken over to a family of three, mother, father and daughter. They were called Gronau, and had driven all night from Thuringia in the south. The warden had told me that this was change-over day, that they never knew when people would arrive, so he liked to give them a hot meal that could be ready at any time. When the 'hot meal' arrived it was one course: a plate of vegetable soup, with a piece of bread. We were, admittedly, offered second helpings.

It was explained that I was from the BBC. The father shrank back, but the warden reassured him: he was at liberty to say exactly what he liked, we were there with the full approval of the government. Within a few minutes we were discussing their enthusiasm for *oben ohne*, and whenever possible *unter ohne: Freie Körperliche Kultur*, FKK for short, free physical culture or nudism.

Outside it was raining. I didn't like to ask about the effect of rain on nudism, but said it was a pity about the weather. They shrugged their shoulders: they couldn't choose when they took their holiday,

Beach chairs at a workers' holiday resort on the Island of Poel in the DDR

they'd have to make the most of it. Frau Gronau told me they really needed the holiday because of her husband being on shift work: it was playing merry hell with their marriage. She worked normal hours, her husband one week nights, one week the late shift, one week the morning shift. It made their life 'very complicated'. Feeling we now knew each other, I asked him what he did for a job. He shook his head and refused to answer.

The workers' holiday home was an old-fashioned white house separated from the beach by a hedge of dull evergreens, with rather municipal flowerbeds and a children's mini-golf course. Down on the sand old ladies were sitting in double-seater, high-backed, covered chairs, sheltering from the rain as they ate their picnic lunch, a party of schoolchildren on a day trip from Schwerin were scampering into the sea with a spartan courage that seemed quintessentially East German, and swans floated beyond the breakers. The warden explained that the swans were a traditional feature on the Baltic coast, and, environmental matters being probably the most talked-about subject in both East and West Germany, added that they were breeding in such numbers they were becoming a nuisance.

The only reminder of the frontier were the byelaws, posted up on glass-fronted noticeboards, forbidding the use of boats after dark, or 'any kind of diving equipment at any time'.

While we were filming the gardens an elderly couple were sitting patiently on a bench in their raincoats. The sun came out for a moment. They took their raincoats off, and we had to ask them to put them back on again for 'continuity'. As I was apologizing I heard for the first time, but not the last, the most interesting word then in use in socialist East Germany. They were not staying at the Holiday Home, but at a house a little way along the coast, *privat*.

The biggest jolt on the Island of Poel came in conversation with an old lady who'd stopped to watch the camera being set up on the beach. I asked her if she'd lived there all her life. No, she'd been born in the 'so-called Baltikum' – the German settlements in Lithuania and Estonia – and had come there in 1942. '*Auf Führers Beruf, heim ins Reich.*' She referred to the Führer and his call to return to the Reich in such a cheerful, matter-of-fact tone it seemed uncanny, like suddenly seeing a ghost.

The fact is, of course, that there is a continuum: even after nearly fifty years of division, the two states are still fundamentally German, and not only in their shared history, literature and language: the yellow post-boxes with the black posthorn on the side, the ringed H for *Haltestelle* at every bus stop, the traditional beer and sausages,

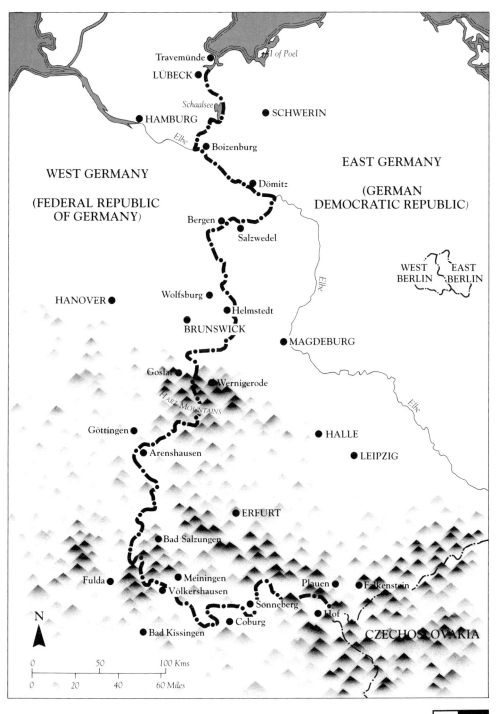

Travemünde
LÜBECK
Isl of Poel
Schaalsee
SCHWERIN
HAMBURG
Elbe
Boizenburg

WEST GERMANY

(FEDERAL REPUBLIC
OF GERMANY)

EAST GERMANY

(GERMAN
DEMOCRATIC REPUBLIC)

Dömitz

Bergen
Salzwedel

Elbe

WEST   EAST
BERLIN   BERLIN

HANOVER

Wolfsburg
Helmstedt
BRUNSWICK

MAGDEBURG

Goslar
Wernigerode
HARZ MOUNTAINS

Elbe

Göttingen

HALLE

Arenshausen

LEIPZIG

ERFURT

Bad Salzungen

Fulda
Meiningen
Völkershausen
Plauen
Falkenstein
Sonneberg
Coburg
Hof

Bad Kissingen

CZECHOSLOVAKIA

N

0   50   100 Kms
0   20   40   60 Miles

the net curtains at the windows of the small, steep-roofed houses, which, except for cross-frontier outcrops of regional styles like the slate-hung or half-timbered houses of the Harz, are identical from the Baltic to Bavaria. Both countries have an organization, now separately administered, called the German Red Cross.

Lübeck, the city east of Hamburg whose ancient rights even during the days of the Iron Curtain still allowed its fishing boats legally to infringe East German sovereignty at sea, is probably best known as the birthplace of Thomas Mann, the one twentieth-century German writer equally respected on both sides of the frontier. After the Second World War he was almost alone in commending the serious-ness of the DDR in their pursuit of socialism. The Germans had often been divided: Catholics and Protestants, Prussians and Bavarians, but Thomas Mann in his youth divided them into *Bürger* and *Künstler*, Reliable Bourgeois Citizens and Artists, those with Soul. It is tempting to apply that division to the two German states: West Germany all realism and glossy achievement, East Germany grimly striving for the unattainable ideal.

In any event the present division, the German–German frontier, was drawn on a map at Lancaster House in London by Sir William Strang in 1944, as a proposed border for the Russian zone of an Allied-occupied Germany. This was adopted in the London Protocol later that year as:

> a line drawn from a point on Lübeck Bay where the frontiers of Schleswig-Holstein and Mecklenberg meet, along the western frontier of Mecklenberg to the province of Hannover, thence along the eastern frontier of the Prussian province of Saxony . . . and the western frontier of Thuringia to where the latter meets the Bavarian border; thence eastwards . . . to the 1937 Czechoslovak frontier.

Conceived in the bitterest days of the war, it was clearly intended as a stake driven through the Vampire's heart.

The fence was built in 1952, principally to prevent further loss of talent to the West – by that time nearly 20 per cent of East Germans had crossed over the old 'green' frontier – but also to establish the DDR as an independent sovereign state. Even moderate West German right-wingers continued to refer to the DDR as *'ein Teil Deutschlands'* – a part of Germany – and West German passports were automatically available to any refugee from the DDR.

Much that was absurd and obscene about the closed frontier could therefore be traced back to the East's sense of fragile identity as an independent nation. Just how fragile it is we were to discover as we

Top Russian soldiers at the frontier at Virtaniemi, the most northerly border crossing between the USSR and Finland.

Above Border posts, painted blue and white for Finland and red and green for Russia, run all the way along the 800-mile frontier.

Above Finnish soldier near the Soviet border
Right Reindeer farm in Lapland. Around four
thousand Lapps live in this area of Finland;
traditionally a nomadic people, they are allowed
to wander across the Nordic frontiers, but not
into Russia.

Left One of the most dramatic symbols of a divided Germany was the road bridge at Dömitz which ran halfway across the River Elbe and then stopped in mid-air.
Below West German road near the German–German frontier

Above A soldier of the British military police guarding the border zone in the British sector of West Berlin shortly before the Berlin Wall was opened.
Right The cleared border zone between the two Germanies, until autumn 1989 vigilantly patrolled by East Germany to stop its citizens escaping to the West.

The grave dedicated to an Unknown German Soldier at Dreiländereck, 'Three Country Corner', where the two Germanies and Czechoslovakia meet.

travelled south. The old closed frontier began in real earnest on dry land, on the beach half a mile east of Travemünde: on the western side there was a ten-foot fence of tight, diagonal wire mesh, with 'barber's poles' – square posts painted in red, yellow and black with a metal plaque announcing the German Democratic Republic. Beyond the fence at this point there was a wilderness: a deer blundered out on to the beach and careered away into the trees again, and along its whole length much of the area between the fences had become an unintentional nature reserve.

In the sixties there were minefields, and later SM70s, shotgun boobytraps. These were removed some years back, and the shoot to kill policy officially abandoned in June 1989. Beyond the undergrowth now were a vehicle track, an area of raked earth, and in some places a line for dogs on long running leads. Watchtowers rose above the trees, permanently manned by guards with binoculars, and at those places where they were nearer to the wire, with cameras. Anyone lingering near the fence was photographed repeatedly with a terrifying Germanic thoroughness, though what purpose the pictures served, or indeed whether there was any film in their cameras, we were unable to discover. On the DDR side was a 500-metre restricted area, into which East Germans were only allowed if they were in possession of a special pass.

DDR frontier guards were legally permitted to patrol on the western side of the fence, working in pairs, and observing a standard drill when they encountered any Westerner: one turned his back and wrote notes, the other photographed the 'suspect'. They never spoke.

Permission to film in East Germany at all before the Revolution had been a struggle to obtain, involving finally a meeting with the DDR Foreign Office in East Berlin, and it became clear that we were either going to do it their way or not at all. Conditions were imposed that would not now be imposed: we were only allowed to interview those put forward by the 'International Press Centre', and a member of their staff was to travel with us and be present whenever we were working.

We were also required, like all tourists visiting the DDR, to stay in the official Interhotels – comfortable by any standards, but expensive by any standards, and accepting only West German marks. This severely restricted our movement and the amount of time we had to work: the only rooms available in the whole of the northern sector, even with eight weeks' warning, were in Rostock, and this meant round-trips of two or three hundred miles to visit the first third of the frontier, returning every night to the Baltic coast.

The few conversations I had with dissidents, usually by chance –
after a concert in a Lutheran church, in the train on the way to
Berlin, or walking in the country – revealed a sour disenchantment
on the part of working people with the incompetence of the regime,
and the existence of a substantial and disgruntled middle class, many
of them bearded, long-haired, looking very like those involved in the
Anti-Vietnam War movement in the West in the sixties. The more
idealistic complained about political repression, the imprisonment of
those who refused to do their national service, the bulldozing of
churches or old buildings, industrial pollution, the shoddiness of life
in general. The great majority were sick of austerity and longed for
the West German Garden of Earthly Delights that most of East
Germany can see every night on television.

The most surprising ideological encounter between East and West
was in the train. A young West Berliner in a leather jacket was
bragging to two East German boys and a girl about life in the West.
They sat very still, occasionally laughing. He flicked the metal lid
of the ashtray, shifted in his seat, his eyes moving all the time. They
had a tape recorder they were obviously very proud of, still wrapped
in plastic. He asked if he could use it, he'd been in Venice the week
before and had dropped his Walkman in the Grand Canal. Whether
or not they believed him their eyes grew wide and sad. He played
his tape, very loudly, to the unprotesting carriage. They should come
over, they were mad to stay. They grinned. Then, for some reason,
he started talking about Christianity. How could anyone believe in
all that rubbish? I noticed them stiffen, and that one of the boys had
a silver cross round his neck. All three, one after the other, then told
him that they were practising Christians.

The Party spokesmen I asked about it was an atheist, but had a
friend who was a Catholic priest, known locally as 'Red Richard'.
The Catholics, he said, gave them no trouble.

East German Protestants however were consistently far from loyal
to the regime. They were, after all, the only national organization
outside the control of the state. The edgiest test of our press advisor's
authority was an incident on the Schaalsee, twenty miles inland,
where we arrived in a thunderstorm, having meant to film the frontier
across the water from the East. The plan was to set up the cameras
in a village churchyard. It contained the tomb of the Bernsdorffs,
an aristocratic family of Protestant Prussian diplomats, semi-derelict
with a broken iron gate. The church itself, and the other graves, were
well cared for.

We sat in the van as the rain hammered on the roof and the sky
over the lake went from purple-grey to black, and had just decided

to give up when two men in their thirties, soaked to the skin, ran up and asked us whether we had permission to film there. Did we realize it was *Privatbesitz*, private property? Our minder from Berlin and the local press officer seemed angry, sitting tight in the dry and saying that it had all been cleared with the local council. One of the young men leaned in to him, and I saw the corners of his mouth go down. Not with the church, he said; we needed written permission. The press officers looked away, refusing to answer. I talked across them, explaining that we weren't going to film anyway, but would of course had paid a facility fee if they asked for it. They relaxed. Did we like the church? They'd just finished restoring it, they'd raised all the money themselves. They were sorry about the Bernsdorff tomb, they were going to do that next, they wouldn't like us to think they were barbarians who didn't look after things.

The older generation of East Germans, certainly, saw the closed frontier as a punishment for German barbarism in the past. After the vast maze of interlocking blockhouses and security barriers at Zarentin, where the Hamburg to Berlin motorway crosses to the East, the most dramatic wound inflicted by the old closed frontier was at Dömitz on the River Elbe.

The old railway bridge was still there, but blasted, rusty and abandoned: the road bridge from the West ran out halfway across the river and then stopped dead. The surface had been repaired, and the barrier to prevent you driving off the end was fitted with coin-in-the-slot telescopes to look across at the other side: marshy meadows, then the grey mesh of the fence, and above the trees to the right the roofs of Dömitz and its church spire. For the West the bridge was a sentimental monument to lost German unity.

Wolfgang Nowe, living in Dömitz, in the East, was more philosophical.

> The frontier itself forces us to think, every day of our
> lives, of how it came into existence. It is after all not a
> frontier we drew ourselves because we wanted it here; it
> is a relic of a tragic chapter in the story of the German
> nation. For Germans, it is a direct consequence of the war;
> they, we – and I include myself, even though I was only
> twelve years old when the war ended – we have no right
> to complain because we must bear the blame for it.

Nowe was an old schoolmaster, a socialist but an active member of the local Lutheran church, and the author of occasional poems in Plattdeutsch, a slightly comic north German dialect still spoken on both sides of the wire. Our walk through the town, its shabby red-brick and timbered houses unchanged since the war, brought us suddenly and dramatically up against the fence. Beyond it, the dogs and the watchtowers.

> A visitor is struck by it, and shaken by it: I've seen that again and again. But for us here right up against it, it's a fact of life that you ... yes, that you get used to, sad as it sounds, that you get used to. I suppose you sometimes think to yourself, if the frontier wasn't there, you might want to stand on the other bank of the river, as you could when the two bridges were still up. Against that sort of thought that just flares up is the reality that says 'History created it, we have to come to terms with things as they are.'

Walking on through the cobbled streets, he talked about his own difficulties: when his father was dying in West Germany in 1974 he was refused permission to go and see him; even now he and his wife are still waiting for a visa to visit West Germany at the same time. He was tolerant of those who had tried to escape. They went for very different reasons: political, psychological, economic or emotional. 'All these different motives deserve respect and consideration. But if you've made your life here, then I think you have a duty to stay.'

Broken bridges apart, the frontier runs for most of its length through farmland and forest: if the wildlife in some cases benefited, the economy suffered both in East and West. What before division had been local market towns were now in a foreign country, inaccessible; villages that had once been on a main road in the middle of Germany had become remote frontier posts at the edge of warring empires. The most extreme example was much further south at Falkenstein, on the Bavarian border, exactly halfway by rail from Berlin to Munich. Before the war it was a place were people came from Thuringia and Bavaria to spend the weekend, with a flourishing hotel and a brewery. By 1989, after forty years of isolation in a crooked corner of fence, the hotel was bankrupt and empty, the brewery in ruins.

Bergen on the River Dumme, a few miles south of Dömitz, is in the West, but could easily be mistaken for the East by the pensioners from the DDR – pensioners were allowed some freedom of movement, being of no further use to the state – who came through the frontier regularly on the bus. There were, it is true, girlie magazines and Coca Cola on sale in the newspaper shop, but its high street, once the trunk road, was extremely sleepy. The mayor, just old enough to have served in the Wehrmacht, remembered walking to school in Salzwedel, now in the East. There had also been a local railway connection. Now both the road and the railway line were overgrown, lost in the woods.

> Before 1945, Bergen was on the so-called Salt Road: we had fourteen old coaching inns. Today there are three, simply because nobody drives through any more. We've lost something like 70 per cent of our income because of the frontier. From 1945 to 1952 you could still roughly speaking get across: lorries went through, cars with the right papers. We used to go across on our bikes to dances. Our papers were checked sometimes by the Russians, sometimes we'd spend a night in the cells, but they were human and they always let us out again in the morning. Until then we didn't know they were even human. We'd been brought up to believe they were subhuman, *Untermenschen*.
>
> Then in 1952 relations between East and West got worse and the DDR gave orders for the frontier to be hermetically sealed. In those days I was working for the electricity board, and Bergen got its power from the DDR. Two days before Whitsun in 1952, at four o'clock in the morning, they turned the power off.

Bergen was without electricity, they had to reconnect it overland to the West, and clearly it would have been dangerous to reconnect to the old eastern grid. He himself had the job of climbing the pylon and cutting the cable to the DDR.

In the East the economic damage done by the frontier was probably greater, but East German socialism could not afford to admit its defeats. The mayor of Salzwedel, five miles east along the old *Salzstrasse*, wobbled about his relatively prosperous old town on a bike with a saddle on the crossbar for his granddaughter, and was full of socialist achievement. 'The state frontier poses no problems to our development. On the contrary we are of the opinion it is necessary for us to have so stable and secure a state frontier, because everything we achieved would only have been possible with such a stable and secure state frontier.'

Talking to him, I found myself unworthily wondering whether

Overleaf Border zone at the village of Zicherie, near Helmstedt, in 1957

there might not be some truth in the offensive graffiti painted on a wall in West Berlin: '*DDR = Der Doofe Rest*' – suggesting that those who remain may be less intelligent than those who have left. When I asked him about refugees to the West he changed the subject, and repeated the argument for the closed frontier often heard in the East, that it is a defence against the neo-Fascism reemerging 'in all the states of the Federal Republic'.

This old Cold War German–German hostility – at least until the peaceful October Revolution – was almost certainly defensive: the more its citizens deserted, the more defiant it became. At the frontier this in the past produced tragic incidents.

In the air-conditioned briefing room of the US Eleventh Armored Cavalry Regiment at Fulda, for instance, we were told how an East German helicopter had begun aping the movements of an American helicopter patrolling on the western side of the fence. The American pilot had carried out increasingly dangerous aerobatics, culminating in a dizzy drop to within a few feet of the ground. The East German helicopter, older and less manoeuvrable, had followed suit and crashed in flames. The Americans had colour slides of the aftermath: senior DDR officers inspecting the burning wreckage, then a smoke screen being laid down. When it lifts all evidence of the crash has been obliterated, even the charred grass replaced with new turf.

But the hostility was not all one-sided: just north of Dömitz, for instance, the 1945 frontier was still disputed, both sides claiming the Elbe. The West German customs thundered up and down the middle of the river in powerboats, throttles wide open, leaving their DDR equivalents, half their size and with a tenth of their horsepower, to bob in the eastern shallows, with only the obligatory cameras or binoculars up to cover their dignity.

Horsepower was what the war was about: all along the frontier the conflict was economic, and every defector was a small victory for capitalism. If, as some newspapers claimed at the time, West Germany gave five million Deutschmarks in aid to the Hungarian government when Hungary was hesitating as to whether it should release the refugees, nobody in the East would have been surprised.

Communist posters in Germany in the twenties and early thirties, before the party was suppressed by the Nazis, show the Workers of the Future seizing the Means of Production, represented in cartoon form as prosperous factories, chimneys smoking, working at full stretch. Seizing the bombed-out ruins in what had been, with a very few exceptions, the poorest part of Germany was, with Russian help, easy. Rebuilding the economy, with or without Russian help – almost all the technology that survived the war was shipped back home to Russia – was a great deal more difficult.

Boizenburg, a boat-building yard whose antiquated cranes rising above the reeds on the eastern shore of the Elbe were viewed with contempt by the West German customs in their patrol boats, was one of the powerhouses of the East German economy. On the face of it, Boizenburg was a concern that many on Humberside and other redundant Western shipyards might have envied. The business had been there for over two hundred years, there were models and photographs in the board room going back to the beginning of the present century, and there was a more confident relationship with the West: because of the height of the bridges over the Elbe, ships for export went down the river for fitting out in Hamburg, sometimes with East German labour, before being taken round by sea to Rostock on the Baltic coast. A giant crane rumbled over the half-completed hull of a cruise ship, rivets glowed red hot under the hammer, and the order books were full, including a river steamer to be built for West Germany in the face of international competition. I asked about subsidies: yes, the yard was subsidized by the government, but its survival depended on long-term orders from the Soviet Union. A board at the gates offered vacancies for every kind of skilled labour. In western Europe it might have been a sign of hope; in the D D R it was only evidence of desertion.

The Sket Engineering Works in Magdeburg were another East German success story. Built on the ruins of the old Krupp factory, they were named after the Communist leader Ernst Thälmann, imprisoned by Hitler in the thirties and secretly shot in Buchenwald. The managing director, Herr Werner, was an unusually engaging man, buck-toothed, eyes twinkling behind his spectacles, full of jokes, and of great humility. When we were shown up to his office he was standing in an overall outside the Gents, offering us a pee before the meeting, and we all assumed he was the lavatory attendant. He showed us round the factory floor, as charming and enthusiastic to his workers as he was to us.

On the walls above the machinery there were morally uplifting slogans printed on red banners, appealing to workers to fulfil the targets set by the Party Congress, and less prominently, chalked on a blackboard round the back by the nude pin-ups, management demands for less absenteeism and less damage to machinery. In an open space between the sheds was a white scoreboard, announcing successes in Socialist Achievement: Sales to Socialist Countries, 112 per cent, Sales to Non-Socialist Counties 109 per cent, and so on. I asked Herr Werner if the figures were genuine.

Of course they're genuine. It doesn't matter what country
you're in, if it's a socialist business or a capitalist business,
you can't mismanage it, get into debt. We can't, you can't.
It has to be economic. If we have to fiddle the figures that
means we're getting it wrong. No, I can understand anyone
wanting to know how we operate, but I'll tell you: we are
proud of what we're doing, it means a lot of work, a lot
of personal initiative, and a lot of overtime.

To compare the Ernst Thälmann plant with the Volkswagen works
at Wolfsburg, due west mid-way down the frontier, would be as cruel
as transmitting commercials for twenty different brands of hairspray
to East German women making do with one kind of state-manu-
factured shampoo. At Wolfsburg robots danced over the assembly
lines, watched by engineers who took their holidays in Thailand, and
a new Golf left the factory every fifteen seconds. There were no
earnest appeals to the workers' better nature, only advertisements
inflaming their basest desires. In a straight economic fight between
puritanism and materialism there was no question which was
winning.

Hence the economic importance, for the DDR, of the closed
frontier. As Wolfgang Nowe explained it.

With you, and this may sound mildly offensive, money
exercises the power, or shall we say the bourgeoisie, the
middle class. What we are saying is that the working class
has a historic mission, which it has accepted and realized
here in the DDR, and this mission has to be protected.

This mission was illustrated on a vast semi-circular bronze mural
behind the larger-than-life statue of Ernst Thälmann outside the
Sket works. The mural showed scenes from the Lives of the Saints,
Marx, Lenin, and Thälmann, the history of the struggle, and a final
panel of a kind of *oben ohne* earthly paradise, in which workers of
both sexes lolled topless in a flowery meadow or bathed in a distant
stream.

That this paradise had not yet been achieved even the most
evangelical East German Marxist would readily have conceded. But
it wasn't entirely Cloud Cuckoo Land. Christian von der Borch, a
leftist radical academic teaching in Munich who lived for a year in
the DDR, argued that the economic comparison was in any event
unfair – you wouldn't, he said, compare two countries like Italy or
Turkey on those criteria – and there was an alternative socialist way

of life in the D D R that many, even in West Germany, respected and saw as threatened.

Hardline materialism, for instance, wasn't all that of an advantage if you compared the two medieval cities of Goslar and Wernigerode. Both were in the Harz Mountains, one in the Federal Republic, the other in the D D R. Both escaped damage during the war.

Goslar's wealth had for a thousand years depended on mining: the last mine closed in 1988, leaving the city dependent largely on tourism. Capitalism had come to the aid of conservation in the usual way: old buildings had been turned into hotels and restaurants, their glass doors emblazoned with credit cards, and there was a hard, efficient glitter to the old town. Expensive cars straddled the pavement, every twist of slated gable was in place, every attic window gleaming. Walt Disney, you couldn't help feeling, would be proud of it.

The two great places of pilgrimage were the Siemenshaus, where the founder of the great Siemens electrical empire once drove his creaking old farm cart in under the carved gateway, and the local equivalent of the Mannekin Pis in Brussels, introduced by our prim middle-aged lady guide as the Ducat Shitter. Medieval debtors were made to stand *unten ohne*, their buttocks exposed, in the marketplace, and then thumped, bottom-down, on a stone until their debts were deemed to be discharged. This was expressed poetically in painted stone by the golden ducats emerging from the little figure's anus.

Wernigerode, by contrast, had a soft, untroubled provincial authenticity. Its narrow streets of old half-timbered houses had been cautiously restored, in most cases by the occupants under the direction of the town's architect. I was surprised to discover that 60 per cent of the housing stock in East Germany was privately owned. Several businesses, too, including a very good second-hand bookshop and a small porcelain factory, were *privat*. The wedding party we watched outside the medieval town hall respected the old tradition of bride and groom sawing a log in half as their first shared task as man and wife, and then drove off in a horse-drawn carriage provided by a private hire firm.

Such a degree of private ownership and gradual privatization, however, only highlighted the fragility of East Germany as a sovereign state beside its booming neighbour. To buy a half-timbered house in the prettiest part of Wernigerode, in the quiet lanes near the church, would have cost the average West German worker thirty hours' work. Owners could then apply for a state loan to restore it of about twenty times that. A similar house a few miles away in

West Germany would have cost perhaps a hundred times that total. To remove the frontier overnight would have been like breaching a dam: the East German economy would have disappeared overnight.

The extent of West Germany's proprietary attitude to the East, its belief that East German soil is still German, that is to say West German temporarily under alien control, became clear to me several days after we had left Wernigerode. We had crossed the frontier, and on returning to the East were shown a cutting from a West German newspaper for which we were held responsible. In fact we weren't, as we hadn't talked to any West German journalists, but the news-paper's attitude was none the less fascinating. Wernigerode planned to sell the so-called Gothic House, opposite the town hall, to a Swiss or Swedish hotel corporation, on condition, if the deal went through, that all the exterior walls should remain untouched. How dare the DDR, the correspondent of the *Frankfurter Rundschau* demanded, behave so irresponsibly with their German heritage?

We also had the opportunity, on the one night we were entirely out of reach of an Interhotel, of staying in flats provided for migrant workers on a council housing estate. Each flat had a fully equipped kitchen, bathroom and bedroom, a good-sized living room with a colour TV, and – always a selling point with German estate agents on either side of the frontier – a balcony. The water was hot, there were adequate towels and sheets, and the entrance hall, if concrete and raw brick, was clean and well lit. What was surprising was the absence of vandalism or any threat of violence: while we were unloading the vans a group of teenagers with bikes gathered to watch us. One of them, braver than the rest, intoned 'Do you speak English?' several times. When we answered in German they laughed, ridiculing the boy who had asked the question and dispersing. From the balcony there was a view of several hundred identical flats, in pale-coloured five-storey blocks, row after row of identical Wartburgs and Trabants parked outside. By a quarter to ten at night there was hardly a sound. Perfect socialist peace.

Arenshausen was a show village, close up against the fence in the last south-western bulge of the DDR before the frontier runs east-wards to Czechoslovakia. Such villages, within the half-kilometre security zone, were peopled, according to the official Western line, only with staunch party loyalists. The little, wooden, model watch-towers tucked away on bookshelves in the mayor's office, Sparta-kus Awards 'For Socialist Vigilance' – certainly did little to dispel

Wedding at the medieval town hall of Wernigerode in East Germany that idea. The mayor's office was still in a group of temporary huts, but the breakfast he provided, both times we visited him, would have been hard to match anywhere in West Germany: mounds of *Hackerfleisch* – raw minced pork, rough pâté, cold meats and different kinds of cheese. He said they had their own butcher – *privat*.

Although agriculture in East Germany was entirely collectivized, the land officially belonged to the individual farmer, and some fringe activities like market gardening and keeping pigs were allowed as private enterprise – hence the private enterprise butcher.

There was no sense of secret privilege about the mayor's breakfast: people from the village came and went as they would in any country community in the West, all greeted by the mayor by name, all looking relatively well off. The village, no doubt because of its front-line status, was unusually prosperous: there was a row of very competent 'self-built' houses in the traditional style lining the main street. The council provided the building materials and craft lessons, and the family, if they obtained the necessary permission, got on with it. There were also two state supermarkets, in the second of which the deputy mayor managed to find me a packet of razor blades as the first was out of stock. Teenagers leaned on their new bikes and ate ice cream outside, all the front gardens were well looked after, and the state nursery exemplary. It had been built, we were told, to supplement the Catholic nursery that had been there since the war. The children sang a song of welcome, presented bunches of flowers and played in their spotless, brand-new playrooms.

During lunch in the pub beside the new village hall the mayor suggested we should do an unscheduled interview in the new cider factory. It was *privat*. Our minder had no objection. Everything was new: showers off the upstairs workrooms, the machinery laid out on the floor, glass jars, bottle racks, filters and pumps waiting to be assembled. The cider maker had bright blue eyes, a firm handshake, and an unaccustomed entrepreneurial energy. He said he'd bought it all himself – second-hand, because he couldn't get it new – from the profits he'd made breeding pigs. 'I'd always wanted my own business.'

The newly-built village hall and community centre was dedicated to the memory of a young East German frontier guard. According to the official commendation hanging next to his picture he was 'assassinated'. I asked the mayor whether he'd been shot by West German frontier guards, and his face grew rigid with contempt. 'He was killed by a traitor who escaped to the West.'

If there was any open, state-approved discussion at all in the D D R, before October 1989, about political ideas in general or the significance of the closed frontier in particular, it was in the theatre. West Berliners were amazed at the German Language Theatre Festival in the spring of the same year to see the East German dramatist Volker Braun's adaptation of *The Three Sisters*, *Die Ubergangsgesellschaft* (Society in Transit), in which the yearning to go to Moscow becomes a yearning to go to the West. To some extent it depoliticized the issue: East Germany *was* quintessentially provincial, the drive that took East Germans to the West was the same drive that took any provincial to the big city. But the fact that the play was being performed, not only inside East Germany but to represent East German theatre abroad, six months before the troubles started in the streets, struck many as remarkable.

The Meiningen State Theatre was equally unexpected. Its director, Jürgen Juhnke, believed that change would come, that the DDR was moving towards 'the establishment of a form of Socialist democracy that will actually be fun'. He was also proud of the theatre's 158-year-old tradition, and revered above all others Duke George the Second, who was a hundred years earlier had put Meiningen on the map as the leading company in Europe.

> He created a new theatrical style: not so much a revolution, or even a reformation: he insisted on company work as opposed to the old star system. If you played the lead in one production you played a walk-on part in the next: what concerned him was form, content, the conception of a piece. You can see it in his stage designs, his sketches for scenes, the way he brought out the conflict between the classes at a time when such a thing was inconceivable. That tradition is our life.

The theatre in the DDR was generously subsidized, ticket prices were kept very low, and, unlike other 'popular theatre', Meiningen seemed genuinely to appeal to a working-class audience. While I was talking to Jürgen Juhnke in a hayfield above this open-air theatre, a line of haymakers was raking its way towards us, and the old lady leading the line, in an overall and with her head wrapped in a kerchief, called over to ask Jürgen if he'd heard that the last director of the theatre had just died of a heart attack. He said that whatever they played she was always in the audience.

The play they were rehearsing was a Hungarian piece called *Report on a Pop Festival*. The open-air theatre vibrated with amplified drums and guitars, and the Stars and Stripes was stretched between two poles above a seedy bandstand. It was the story of two Hungarian refugees in the United States, appalled by the drugs and general decadence. The hero, in long hair and jeans, was working with the director on the best way to hurl a drug peddler across twenty feet of open stage, roaring 'This is your society!'

Coming through the frontier again, to the drugged punks sprawled round the fountain in the ancient university city of Göttingen, I couldn't help feeling they might have had a point.

But despite growing pressure for change, the cautious encouragement by the East German government of private enterprise, and some freedom of speech in the theatre, the hard-liners clearly continued to dominate. I talked to the major of Sonneberg, an old toy-manufacturing town that looks across at Coburg in the West: despite a factory that exports model railways all over the world, the local toyshops were bare, the streets gloomy and deserted. Why the closed frontier, why the dogs and the watchtowers?

'The open frontier did our development a great, great deal of damage. Economically, and politically, and in many other areas. Once that interference factor was eliminated we were able to get on with developing a socialist society.'

What about those who weren't so keen on developing a socialist society?

'Our citizens have absolutely understood that there have to be regulations at the frontier. Anywhere on earth there are frontier regulations, between capitalist countries as well. There must be regulations. Our citizens are for peace and order, and that includes knowing this is where the socialist German Republic ends, and this is where the capitalist Federal Republic begins!'

On the western side, at least, they would have preferred that no such distinction had ever existed. At Lauenheim they lit a bonfire every year to remind East Germans of the day in June 1953 when East Berliners rose in protest and there was rioting in the streets, suppressed by Russian tanks. The farmer in whose field the bonfire party was to be held drove me down earlier in the evening to look at the frontier: a broken railway bridge that used to bring materials across for making of Hitler's V2 rockets, deer rustling beyond the wire, the grey mesh of the fence among the trees, the place where only months before an East German had succeeded in breaking through with a bulldozer, and had got stuck in a ditch just this side of the wire. He had been shot in the back before anyone could reach him, and dragged back into the DDR.

He talked about the struggle of farming on border subsidies.

Young people were leaving the area, there was nothing to keep them. When we got back to his battered old car flies were swarming on an oil leak, and on the way up hill again the car was full of flies.

Two trestle tables had been put up on the hillside, looking across into the forested hills of the DDR. There was beer and sausages, and a murmur of country conversation. A young man introduced himself: he'd just escaped from the DDR. I asked him how he'd come. Through the Hungarian border. This was in June: the wire had been down only a few days, all he'd had to do was avoid the Hungarian border guards. It was almost certainly stories like this, getting back to the DDR, that triggered the great exodus two months later.

As darkness fell the bonfire was lit, sparks crackling against the moon, and I looked out into the darkness of the DDR to see if there was any answering light. Apart from what could be a remote street lamp, there was nothing. I asked one of the organizers how many people he thought could see the beacon in East Germany. He said probably nobody. What he did not say was that West German television was blazing out across East Germany every night of the year, doing the same job less sentimentally but with infinitely greater impact.

But official East German reserve was evident at the Lace Festival in Plauen, in the DDR, to which the mayor of Hof, just on the other side of the frontier, had for years taken his brass band in the cause of German togetherness. A local marching band with quaint silver horns marched by, Czech drum majorettes with wonderful legs kicked past, the Russian army band strolled through playing German marches, grinning DDR Bürgers clattered by on horseback in vaguely medieval costumes under a banner recalling 'The First German Settlers', and finally the West German brass went through in their scarlet tabards and Three Musketeers hats. Then the mayor of Plauen got up to talk about socialist achievement and security, and there was a strong impression that, in official East Germany at least, the German Federal Republic was just another foreign country.

I suppose my most poignant memory of East Germany is the mining village of Völkershausen, again very close to the wire and the watch-towers. West Germans were blaming a nearby chemical works, clearly visible from the West smoking away like a painting from the early days of the Industrial Revolution, for polluting their river.

Völkershausen had a more serious complaint. According to the protest note delivered to Bonn by the East German government

Tractor at the *Spitzenfest*, or Lace Festival, at Plauen in East Germany

in the spring of 1989, West German mining engineers setting off explosions underground created the equivalent of a major earthquake. Several old houses in Völkershausen collapsed, others were wrecked beyond repair, and the onion-towered village church, built in 1711, was split from its foundations to the belfry. Miraculously no one was killed.

Local opinion was divided, although everyone agreed it was mining, one side or the other. But whether the West literally undermined the East in this instance, it would be hard, looking round the wrecked village, to find a more potent symbol of the effect that West Germany was having on the fragile sovereignty of the German Democratic Republic.

So, before they opened the Wall and allowed free travel, life continued in the Two Germanies. Everywhere in the D D R felt somehow like the late forties: it may have been the lack of traffic, the fact that there was no advertising, the shortage of money that had made them repair rather than rebuild.

To find yourself in the West German watering place of Bad Kissingen was to experience a sense of time travel of a more extreme kind. Under the royal coat of arms of King Ludwig of Bavaria, carved in stone against the blue of the sky, perfectly tended flower-beds stretched away in ordered perspective under the arching white water of decorative fountains; a deferential organ-grinder in a grey topper and morning dress – the German equivalent of the RSPCA had suppressed his monkey – played ageless, piping, German folk-songs, affluent old capitalists sunned themselves on seats along broad sandy avenues, self-made industrialists in expensively cut blazers and their ageing, sunblasted mistresses in even more expensive silk dresses promenaded under marble arcades. It could have been the set for a film about the Belle Epoque.

At Bad Salzungen too, fifty miles to the northeast, turn-of-the-century cherubs spouted salty steam, but the money had run out like water out of a cracked reservoir.

Bad Kissingen flaunted its materialism, its shameless worship of the Golden Calf, Bad Salzungen practised poverty and Socialist piety. Under the steep cathedral roof of a long wooden barn, open at the sides to shabby gardens and patches of unmown grass, the wooden outer colonnade was so rotted away by the sulphur-smelling atmosphere that its pillars were soft to the touch and came away as lint. Water trickled from the roof down a central wall of dripping, salt-encrusted birch twigs, and the penitents processed round and round, dressed in white monastic habits to protect their clothes from the all-pervasive salt, the only sound the tramp of their feet on the wooden floor, the last of German Communism's old believers.

The frontier between West Germany and East Germany ends at the *Dreiländereck* – Three Country Corner. A meadow to the south is already Czechoslovakia. A shallow brook slides by over bright pebbles, beech trees cast a dappled shadow, there is birdsong and the smell of the forest. Behind a low fence is a grave with a wooden cross and a Wehrmacht helmet. It is dedicated to the Unknown German Soldier.

RICHARD RODRIGUEZ

NIGHT AND DAY

Mexico–USA

*W*HEREVER, on the American side, there are houses
and roads and a rash of lights, you will find answering
signals on the Mexican side and a fence between. Wherever
there are lights, there are Mexicans waiting in the dark to steal
across to the American side. Whenever there is darkness, there are
Americans with floodlights trained to surprise the encroachment of
Mexico.

Each night hundreds, perhaps thousands, of Mexicans slip over
the border illegally. America officially deplores the night-time scrim-
mage, but America cannot lose. Farmers and businessmen in the
south-western United States have profited for years from cheap
Mexican labour.

Mexico is a proud country. Mexican officials are embarrassed that
so many Mexicans are leaving for the United States. Modern Mexico
is an economic failure. But Mexico measures her stature by memory,
not by an economic rule. Mexico disparages those who would leave
her as betrayers of memory.

Mexicans who cross into the United States are eluding two countries. They come privately, invisibly. They think they are invisible
because they come beneath the law, beneath the fence, beneath the
wave of history. No one is supposed to notice their comings and
goings. So long as they slip through the canyon at night, so long as
they ferry across the river at some insignificant point and at some
diminutive hour, the law – the edifice of the law – has been upheld.
For the law is sterling, *si señor*, as it is in Mexico. The law is a fine
thing. And necessity is a private venue.

Richard Rodriguez

Privately, the US border patrolman will admit that if his kids were starving he would do the same thing the Mexicans do. But the law is the law. Arresting Mexicans is his job.

'Poor Mexico, so far from God, so close to the United States.' The commonplace represents Mexico's lament, her excuse for over a century. We must be careful to attribute the *mot* to Porfirio Diaz, the Mexican president who sold more of Mexico to foreign interests than any other Mexican president. *Poor Mexico* is the Mexican national sampler, as *God Bless America* is the American device.

Lose a battle and Mexico will erect a statue in your honour, Mexicans say. Mexico has formed a national identity as an exoskeleton over defeat. Mexico's pearl is grievance. The nineteenth century should have been Mexico's time: after three centuries of colonial rule, Mexico declared her independence from Spain. But royalist Spain had bequeathed to Mexico notions of authoritarianism that were already obsolete in Europe. With independence, Mexico was left to argue with herself about the kind of country she would become, the kind of ideology she should espouse.

The pageant of nineteenth-century Mexican history was a confusing succession of ideological banns. Mexico was the richest daughter of the King of Spain. Mexico had many suitors. The French invaded Mexico in the nineteenth century. British bankers inveigled Mexico in the nineteenth century. An Austrian archduke came to marry Mexico with full panoply of candles and bishops. All the while, America reached under Mexico's skirt every chance we got.

Mexico's ruffled skirt extended over what is now the south-western United States – California, Arizona, New Mexico, Texas, Nevada and Utah, as well as parts of Colorado, Kansas, Oklahoma and Wyoming. In the early decades of the nineteenth century America, the younger, the brasher country, was the lesser country. But adolescent America was beginning to discover extroversion. 'Eminent domain,' we called it – a God-given right – and by that we meant the reach of our arms. Rough-mannered trappers, as sordid as the skins they wore, wandered into Mexico's northern territories to poach. And American settlers sailed westward over the plains in four-wheeled prairie schooners.

In time there was a war between Mexico and America. Mexico lost the South-west. Americans claimed that Mexico scarcely held the region in any case: it was empty land, poorly garrisoned, incompetently defended. Americans have never been particularly proud of the war; Americans have inclined to consign the memory of that time to amnesia or to attribute their gain to inevitability. How can you stop an epic movement of peoples?

America is an arrogant country. Mexicans notice the gringo's appropriation of the name of the hemisphere to his destiny as typical of the gringo's arrogance.

After the Mexican–American war, Mexicans who remained in the south-western United States became US citizens, but their ancestral claim on the land was lost. Spanish, the great metropolitan language of the region, was reduced to a foreign tongue, the language of the

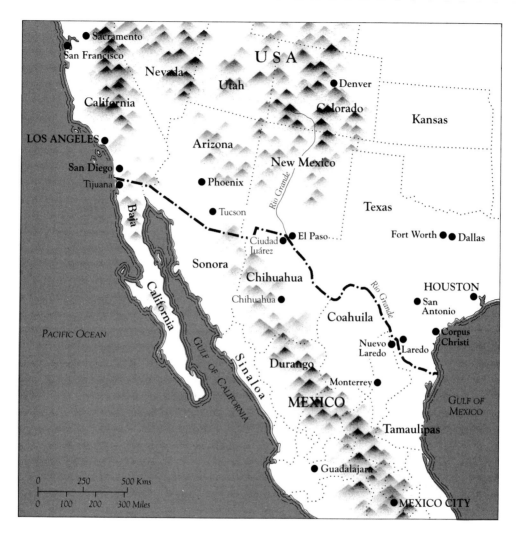

outskirts, the language of the gibbering poor, thus gibberish; English, the triumphal crushing metaphor.

In the American South-west, 'Mexican' became the name for the loser (spic, greaser). 'Gringo' was what Mexicans called the American – or, in polite company, the American was called 'Anglo'. Polite people did not say gringo. Polite people did not say Mexican either. The euphemism for 'Mexican' in the South-west was 'Latin' or 'Spanish'. To those Mexican Americans who claimed to be Spanish, who could seem to antedate strife or Indian tincture, came admission

Overleaf Mexican day workers returning home at the El Paso–Juárez crossing

to circles of civility and the possibility of social mobility and inter-marriage. Plain Mexicans, on the other hand, were poor people who came up from the border to do the dirty work of the region. Mexicans picked fruit. Mexicans dug ditches. Mexicans lived on the wrong sides of towns. Many places of congregation – theatres, restaurants, public baths – were segregated between Mexicans and Americans.

In good times for America – rich times, harvest times – America invited Mexican labour. The American expectation was always that Mexicans would disappear after the work was done. In the 1930s, the Depression years, Mexicans were rounded up by US immigration officers and thrown back over the border. But already, by the 1930s, the path between the two countries was well-worn. America had become a rite of passage for Mexican males.

Poor America! If only America were like Australia, an island country, alone in the sea. But America shares with Mexico a two thousand-mile connection; the skin of two heads. Everything America wants to believe about itself – that it is virgin country (a country of virgins), colourless, odourless – the epitome of optimism and innocence – is corrected, weighed upon, glossed by Mexico, the ballast of Mexico, the envy of Mexico, the memory of Mexico. Mexico is an old country. America is not accustomed to thinking of the New World as old or in decline. When Americans speak of the 'old country', we mean Europe.

For three or four generations now, Mexican villages have lived under the rumour of America, a rumour vaguer than paradise. America exists as a possibility in thousands of Mexican prayers. Everyone knows someone who has been.

What do you expect to find?

The answer is always an explanation for the journey: 'I want to make enough money to be able to return to live with my family in Mexico.' Proofs of America's existence abound in Mexican villages – stereo equipment, Mickey Mouse T-shirts, broken-down cars – but these are things Americans picked up or put down, not America.

Among twilit Mexican men, waiting along the levee in Tijuana to cross over, America is described by its proper name: *oportunidad*. A job. Nothing more.

Mexicans know very little of the United States, though they have seen America, the TV show, and America, the movie. When Octavio Paz, the Mexican poet, writes about the border, the United States becomes a philosophical idea of no characteristic mansion or spice. Paz has travelled and taught in America, but his writings relegate America to ineluctability – a jut of optimism, an aerodynamic law.

Compared to pulpy Mexico, grave Mexico, sandstone Mexico that takes the impression of time, the United States and its promise of the future must seem always hypothetical – occasion more than place. When I ask a middle-class Mexican what he admires about the United States (a provocative question because, according to Mexican history and proverb, there is nothing to admire in the United States), he finds only one disembodied word: organization. When I press the man to anthropomorphize further, he says, 'Deliveries get made, phones work, breaks are repaired' (indirect construction, all as if by the consent of unseen hands).

My father, who is now in his eighties, was born in Mexico, but has lived most of his life in America. America barely exists for my father. There is too much diversity, he says; no common purpose; too many permissions.

Both my mother and father came to America for political reasons more than for economic reasons. They came separately but within a few years of each other – she as a girl with her family; he as an orphan, alone. Both my parents fled the civil war that Mexican politicians prefer to describe as Mexico's Revolution. When the dust of Revolution settled, Catholic Mexico had an anti-Catholic government; my mother and father were missing.

In the United States there are, officially counted, twelve million persons who are Mexican-born (like my parents) or of Mexican ancestry (like myself). But who can say how many of us there are? There are many Mexicans illegally here whose business it is to elude any count. And there are Mexicans, some of my own relatives, who have lived on this side of the border most of their lives, but have never bothered to apply for American citizenship.

The cliché about Mexican Americans is that they are unlike other immigrants to the United States. Mexicans won't speak English, Mexicans don't vote. Mexicans don't try to change. The cliché explanation for Mexican–American reticence is the proximity of Mexico. Most Mexican Americans live within two or three hours of the border, which is within the possibility of recourse to Mexico, or within the sound of her voice. By contrast, the conventional American immigrant myth describes an ocean – amnesia – immigrants from Europe leave behind several time zones and all the names for things. The traditional assumption of America is that immigrants will change.

The other night I met a man from Hungary. He speaks American with a European accent – unconfident dustcovers muffle his words, and many words not yet unpacked. He speaks only English now. Though his native Hungary is near the epicentre of political change in Europe, he says he avoids reading despatches from Budapest. He is training his imagination upon the United States, and he fears losing concentration.

You will look a long time before you will find a Mexican immigrant who professes such an imperative to close off the past. Mexicans new to America may be as bewildered as other immigrants, but they will never admit that the scaling of America requires them to relinquish any burden of the past.

Coming from Mexico, a country that is so thoroughly *there*, where things are not necessarily different from when your father was your age, it is no wonder Mexican immigrants find America transparent. No wonder Mexicans are unable to describe America as more than an idea. No wonder Mexicans are unable to puncture the abstraction. Mexicans are not willing to submit themselves to abstraction. For Mexicans, even death is less abstract than America.

In the Central Valley of California where I grew up, Mexican farmworkers regularly commuted between the past and the future. Every autumn, after the tomatoes and the melons and the peaches had been picked, Mexicans would take their children out of American schools, load up their cars and head back into Mexico for two or three months. The American schoolmarm was scandalized by what she took as the Mexicans' neglect of their children's futures.

The theme of America is discontinuity. America's national faith is Protestant. Americans believe in conversion, in Pauline rebirth. You can escape your father's eyes. You can escape your father's sins. You can escape your father. You can – you should – earn more money than your old man. You can escape history. All that the past had in store for you should be dissolved.

Between immigrant parents and their native-born children, silence elongates like shadow upon a wall. Children no longer speak. It is such a drag to have to explain everything to your parents.

Parents say, eh, eh, what do you say?

America's most forbidding proverb is 'You can't go home again.' But Americans are a pragmatic people. We refuse to worry about what cannot be repaired. Estrangement from the past is the only inevitability. On the other hand, there isn't much that cannot be repaired in America. You can even get a new heart in America.

Mexican teenagers waiting on the levee in Tijuana are bound to be fooled by the United States because they do not yet realize that the future can be as binding as the past. Abstraction exerts positive force in America. Mexicans do not understand that once they land a job, they have landed in America. Americans use work to overturn the authority of their fathers. You leave one job only to find another, better. As you earn more money you become a person of choices, a self-made man. In America you are rewarded individually. The American job will introduce the Mexican to an industry, an optimism, a solitude nowhere described in Mexico's theology.

How can two Mexican teenagers know this, clutching the paper bags their mamas packed for them this morning? The past is already the future, for the bags contain only a change of underwear. These two may have seen *Dallas* on TV and they may think they are privy to the mind and locution of America. But that is not the same thing as having twenty American dollars in their own pockets. America seems not to pose any obstacle to their private purpose. How can something that is not there keep them from returning to Mexico?

Ask an American to define America and you will hear something as abstract as anything you'd hear from a Mexican, though couched in words of positive rather than negative connotation: America is the land of the free, the home of the brave.

How do you film that? What do you show? The Grand Canyon? Grand Central Station? The flag at Iwo Jima? The Statue of Liberty?

If I were to show you America, or try, I would take you to the restaurant – OPEN TWENTY-FOUR HOURS/BREAKFAST SERVED ALL DAY – on Frontage Road, alongside a freeway, any freeway in the USA. The waitress is a blonde or a redhead – not the same colour as at her last job. She is divorced. Her eyebrows are jet-black migraines painted on, or relaxed, clownish domes of cinnamon brown. Morning and the bloom of youth are painted on her cheeks. She is at once anti-maternal – the kind of woman you're not supposed to know – and supra-maternal, the nurturer of lost boys. She'll call you hon.

She is the priestess of the short order, curator of the apple pie. She administers all the consolation of America. She is brisk. She'll tell you she has no illusions. She knows the score. She knows what you like. She's never seen you before. She'll never see you again. She hands you the oversized menu printed on plastic.

Your table may yet be littered with bitten toast and spilled coffee and a dollar tip. Now you will see the greatness of America. As one complete gesture, the waitress pockets the tip, stacks dishes along one strong forearm, produces a damp rag soaked in Lethe water which she then passes over the formica tabletop.

There! With that one swipe of the rag, the past has been obliterated. The waitress has removed all trace of customers who preceded you. The formica gleams like new. You can order anything you want.

My father expected to sail past pragmatism to romance – he once heard a German sailor boast of Australia. My father from Mexico never made it to Australia. The Australian Consul-General in San Francisco discouraged him from going any further. There were no jobs in Australia – well, none for a Mexican – so my father settled for America. He ended up, by accident, making false teeth in Sacramento.

I remember my father, still a young man, in a white coat, in a white room, surrounded by shelves of grinning false teeth. But this is not an ironical portrait of my father as he then was. Irony had no power over my father. My father had a job. The assurance of my American childhood was that I would not end up making false teeth in Sacramento.

Growing up in Sacramento I fell in love with the idea of America, but not at first as an idea. At school, during most of the year, America was an abstraction, a concept for the civics class or a Pledge of Allegiance. In summer America was palpable. Days were long and warm and free and I could make of them what I liked. For almost any American child, the abstraction of freedom is clothed in the leaves of summer. Summer is the season when an American child is free of the constraints of lessons, of history, of memory. Because I was excused from participating in America, I could notice that America really existed. America tickled my feet and warmed my back. I drank it and swam in it and lounged around on its prickly green, confident America would take me wherever I wanted to go. America rose in summer, even as the grasses, even as the heat, even as planes rise. America opened like a sprinkler's fan or like a book in summer. At the Clunie Library in McKinley Park, the books that pleased me most were books about boyhood and summer and America; synonyms.

Huck Finn could change his identity in the light of every lantern along the Mississippi River. America was that large and that generous. Huck could pass as a girl, or the two scalliwags he met up with could pass themselves off as English nobility. (America is a place where you can name yourself. You can be anything you want to be.)

I'm going to be a fireman. I'm going to be a nurse. American children are encouraged very early to name what they will be. Say whatever you want. America will not laugh. America will regard you with the gravity of a Puritan father and give you its blessing: you must only work very hard.

In the nineteenth century, the United States opened itself to

School for illegal immigrants in Houston, Texas

immigrants from non-Protestant, southern European countries. Then there were outbursts of nativist violence in America. But America resisted the impulse to closure. And by remaining open to outsiders, America discovered its Protestant virtue.

When I was a university student in England a few years ago, I fell in with a Pakistani student from Birmingham. The Pakistani was curious about my American face. My face was nearly his face. Which is harder, he finally must ask, being brown in Britain or being brown in America? I couldn't say about England. I hadn't really needed to meet England. I'd met professors and graduate students and people at the box offices of plays. But I could answer that the outsider is the quintessential American. The outsider in the USA may be taunted for being different, for being brown, for being 'foreign' – reticent in manner or voice. But America is, by self description, an immigrant country and Americans must recognize their ancestors in the latest, newest comer.

Growing up in California, what was my oppression? A few strangers, mainly children, shouted out at me a handful of times: 'Dirty Mexican!' And in the world of schoolboys I had to learn a game of ethnic name-calling, analogous to butt-slapping in what passes for good male fun. I accepted the fiction of sacrificial slurs. The reminder of my difference was intended as proof of my acceptance. In turn, I gave as good as I got. What else? The billboards were blond. Story books were blond. The faces of politicians were pale. I never doubted, though, that I belonged in America. I knew enough about America to realize that my parents, with their accents and their Mexican manners – but with their refusal to betray any embarrassment – had purchased America for me.

I never once bought into the romance of small-town America – the white Protestant church on the square, the drugstore, the Elks building. My version of America was never settled or homogenous. It was always big. Big city. New York, Chicago, San Francisco. Impossible cities of tumult and pulse.

Los Angeles seems to me today the most American of America's cities. When I am homebound from some other part of the world, from Europe or one of those sterile, circuit-soldering cities of Asia, I always try to arrange a flight that will take me non-stop to LA. My eyes smart with recognition as the plane begins its descent – the smog, the corrosive atmosphere, the freeways.... And nearer: the Protestant backyards, little Puritan squares of green, the winking swimming pools.... And nearer still: the billboards, legible promises upholding the highest per capita and an unstable chic. Los Angeles is an impossible city of individual ambitions, like eighteenth-century

Above Slums in
Tijuana
Right Homeless
mother
On the US border,
Tijuana is one of the
fastest growing cities
in Mexico, with a
population of a
million or more.

Above A game of volleyball played over the
fence which divides the US and Mexico
Right Tijuana street scene
Overleaf Undocumented aliens caught trying to
enter the US illegally are rounded up and
returned to Mexico.

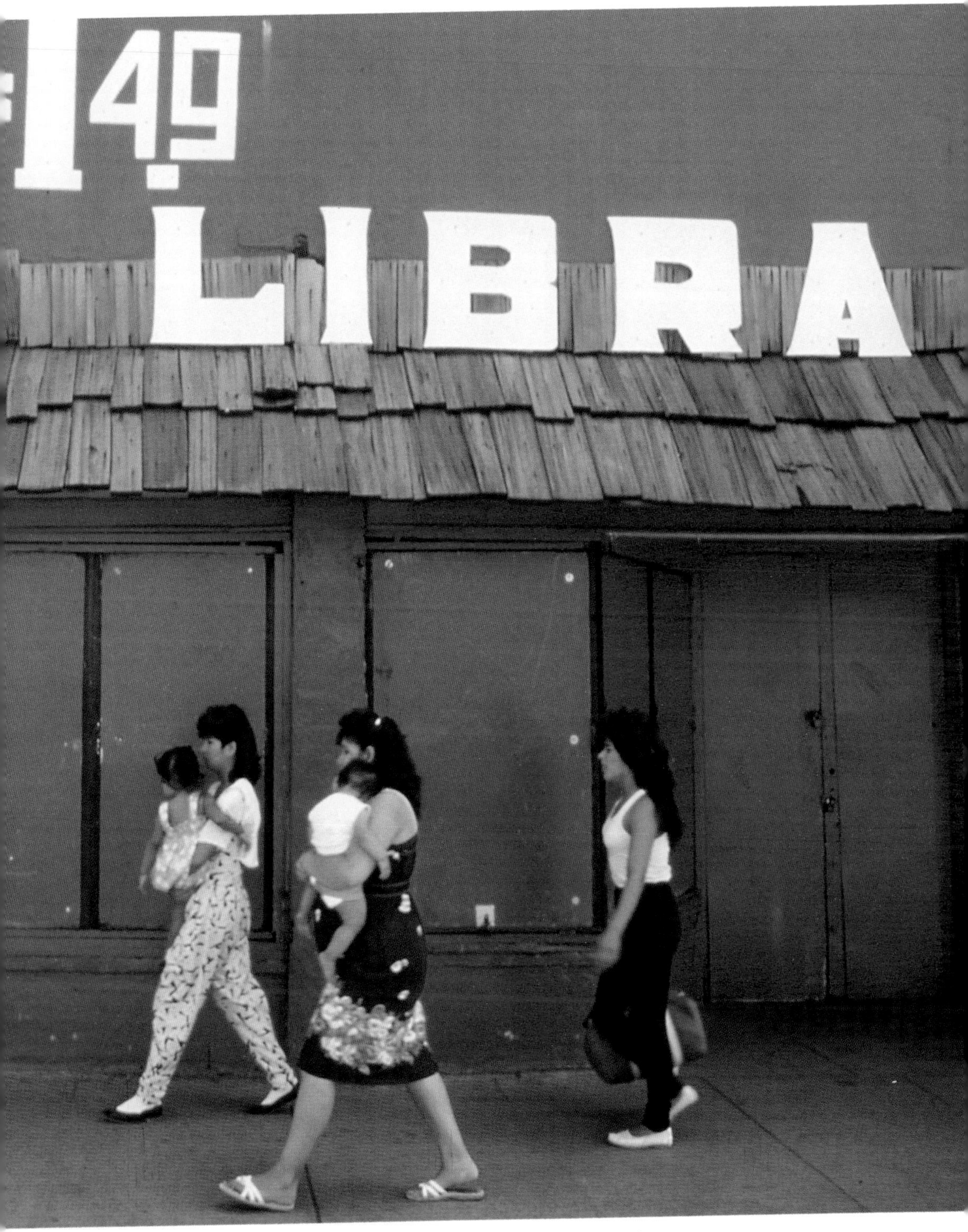
LIBRA

The Pyrenees **(left)**, the most natural of
frontiers, divides France and Spain. But the
frontier has many anomalies, among them the

Val d'Aran **(above)** which has belonged to
Spain since the thirteenth century although it
lies on the northern side of the mountain range.

Above Basque graffiti. Wall paintings depicting Picasso's masterpiece *Guernica* decorate many public places in the Spanish Basque country.

Below Graffiti of the Catalan separatist movement in Barcelona. The star and stripes in the left-hand corner represent the Catalan flag.

London. People are beginning to say that it doesn't work any more; LA doesn't work any more.

But it will in the future. If traffic standstill occurs first in L A – maybe as early as next Monday morning – so too will some austere, some outlandish solution.

Internationally Los Angeles is famous as a loony-tune town. Los Angeles is still described by the union of orthodox states as 'laid back', 'far out' – a tribe of fantasists, utopians, lotus-eaters. Unlike the East Coast cities, Los Angeles has been the creation of 'internal immigrants', of people fleeing American constraint elsewhere – Brooklyn, Granville, Cedar Rapids – for year-long summer, the perpetual assurance of freedom. Here America recreates America.

Now Los Angeles is, as well, the immigrant capital of the USA, the new New York. Los Angeles is filling with Thais and Syrians and Koreans. More numerous than any other immigrant group are Mexicans. Los Angeles has the second largest Mexican population in the world, second only to Mexico City – the new Mexican's city.

On US maps of my schooldays, I remember Mexico was often designated 'OLD MEXICO'. This whim of map-makers was, in part, romance. If America was asphalt, Mexico should be parchment. But partly it was America's way of distinguishing Mexico (jaundiced yellow) from the evergreen United States. New York, New Jersey, New Mexico – 'new' is the adjective Americans trust. I did. I was repelled by Mexico's association with the old. In my imagination Mexico was a bewhiskered hag, huddled upon an expanse of rumpled canvas, which bore her legend: OLD MEXICO. Mexico betrayed an inimical regard of me. She claimed knowledge. She claimed intimacy. But Mexico couldn't claim me. Mexico was nothing to do with me. I wasn't born there. I'd never been there.

Where you from?

Eventually I answered, 'Mexico'. Initially, in order to confound what I took as my interrogator's attempt to demoralize my sense of belonging to America, I gave the straight answer: 'San Francisco, California.' Maybe I understand the question better now, maybe not. But I wasn't from Mexico. I was an American child. I was an heir to Protestantism.

Though I was a Catholic schoolboy. Very early, certainly before I could distinguish between Methodists and Baptists, I was introduced to the idea of Protestantism. Protestants were people unwilling to put on the full flesh of communal Catholicism – which included tragedy – preferring a brighter, plainer, disembodied faith. They didn't go to confession. They didn't fall to their knees. They sang with clarion voices. I loved to hear Protestant hymns as I bicycled

225

Confirmation ceremony at Tijuana

past their churches on weekday nights or on Sunday mornings. Protestants went to church in suits and ties; Catholics went as they were.

Puritans first appeared to me in transparent guise – as smiling, doll-like figures with lacy collars and buckles and muskets – figures to colour at Thanksgiving time. America's Founding Fathers never seemed dour to me, they seemed optimistic and without precedent, open to interpretation. Hadn't English Puritans cut themselves loose from the Old World? They stood alone before God and believed, as latter-day Californians also believe, that history can be re-invented. I believed these optimistic people would protect me from Old Mexico.

Mexico is a proud country. Mexico regards herself as America's cultural rival and moral superior. Outside the great porous churches of Mexico are signs reminding tourists to behave with dignity. *Please to cover your head. Please to observe silence.* The signs are in English.

Mexico is embarrassed by her dusty border towns; even more embarrassed by her booming border towns along the US line. In the opinion of Mother Mexico the border states incline too much towards the north. Border Mexicans speak vulgar Spanish – mongrel, really. They hear too much American music. They watch too much American television. Their politics are too much of the gringo. They are

Selling souvenirs at the Tijuana–San Diego crossing

not rooted in history, in memory, in Mexico. Mexico would warn visitors not to make too much of the border. Real Mexico, its great, watery heart, lies elsewhere.

The best travel books about Mexico in English have been written by the British, not by Americans. Americans think they know what Mexico is. (Mexico is the absence of America.) In Puritan culture, wealth is a sign of election. And God Almighty, look at the squalor of Mexico! Since the nineteenth century, Americans have describd Mexico as a shambles.

Whereas for Graham Greene, D. H. Lawrence, Sybille Bedford and Evelyn Waugh, Mexico has much allure. Mexico has five senses and an enormous, unwieldy, medieval soul. In his recent travel account of Mexico and Central America, *So Far from God*, Patrick Marnham dispenses with California ('that part of America that is so far into the future that it is practically detached from the continent'). The United States cannot impede this British traveller – America, in Marnham's view, is only Britain's 'monstrous child'. (The English think they know what America is.)

I think the reason the British have been so interested in Mexico is that they have recognized in Mexico the other. Mexico is opposite the English Protestant experiment. Mexico is the incarnation of Renaissance England's sixteenth-century antagonist – Mexico is

Spanish, Mexico is the duskier New World possibility.

In North America, English settlers and Indians stood apart, and they have remained apart through centuries. The Spaniards came to plunder, to prop up the Old World order. But the Spaniard came also to convert the Indian. In the history of colonialism few ideas are as remarkable as Spanish Catholicism's insistence that Indians had souls, and were, therefore, spiritually the Europeans' equals.

Temples were overturned in Mexico. Blood was spilled. Women were ravished. But the rape of Mexico became a marriage. The generous impulse within Spanish Catholicism – Spaniards as baptists – found a corresponding curiosity within the Indian – Indians as contemplatives.

Mexico is mestizo. Today 90 per cent of the country is of mixed blood, Spanish and Indian. In its language, as in its architecture, as upon the plaza – the stretched soul of Mexico – it is impossible to say where the Indian survives and the Spaniard surrenders.

In America, Indians were sequestered as a separate nation. In many south-eastern states, miscegenation was declared illegal (to ensure that any transaction between black and white should remain abstract and not take flesh). How could America, with its ideal of individuality, understand the mixture of Mexico? In America's eyes, Mexico was a crime. Mexico was a joke. During the Mexican–American war, Americans perceived Mexicans as inept, cowardly, weakened by their mixture.

Mexicans invariably speak of Spain as bearded, leathery, coarse. Mexicans invariably speak of Mexico as mother, taking the Indian part. Politically, Mexico has always seen herself as the virgin set upon by brigands at a clearing in the woods. The metaphor lent Mexicans a convenient excuse for political incompetence. Though the entire political rhetoric of Mexico is predicated upon victimization, Mexico is in fact both Indian and Spanish. And it is this union – the capacity of Mexico to join two races as one flesh – that I would call a truly feminine or maternal genius. Miscegenation is Mexico's Gioconda secret, her glamour, her royal trump over the little Puritan up north.

America's transparency does not lend itself to sexual metaphor. George Washington is the father of the country. We speak of the Founding Fathers. But the legend ascribed to the Statue of Liberty is childlessness. America is an immigrant country. Motherhood is less our point than adoption. If I had to assign gender to America I would notice the consensus of the rest of the world. When America is burned in effigy, a male is burned. Americans themselves speak of Uncle Sam.

Like the goddess of Liberty, Uncle Sam has no children of his own. He is the personification of conscription. He steals children to make men of them. Uncle Sam is a hectoring Yankee, a skinflint uncle, gaunt, uncouth, unloved. But he is always right. He is the American Savonarola – hater of moonshine, destroyer of stills, burner of cocaine. Free enterprise is always an evasion of Uncle Sam, and in a way he represents necessary evil to the American imagination. He is implacable. He will nail you in the end. He is the Fed.

You betray Uncle Sam by favouring private over public life, by seeking to exempt yourself from the commonweal; by cheating on your income taxes; by avoiding jury duty; by trying to keep your son on the farm. These are legal offences.

Betrayal of Mother Mexico, on the other hand, is a sin against the natural law, a failure of memory. Mexico has a name for those Mexicans who cross over the border for the gringo and grow estranged from her: *pocho*. The Mexican who forgets his mother is a *pocho*.

I was a *pocho* from boyhood. People used to say to me, 'Be proud of Mexico, be proud of your heritage. Don't lose your Spanish. It is a wonderful thing to speak two languages.' But nobody told me how to reconcile countries as different as day and night. And I never confessed that I was afraid of the dark.

America seemed to me a country of daylight. Mexico belonged to the night. When Americans first meet, they ask one another's occupation. 'What do you do?' (What do you do in the light of day?) Americans do not as readily enquire about family ties or about place of birth. They assume they have no right to know. Identity in America is active.

In Mexico people work very hard. There is a frenzy to Mexican labour. But in contrast to America, where work ennobles, in Mexico work degrades. Mexicans work quickly because work is evil. Mexicans are made for leisure, for eternity. Work is the result of man's sinful condition, his expulsion from Eden. One must work to live, but work is not life. Work is a curse.

As night approaches the Mexican turns towards home, the last vestige of paradise. In Mexico, identity comes from being recognized. It is within the realm of leisure, within the company of family, that one is recognized.

I met an old woman in Mexico who seemed to me more alone than anyone I had met. She was a beggar woman in a slum market in Mexico City. The aisles of the market were covered with canvas and on either side of these tent walls hung chickens and flowers and pineapples. Within the transept of the market, against a stone wall, the old woman ('*madre*', everyone called her) kept her anchor-hold.

Hair grew out of her nose like winter breath. Her only reply was 'No'. No husband. No sisters. No brother. Her son was dead. She had no children alive and that was her tragedy. If there was no one to recognize her, no one to claim her from the past, then she was unalterably separated from life. She lived in eternity, but not as a nun lives, or a devotee of Krishna, but as Job lived. Even the poor neighbourhood people, the poorest of the poor, could spare a few pesos for the mother of tragedy. People were in awe of her, for she was without grace, which in Mexico is children.

Americans eat early. Mexicans eat at about the time Americans get ready for bed, though both peoples inhabit the same time zones. Mexicans are people who move as naturally and comfortably in the dark as cats or wolves or owls do. Mexicans take their famous promenade around the plaza at night. Mexicans gossip beneath the lamppost. Mexicans get drunk and sing like cats beneath the moon. Mexicans take their meaning from the dark.

Though Mexicans are hired to do the dirty work of America, Mexicans are otherwise ridiculed in the United States as people who sleep during the day – witness the famous siesta, a paradisical habit, surely. The figure on the ceramic ashtray, the figure that forms the bookend – the Mexican figurine is always taking his siesta, propped against a cactus, shaded by his sombrero. Mexicans are always late, or, refusing to be circumscribed by time, they resort to *mañana*. Don't worry. It is the Mexican's gloss on the light of day. *Mañana*, by definition, will never come. *Mañana* intends to undo all the adages of the English language. Waste not, want not. Don't put off till tomorrow. A stitch in time.

Americans take short shrift from sorrow, reassuring one another that tomorrow is a new day; or time heals all wounds. The genius of American culture and its integrity comes from fidelity to the light. Plain as day, we say. Happy as the day is long. Early to bed, early to rise. American virtues are daylight virtues: honesty, integrity, plain speech. We say yes when we mean yes and no when we mean no, and all else comes from the evil one. America presumes innocence and even the right to happiness.

The Mexican presumption is the Catholic presumption of guilt.

The British journalist Alan Riding observes, in *Distant Neighbours*, that in Mexico 'the concept of commonwealth barely exists' – though all the forms of commonwealth are in place, from traffic lights to voting boxes. Mexico City is chaos. The air is the colour of the buildings of Sienna. People drive on the sidewalks. Telephone connections are an aspect of the Will of God. But Mexico manages to live withal and Mexican politicians wear dark glasses. It is Mexican custom to listen to the politician's amplified promise and to assume the reverse to be true. Cynicism is an aspect of the Mexican habit of always seeking the shade. In daylight nothing is what it seems. The listed price is subject to barter; the jail sentence can be commuted with a bribe.

At night, Mexico City will fool you with its beauty, its crowds, its perfume. Mexico is a nineteenth-century country arranged for gaslight. Once brought into the harsh light of the twentieth-century media, Mexico can only seem false. In its male, in its public, its city aspect, Mexico is an arch-transvestite, a tragic buffoon. Dogs bark and babies cry when Mother Mexico walks abroad in the light of day. The policeman, the Marxist mayor – Mother Mexico doesn't even bother to shave her mustachios. Swords and rifles and spurs and bags of money chink and clatter beneath her skirts. A chain of martyred priests dangles from her waist, for she is an austere, pious lady. Ay, how much – clutching her jangling bosoms; spilling cigars – how much she has suffered.

Mexico is a country of nuance and mascara. The language is an architecture of exquisite insincerity, excessive protestations of affection or interest. Transposed into the sunlight of an American street corner, displays of Mexican machismo seem much too theatrical – ridiculous struttings and posings. American feminists loathe machismo. But Mexican machismo, like Mexican politics, needs its *mise-en-scène*. In fair Verona, in doublet and hose, it might yet play. Machismo is not simply an assertion of power or potency. It is a rite of chivalry. The macho is a protector of the helpless and the needy.

True Mexican *machismo* is more akin to *gravitas* than volatility. In the 1950s, Mexican men came up to California to work as contract labourers in the fields. Every Saturday they would come into Sacramento and I would see them crowding the Western Union office, waiting to send money back home to Mexico. The Mexican male is taught that to remain male he must not abandon those who depend upon him. He remains a faithful son, always the son, a faithful father, a faithful husband (though otherwise famous for his infidelities).

Poor Mexico! The lament is false to the extent that it is convenient as a political excuse; but 'Poor Mexico' does rhyme with a tragic disposition of Mexicans, older and deeper than politics. Mexico's tragic sense is both Indian and Spanish, and it is as manifest in the stone faces of Indian gods as upon the bloodied crucifixes of Mexican churches. Mexicans are famous for their pastry skulls and their skeleton figurines. Many such death-ridden kewpies and pre-occupations converge in the phrase used by philosophers and tourists to describe Mexico: Mexican fatalism. Mexican fatalism is not

231

Top Migrants gather on the Mexican border waiting for dark to run
across to the USA
Above An undocumented Mexican day worker is carried over the Rio
Bravo near the El Paso–Juárez crossing
Right US Border Patrol rounding up illegal migrants during the night

despair, as you might expect. Mexican fatalism is humour. Mexicans delight in levelling farce – developments unforeseen – which nevertheless reinforce inevitability. Mexicans can see in the dark: the priest with his whisky bottle; the lover beneath the bed; the skull beneath the skin.

There is nothing new under the Mexican sun. Individual assertion is beside the point. Mexicans learn to live with limits and to seek (and to forgive) consolations. Tragic cultures serve up better food than optimistic cultures. Mexico has better food and darker beer than America, and bigger families with politer children. Mexican children are never protected from life's largest lesson.

My mother's favourite proverb is almost a curse: 'As you see yourself, I once saw myself; as you see me now, you will be seen.' (*Como te ves, me ví; como me ves, te verás*). My mother is arthritic, her joints are swollen, her shoulders are heavy with time. Still, she laughs at the proverb. In tragic cultures the old have something to teach the young. And they are believed.

My father watches America from his living room window. He always remarks on the American expectation of repair. Not: Can it be fixed? Rather, How long will it take? How much will it cost?

Americans believe that most things can be fixed. When the tree branch falls or the pavement cracks, someone comes out from 'the city' to repair the damage.

The American expectation of commonwealth turns shrill when it goes on tour. The trouble with gringo tourists, the Mexican hotel manager confides, is that they are always complaining. Usually about the water. The water! Nothing wrong with the water, the Mexican says. I drink it all day, the Mexican says. But the gringos won't drink. They won't swim in the pool or sing in the shower. They go to restaurants and they refuse to eat. Is it clean? Is it safe?

Along the US–Mexico border, Americans cross over the line after dark. Traditionally, Americans have gone to Mexico for whores or for *cerveza* or *cualquier cosa*. Mexico has always obliged, for a price, though in the light of day, both partners deny everything.

My mother became an American secretary. California met my mother's ambition (an ambition unnatural in Mexico for she never wanted to become a seamstress like her mother). I remember my Mexican grandmother when she was in her seventies, dressed all in black, sewing in the pale afternoon light of California. When my grandmother's eyes got so bad she could no longer sew, she sat still and waited for death to find her.

Now my mother is late in her seventies. Every night my mother does her 'exercises'. My mother revolves her arms. She lies on her back on the prickly green carpet and slowly she raises her legs, first one, then the other. She is considering purchasing an exercycle – a bicycle that doesn't go anywhere, an American bicycle designed to outrun death.

What, after all, shall Odysseus do after he returns to Penelope? How shall the life that takes its meaning from action find coherence in retirement? Americans are bound to be better readers of the *Odyssey* than of the *Iliad*. We trust the comic epic's description of the active life and of the journey, and just as the *Odyssey* devolves in anti-climax, so America exists only so long as it remains unresolved.

In the United States, where life takes its meaning from new beginnings, it is crucial that the elderly keep young. In America, men as old as Laertes run marathon races. Grandmothers lift weights. If you do not keep busy in America, you are beside the point in America. The silent old woman sitting in front of her TV all day – or who knows what she does? – in her fiercely flowered housedress, is beside the point. It's not that she doesn't have children. She's a burden on her children – she is weighing them down.

What happens to the idea of America when Americans no longer feel young?

My parents have ended up in America with a big house. They fall asleep watching the colour television in their bedroom. On top of the TV are portraits of their middle-aged children and their grand-children, 'as tall as movie stars'. America has worked for my parents the same way America has worked for millions of other immigrants. But even my parents, those two voyagers, have begun – just once in a while – to regret changes in their neighbourhood wrought by those 'newcomers'; the old stores going out of business; the old neighbours moving away.

Americans are caught in a labyrinth of their own desire. Americans realize that the nation's energy, its very identity, comes from immi-grants. Still, Americans often come to resent new immigrants, perhaps out of envy, perhaps from fatigue. It is unsettling to live in a country that leaves itself open to constant recreation, constant change. Something in the soul wants the assurance of settling, the calm of a finish. In the nineteenth century, American nativists wished for a country that would remain Protestant, northern European in character. A century later, the issue is Europe. Shall America remain a European idea? America is crowding now with faces from Asia and Latin America. American cities and states that feel themselves most 'threatened' by immigrants have voted to declare English 'the official language of America'. English is, of course, *de facto* the official language of the United States. The vote is intended as a reminder to newcomers – mainly Hispanics – that there are, after all, limits to America's willingness to accommodate the newcomer.

But it is not merely nineteenth-century xenophobia that makes Americans wary of the Mexican border. As the twentieth century closes, Americans realize there is not enough room in the United States for everyone in the world who would come.

A new tragic sensibility is beginning to inform America. I hear it most clearly from within the environmental movement. What the environmental movement is telling Americans is that we may have already exhausted the future. Tomorrow is a smoggy day.

Try to keep fit, the Puritan father now counsels. Hope for the best. Lose weight. But you'll have to wait in line to buy a house. And you'll have to pay a lot more than your father did.

The traditional cult of the American first-person pronoun is challenged by new immigrants from Asia and Latin America. Today's non-European immigrants come from highly communal cultures. Americans have watched the post-war economic ascendancy of Asia with disbelief. For Americans have always assumed that our economic invincibility came from individualism – the Excalibur 'I'. Asian examples suggest the reverse: economic vitality can be forged from a corporate 'we'.

From Latin America, meanwhile, from Mexico, from poverty, comes the chaotic, the effusive, the glamorous example of the plural pronoun. If there is much in the Latin American and Asian 'we' that Americans resent ('First one comes over, next thing the whole damn family is here'), there is also some tantalizing possibility of a new frontier.

Americans have taken to eating sushi. Perhaps it will make us lean, corporate warriors. Perhaps Mexican Combination Plate #3, smothered in mestizo gravy, will burn a hole through our hearts.

CLANK. CLANK. All day and all night the turnstile whirls at the US–Mexico border crossing. The turnstile must be broken. Is that why it clanks? The San Diego-Tijuana border crossing is the busiest on earth. The poorest Mexicans and the gaudiest gringos cross paths at what must surely be one of the most remarkable points of irony in the world. The US tries to keep a tally of how many people enter the United States here annually. Forty million, fifty.... CLANK. CLANK.

If America still looks pretty fit in middle-age, look at Mexico: like the story-book crone who throws off a ragged cloak, ancient Mexico has grown so young. She is wearing a Mickey Mouse T-shirt. Half of the population of Mexico has yet to reach puberty. The average Mexican is fifteen years old. Mexico is memory. But what is the prognosis for memory in a country so young?

Even as Americans blame illegal immigrants for undermining America's 'quality of life', Mexicans are on the move. Since the Second World War, there has been an epic migration within Mexico, which is the movement from the medieval village into the twentieth-century city – Mexico City or Tijuana. The cities of Mexico have become crowded with ambition, swollen with desperation. Consider Tijuana. Forty years ago Tijuana was hardly more than a hootchy-kootch curtain. Today Tijuana is a city of a million, perhaps two million people. There is movement. There is money. There is youth. There are factories. There are car repair shops!

One night in Tijuana I go to a new nightclub district that attracts the sons and daughters of the city's upper middle class. These nightclubs are built in an architectural style that resembles an eighteenth-century colonial village (which Tijuana never was). Each club or restaurant has a different international theme. Down one lane you will discover a Greek restaurant. Across the way is a bodega with a flamenco soundtrack. The sons and daughters of *parvenu* Tijuana wander here and there, dressed in international idioms of Milan, New York and Tokyo. These children seem to me as rootless as any American children, quite unlike any Mexicans I am used to seeing. There is even a restaurant where Mexicans can sit and eat traditional Mexican cooking; a floor show features folk dances of Mexico, awkwardly executed.

Civic leaders in Tijuana are embarrassed by the lewd tattoo on the reputation of their city. Progressives refer to the honky-tonk past of Tijuana as 'the dark legend'. Tijuana would rather you notice its skyline of office towers, its industrial parks – the daytime city. Meanwhile, the Mexican government spends millions to lure Americans south. Come to the sun, the Mexican advertisements say, though Mexico's allure to the Americans has always been as the dark.

That same night, over by the border crossing, thousands of American teenagers, under-aged and not, and marines and sailors, and rah-rah collegians, and lone men on the prowl are slipping into Mexico. Traditionally Americans have used Tijuana to relieve their virtue in the dark.

'It's just cool to get drunk in Tijuana,' one woman tells me. She is in her twenties. She comes from northern England.

CLANK.

America grows older; Mexico has acne. Americans yearn for a plural identity; Mexicans leave home in search of individualism.

Each country changes into a parody version of the other. And so even as they change, Mexico and America are fated to remain antagonists. America is entering a post-modern, post-American phase. Mexico is beginning her eighteenth century. The population of Mexico is stirring; young men and women are embarked upon the high road to London.

CLANK. CLANK.

The danger is that both countries will regret what they will become. Great political power awaits the rhetorician in Mexico who can tap the rural nostalgia of Mexicans who find themselves alone, lost in the chaos of the city. Americans, for their part, may turn against the traditional notion of their country as an immigrant nation, may seek to protect the future by limiting it.

The US Border Patrol has erected tall standards atop which spotlights are fixed. At the line separating the two sovereign countries, the poor gather at dusk. Old women cook skinny chickens on open braziers to sell to the people who will travel this night. Pedlars sell torn coats and sweaters for evening has turned cold. Bandits pass among the pilgrims, appraising with their eyes the *pollos* – the chickens – victims in Tijuana slang. Fagin, Sikes, the Artful Dodger – all alive, all present. And innocence is here as well – a father, a mother, two daughters wait patiently near the fence as if they are to have their picture taken. Two teenage boys clutching paper bags are following their father and their grandfather before them. Odysseus, Laertes. In the morning, they will be Americans in an America that may no longer exist.

A young migrant from southern Mexico at the Tijuana border

FREDERIC RAPHAEL

NATURAL BREAK

France–Spain

*O*F ALL THE FRONTIERS OF EUROPE, which seems more natural or more inevitable than the Pyrenees? Only the English Channel appears, as John of Gaunt suggested, so divinely ordained. On the towering face of things, the Pyrenees have indeed kept France and Spain from each other's throats and territories for over three hundred years, apart from the interlude when Napoleon attempted to impose French hegemony in the inadequate person of his brother Joseph. The disasters of the war which followed were rendered unforgettable by Goya's indelible icons of the invaders' savagery (and of the Spaniards' savage response to it). Goya's mordant patriotism did not, however, inhibit him either from working, at one stage, under Joseph's patronage or from spending the last years of his life, in flight from restored Spanish absolutism, in France. He died in Bordeaux in 1828. Distinctions and allegiances are rarely quite as hermetic as diagrams and definitions insist.

Nevertheless, who can deny the specific character and landscape of the Iberian Peninsula? Its Latinate languages certify that it was once part of the Roman Empire, but ever since Spain ceased to be the greatest power on earth – as it was under Philip II in the sixteenth century – it has glowered and gloried in unsmiling detachment from the northern European style. The Pyrenees furnished a rampart behind which Spain went its own way or, more frequently, made a virtue of immobility. While France vaunted itself as the home of intellectual refinement and social progress, Spain – supposedly sharing a common religion – maintained the lineaments of censorious

Frederic Raphael at the Franco-Spanish border in the western Pyrenees

and coercive authoritarianism. Paris and Madrid were poles apart: the Pyrenees formed the high net over which their diplomatic game was played.

It is tempting, even amusing, to imagine what the situation might have been had the mountains not existed. Toulouse would be as accessible from Madrid as from Paris. Barcelona might well have curtailed, or even pre-empted, the prosperity of Marseille. Who, in fact, has been protected from whom? Without the phonetic filter of the mountains, would they now speak French in Malaga, or Spanish in Lille or Liège? Had Philip IV, and his great minister, Olivares, been able to supply their forces in the Netherlands more directly, and to have better *cabezas* to command them, might Spain have held her dominions in northern Europe? It is, of course, also possible that – had communications been less hazardous – the commanding language in both Malaga and Lille would today be Arabic.

At the time of the great Moorish invasions of the Iberian peninsula, neither Spain nor France existed as a nation-state. Islam spilled across the Straits of Gibraltar in virtually unimpeded spate. When, from their exquisite domains in Andalucia, the Arabs rode north against a Christendom ill-organized to resist them, the Pyrenees detained, but did not hold them. Not until Charles Martel rallied the Franks and smashed the Arab armies at Tours, in 732, did the Pyrenees become a line of demarcation to which both sides, in defiant prudence, were disposed to cleave. In elegance of architecture and in constructive civility, the Moors set standards which the Franks never attained (traces of their influence on the 'wrong' side of the frontier can be seen, for ravishing instance, in the little church of L'Hôpital St Blaise). In intellectual curiosity and – with cruel exceptions – in social organization and religious tolerance, Islam was superior to Christianity. For centuries, enlightenment could more plausibly be attributed to Cordoba or Granada than to Paris or to London. If the Pyrenees helped to ensure that the church and the cathedral, rather than the mosque and the minaret, became the routine badges of European civilization, it would be vanity to attribute Charles's hammering of the Moors to divine partisanship. After the Battle of Tours, and the Arab retreat, the Pyrenees peninsulated northern Europe from gracious as well as from aggressive influences; they also deterred the northerners from ruinous intrusion. The Moors' irrigation systems made Andalucia a fecund wonderland; it became arid only when 'liberated' by the Catholic monarchs.

The Pyrenees may have provided convenient intimidation to forces on both side of their divide, but how acceptable is the division for those who actually inhabit the region? France and Spain have ratified the steep definitions of geography, but neither the Basques nor the Catalans have proved equally obliged. And who are they to question the decisions of national governments? Well, the Basques claim to speak the oldest language in Europe; the Catalans possess the oldest national flag (it originated, they say, in bloody fingers dragged down a golden shield). Both of these Pyrenean peoples have a demanding pride which spills over the mountains to unite brothers and sisters who, in theory, are citizens of alien states.

The Pyrenees, on closer inspection, form no strict barrier: they are as much like lock-gates – facilitating the flow of certain traffic – as they are like locked gates, preventing it. They are full of crannies and secret valleys, of rock-pools in which the tides of history have stranded all kinds of barnacled and improbable life. Sometimes that life has become fossilized, pressed to death by forces which neither remoteness nor self-denial could appease. The Cathars (sometimes called Albigensians), whose fastnesses were in the eastern part of the mountains, are the most notorious victims among these who took to the hills, but found no impregnable refuge there. There is little so inexcusable or so implacable as the determination of great powers, secular and theocratic, to allow no exceptions to their rule.

Yet campaigns to eliminate distinction, however crushing, seldom fail to leave uneasy traces. The creators of Spanish unity were, of course, Ferdinand and Isabella, *los reyes Católicos*. Their marriage of the crowns of Aragon and Castile – previously adjacent and fractious kingdoms – presaged the enforced amalgamation of all Spain under a central monarchy and creed. Early in the process Ferdinand and Isabella seized Navarre, an overwhelmingly Basque province, under the pretext of healing a religious schism. The Crown, although irresistible, was constrained, by pacifying prudence, to endorse the ancient *fueros* – local rights – which gave (and give) the Basque provinces that abiding nostalgia for autonomy whereby hangs many a bloody tale.

The ancient capital of the Basques is Guernica. It is well to the west of the Pyrenees, in the province of Vizcaya, but its symbolic significance gives it a central place in any assessment of the meaning of the frontier. It was at Guernica that the Basques and the Spanish kings met in order to endorse their reciprocal duties: the *fueros* were granted by the new king and allegiance sworn by the Basque leaders as between putative equals. If today's Guernica is of no venerable charm, its perfunctory modernity is the result of what happened on 27 April 1937, a market day, when the old town was clamorous with activity. The Spanish Civil War was in its first year. The Basques were strongly pro-Republican, although their idea of the Republic scarcely chimed with that of the Popular Front politicians who prevailed in Madrid. The Basques were fervent Catholics, unmodernized by the anti-clericalism of other Republicans: their priests identified with the people and were to suffer greatly under Franco, sometimes with their lives, for their supposedly heretical faith. If their courage and competence were valuable to the Republic (engineering and shipbuilding remain among their special skills), the

Basques backed the Republic with a certain dissident solidarity. They hoped eventually for a victorious dividend which would restore their antique independence.

When, on that April market day in 1937, the Condor Legion – sent to Spain by Hitler in order to rehearse the tactics of terror on behalf of Francisco Franco – bombed the old city and killed some three thousand people, the shape of things to come was declared. Picasso's instant masterpiece provided a screaming advertisement of Fascist vileness. His *Guernica* was exiled from Spain as long as Franco remained in Madrid; the painting is now back in the Prado, but its meaning for Basques transcends the scandal of massacre from the air. In Vizcaya and Guipuzcoa, meticulous or sketchy reproductions of Picasso's work regularly adorn public places and draw attention not so much to Franco's demise as to the Basques' unappeased claims to their ancient *fueros*.

If their aspirations are no less sincere for being founded in loud fictions of dispossession, the Basques have never, in truth, had their own country. The myth of national identity is most eagerly trumpeted (and overstated) by Herri Batasuna – the extreme national party – and ETA, the secret army with whom it sympathizes as Sinn Fein does with the IRA. Before Franco's death, ETA often appeared, in foreign eyes, as an organization bravely continuing a lost struggle against Fascism. The ruthlessness of its repression gave long proof of the Caudillo's malign character. The accession of King Juan-Carlos and the arrival of democracy did not change the aims or character of the Basque separatists, but it greatly affected their reputation abroad. To kill Franco's men, whether Guardia Civil or senior military officers, might appear progressive; to continue the same tactics in the context of a free society looked like crackpot particularism. French governments had been indulgent when it came to harbouring (or not too officiously seeking out) Franco's Basque enemies, if they sought refuge on the safe side of a border that their own mythology disowned, but in recent years Paris has been less disposed to a liberal reading of ETA's manifesto. As a result, French interests in the Spanish Basque country (and the cars of French tourists) have become targets for exemplary reprisal.

The grievances of the Basques do not immediately recruit an outsider to partisanship. The scandal of Guernica has understandable centrality in local history, but today the provinces are both prosperous and well-run. If Franco sought to repress the language, by

A reproduction of Picasso's painting *Guernica* outside the City Hall of Guernica commemorates the destruction of the city by Hitler's bombers insisting on all public instruction and documentation being in Castilian, the new democracy is tactfully placatory. Even the police parade in costumes and red berets deferential to local style. Yet to the extremist all concessions are duplicitous, all compromises sell-outs.

I talked to 'John' in the shadow of the restored parliament house, near the hollow remnant of the old sacred oak, which now looks like a sapless sentry-box, leafless and bone-dry within its hoop of iron fence. If he agreed that the Basque parliament, which now meets at Vitoria and in which Herri Batasuna has fourteen out of seventy-five seats, was scarcely a corrupt mockery, John could not bring himself to denounce ETA. ('I would not call them terrorists,' he said). John was a handsome, lively and typically bearded zealot in his early thirties; he was not, like more bardic enthusiasts for the mythical past, a manifest vessel of obsolete sentiment. Yet he, like many Basques both young and old, stood by the slogan 'Four plus Three equals One', the intransigent (and almost certainly fruitless) proclamation of the unity of the four Spanish (Vizcaya, Guipuzcoa, Alava and Navarra) and the three French (Labourd, Basse-Navarre and Soule) Basque provinces, for whom the interpolation of the Pyrenees is more effrontery than frontier.

No one can deny the authenticity of the Basque consciousness or the persistence of their customs (honoured in weekend festivals of folkloric repetition and improbably sweltering costume, as if this were a nation of cross-gartered Malvolios), but an outsider sometimes wonders whether the more hectic of the nationalists are not taking refuge in a parochial parade which may keep them the first men in the village but which almost too cosily embargoes them from competing for more difficult priorities elsewhere. However, the Basques can fairly insist that the 'immutable' frontiers of Europe – especially the one which divides them from their French cousins (very few of *them* fanatical separatists) – seldom have so long a history as modern atlases and chancelleries appear to maintain.

The Pyrenean boundary was not settled until 1659, when the representatives of the French and Spanish kings, Louis XIV and Philip IV, met on the Island of Pheasants, in the mouth of the Bidassoa River, at the southern limit of the border town of Hendaye, in order to put an end to a war which had exhausted Spain and impoverished France. The French were in a dominant but scarcely a dictatorial position as the plenipotentiaries passed over the bridges which temporarily moored the ship-shaped island to the adjacent banks. The proceedings ended with the diplomatic division of the island itself into a symbol of reconciliation: it was declared to belong for half of the year to Spain and for half of the year to France. It is

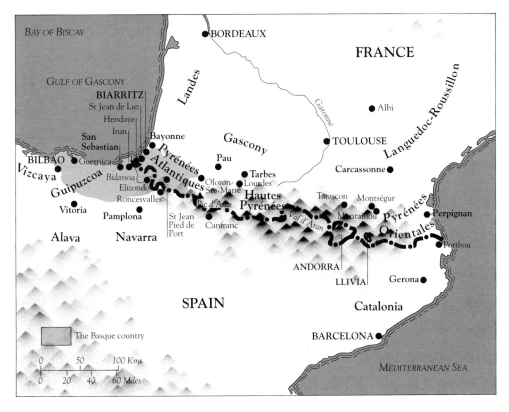

still administered by alternating viceroys. I was lucky enough to enjoy the guidance (and the launch) of the commander of the Bayonne naval base, who doubles as France's governor. Since the island has no inhabitants, Frédéric G.'s responsibilities are scarcely tumultuous: there is grass to mow and trees to trim and a pretentious statue, erected by Napoleon III, to be maintained. The dyarchy is a nicely somnolent matter of antique courtesies and expressions of mutual esteem when the time comes for ceremonial alternation. However, if peace has permanently broken out between Paris and Madrid, the frontier is not without contentious blips, even if one discounts the Basques. Spanish and French fishermen are loud with mutual accusations of malpractice. The French insist that they adhere to Common Market regulations and that the Spaniards break the rules by attaching many more hooks to their lines than the indulgence granted to their 'traditional methods' was ever meant to allow. These eruptions of partisan indignation do not inhibit the easy commerce which rolls through Hendaye and Irun, although a lack of wholly harmonious relations is symbolized by the fact that French and Spanish railways continue to function on different gauges (insti-tuted in the last century to deter the passage of troops trains). International trains from Bordeaux to Madrid are lifted bodily, and with some facility, and imposed on new sets of bogies before continuing to alien destinations.

The charm of the rituals of the Island of Pheasants (on which no eponymous birds have been recorded for many decades) lends a deceptively cloud-cuckoo-landish complexion to a frontier which has a new and charmless problem. French cynics (rarely in short supply) maintain that the drug barons who are now installed on the northern Spanish coast were covertly encouraged, at one stage, by those who hoped that their narcotic influence would sap the separatist energies of the young Basques. The predictable futility of such a plan has been compounded by the lawlessness it has imported. The Colombian Connection owns speedboats which outrun those of the law, while the laundering of dirty money has corrupted the local Spanish economy; the contagion threatens to spill across the border. The French, not unreasonably, regard this development *d'un mauvais oeil*.

Hendaye has had its moments of shame as well as of diplomatic sumptuousness. In 1940 Adolf Hitler came to the frontier, at the height of his power, to claim his reward from Franco. Guernica was, to the Führer, a due bill. He wanted access to Gibraltar and the stranglehold it offered to British influence in the Mediterranean and beyond. If he assumed that his fellow dictator would be at least complaisant, he was to be disappointed. Franco proved as welcoming as a head waiter who, with fawning regret, has no available table. The Caudillo's ingratitude may have been primed by whatever hint of menace the shaken democracies could deliver, but it was also of a piece with the hermetic Spanish suspicion of outsiders, whatever their political sympathy. The 'racial' vanities of the traditional Spanish grandee may, to some degree, be analogous to the Aryan fantasies of the Nazis, but no genuine common attitude existed between the cautious and conservative Franco and the gambler who had used his country as a practice ground for *Blitzkrieg*. Hitler left his rendezvous on the Pyrenees saying that he would sooner have two or three teeth pulled than go through anything like it again. One is left with a twinge of sympathy for two of the most unsym-pathetic men ever to have strutted on history's stage.

The 1659 negotiations on the Island of Pheasants were followed, in the dynastic way of things, by the marriage in 1660 between the young Louis XIV and the Infanta Maria-Teresa of Spain. Louis was not eager for matrimony, since he was in love with another, ineligible woman, but duty encouraged what appetite denied. Maria-Teresa proved, in fact, more nubile than the prince feared: on a secret trip to Fuenterrabía (the adjacent Spanish fortress whose fall to Richelieu's forces had disposed the alarmed Spaniards to diplomacy), Louis was given a secret sight of his intended bride and was apparently converted to majestic enthusiasm. The décor for the marriage was entrusted to Diego Velasquez, among other designers, but the great painter died of a chill, incurred during the preparations, and never saw the wedding. It was celebrated first, by proxy, in Spain and then in person in St Jean de Luz, where bride and groom were accommodated in palaces separated by a waterside square (now the Place Louis XIV). St Jean de Luz had been prosperous in the whaling trade, but stocks had shrivelled. A convenient legend declared that, if a whale were caught before the wedding, Spain and France would remain at peace. Three days before the consummation, an appropriate victim was harpooned. Peace and blood have their sly conspiracies.

Louis XIV famously asserted, after the Treaty of the Pyrenees and his own personal investment in its endurance, '*Il n'y a plus de Pyrénées*'. Had it had been true, would it have been worth saying? The royal marriage was no less happy or successful than many of its kind – it is sentimentally venerated still (Frenchwomen are not uncommonly called Marité) – but the Pyrenees lasted longer. So indeed did some of the incidental consequences of the treaty: both the principality of Andorra and some of the more charming oddities of the frontier derive from blithe decisions made by negotiators keener to return to Paris or Madrid than to spend chilling days in the refinement of arrangements which would affect only nameless peasants in remote valleys.

The broad rule accepted in 1659 was that the mountain watershed should determine the frontier: where the water flowed south, the valley was Spain, and where it flowed north, France. Not the least of the problems created by this solution was that neither the waters nor the topography proved congruent with the polarities thus laid down. More serious still, neither the Basque nor the Catalan languages (nor the people who spoke them) honoured the putative neatness of nature; they continued to flow down both sides of the range.

Whatever Paris or Madrid agree, or divide, the Basques determine the culture of the western Pyrenees on both sides of the frontier. Even the least fervent households take pride in the tradition which, until very recently, has honoured the 'domus' system. Whole families are accommodated in a single, often very big and always very

Basque farmhouse in the French Pyrenees

solemnly constructed, residence. Basque farmhouses – with their
heavy gables and their monumental granite lintels – are frowning
symbols of unbudging solidarity. The language, spikily deterrent
with a plethora of 'x's and 'k's, is rarely learnt by outsiders or
forgotten by natives. Its cousinship with Welsh attests to its deter-
mining (and limiting) place in the consciousness of its adepts; it has
no large literature and it underwrites a cryptic parochialism. The
Basques' sense of grievance is probably as much of a comfort as of
an irritant to them. There may even be an element of bluff in their
pronounced resentments: they are, for all their stolidity, addicted
gamblers. Can we read their rhetoric as a way of raising the political
stakes? To attend one of their pelota festivals is to see their passions
in the raw. Betting is possible (and maintained) until the very last
strike of the ball, even if it concerns simply how long the rally will
last. The *fronton* court in the little town of Elizondo – adjoining one
of the oldest bars – suggests, in the liveliest possible way, that
businesslike sobriety is only part of the local story.

Humour, on the other hand, is no evident component of the Basque
character. There is much pepper in their diet (strings of drying
pimento hang in the autumn air, for use in winter's *pipérades*), but
less salt: wit is not their style. Self-criticism is limited to complacent

folklore, but the culture conceals a secret of dark significance. The Basque monolith has its tragic flaw in the existence of the *Agotes*, as they are called (in a whispered tone) on the Spanish side, or *Cagots* (as the French-speakers say). The *Cagots* are a fraction within Basque society which has been rejected with a disdain akin to that shown to India's untouchables. The *Cagots* are variously said to be descended from German or Visigothic aliens or from lepers. They are alleged to be blue-eyed (unusual in a pariah) and to have no lobes to their ears, something they have in common with the Duke of Wellington — whose men passed this way after evicting the French from the peninsula — and with Lord Byron, who exempted the Pyrenees from his peregrinations.

If the *Cagots* suffered all the humiliations of outsiderdom, not even their persecutors could deny that, in language and religion, they were indeed Basques. They were that sociological oddity, a rejected but integral element, victims of what Freud once called 'the Narcissism of small differences'. An informant in St Jean Pied de Port promised me that the Catholic clergy were among the most vindictive of their enemies. *Cagots* were not refused the sacraments, but they were administered to them at arm's length and, on occasion, through a special hatch in the church walls, so that the rest of the congregation would not be contaminated. If the fear of leprosy (long extinct in these parts) begat their ostracism, it long outlasted the risk of contagion. The *Cagots* lived in ghetto-like streets and villages where they practised trades typical of the outcast: metallurgy and similar works of domestic darkness. If they attempted to intermarry with other Catholics they were violently rejected and sometimes killed. We walked around a reputedly *Agote* village near Elizondo. The nervous — but not remarkably lobeless — inhabitants no longer fear for their lives but have small inclination to welcome strangers. There is no café.

Hoping for inside information, I spoke about the *Agotes* to Alejandro, a lecturer from Bilbao University who had made a theoretical study of them. Alejandro was attending the Basque festival at Elizondo and wore the dark beard and aggressive beret of his clan, although his amused eyes betrayed a somewhat larger intellectual horizon. He gave me a Marxist analysis, as plausible as it was specious (based on the notion of a scapegoat created by the bourgeoisie to divert proletarian indignation). After a few beers, I was emboldened to put it to him that his 'explanation' was merely a partial redescription of the phenomenon. Disarmingly, he more or less conceded the point, admitting that he had never got close enough to any actual *Cagot* to discover what they were like or how they perceived

251

themselves. They seem wholly to have internalized their shame and have produced neither poets nor politicians to articulate it. As for the Basque majority, it seems to have found it reassuring to define itself not only as superior to the external and threatening out-groups (whether of Frenchmen or of Spaniards) but also as distinct from – and outnumbering – its own internal race of unassimilable sub-humans, the dark reflection of its own character.

The barrier of the Pyrenees, you soon discover, was never hermetic. Long before the Economic Community there was, of course, a spiritual community which idealized Christendom into a single entity whose common currency was the Gospel. The lines of tourists who cross from northern Europe into Spain are pilgrims of pleasure who echo, more or less knowingly, the penitents who – from the Dark Ages onwards – walked, or crawled, their way to the supposed tomb of St James at Compostela. Where Crusaders pranced in knightly vanity, and often greed, the pilgrims went in pedestrian piety. St Jean Pied de Port was one of their favourite entry points on the long road. They wore shells – *coquilles St Jacques* – as badges of their

The old town of St Jean Pied de Port

purpose. (Gastronomes can enjoy the hedonistic version at the excellent Hotel des Pyrénées, properly commended by the viceroy of the Island of Pheasants as one of the finest tables in the south-west.) Modern pilgrims are still welcomed, along with less self-denying visitors, within the walled city, above which Louis XIV's indefatigable military architect, Vauban, built one of his typically elegant and practical fortifications. (The king refused Vauban retirement, when he craved it, so irreplaceable were his engineering talents.)

On the steep unspoiled street of the old town, I met a Belgian pilgrim who had wheeled his pushcart all the way from Brussels although he lacked the mermaid with which one of his compatriots was said to have made a similar journey. He had his 'passport' stamped by the lady, Madame Debrill, who makes it her unpaid business to play the gatekeeper of devout souls, before heading for Roncesvalles, on the Spanish side of the border, where Padre Navarro offers beds to genuine (unmotorized) pilgrims on their way to 'St Jacques'. Roncesvalles is a typically grandiose Spanish structure, with a seductive medieval cloister and a corrugated iron roof. Padre Navarro was wary of journalistic interlocutors but he proved considerably less of a Trappist than he had threatened to be, not least when deriding the demanding habits of German pilgrims who expected to be able to make reservations although the rule of the hostelry was strictly 'first come, first sheltered'.

The high pass of Roncesvalles is pompous with a memorial to Roland, who – epic insists – commanded Charlemagne's rearguard when the Frankish army was retreating from some righteous business on the far side of the mountains. Who does not believe that Roland echoed Achilles in his valour and that he sounded his horn for help, alas too late, only when the treacherous heathen outnumbered him a thousandfold? Well, myth is myth and truth, it seems, is something else. Charlemagne's army, we are now assured, was not returning from any Christian mission; it had been hired by one set of Arabs to settle the hash of another. In fact, however, Roland and the other heroes had preferred the easy pickings to be found from sacking Pamplona (already a Basque and Christian city) and never engaged the infidel at all. In this they resembled later Crusaders who, under the blind Doge Dandolo, chose to sack Constantinople rather than proceed on the Fourth Crusade. Roland's rearguard lagged behind as much because they were heavy with booty as because they had been deputed to play the heroic part. It was not a horde of Arabs but vengeful Basques who cut them off and then cut them up. The *chansonniers* turned prosaic greed into poetic self-abnegation. A greater hero than Roland remains unsung, if handsomely entombed,

Memorial to Roland on the high pass of Roncesvalles

at Roncesvalles: Sancho the Strong, a man as tall as a basketball player, has his effigy at the monastery. Sancho indeed conquered the Arabs, at Navas de Tolosa in 1212, and drove them back to Andalucia, where they lived for another two and a half centuries. Sancho was one of the first Spanish kings to unite Navarre, Castile and Aragon, although even his strength could not cement their alliance once the Moors had been defeated.

It is, I suspect, the fractiousness of the Spanish which disposes them to such repeated proclamations of unity, whether religious, racial or political. If they were as confident of their own cohesion as their exclusive rhetoric insists, would they have been obliged to evict the Jews and the Moors (ruining the country in the cruel process)? If their Faith were as great a consolation and as manifest a truth as its zealots asserts, would they have had to be so intolerant of those who failed to share its benefits? The Hispanic dread of outside influences is an acknowledgment, I was once promised by an old scholar in Cordoba, of the Spaniards' repressed awareness that their culture and their blood are alike irremediably hybridized. The purity of the race is as mythical as Roland's (or Francisco Franco's) Christian purposes.

Fear of strangers can lead to amiable gestures no less than to surly battlements. When neighbours such as the French and the Spanish mayors who live in the shadow of the Pic d'Anie clamber up to celebrate, as they do every 13 July, an annual rite of mutual friendship, we may depend upon it that ancient animosities are being sublimated. The ceremony goes back to 1375, more than two hundred years before the Great Armada. It followed a border squabble between shepherds (a profession little disposed to honour formal boundaries if the grass is greener on the far side). The Frenchmen shed blood, probably over access to a spring, and a vendetta was avoided only by what came to be called 'The Three Cow Tribute'. The Frenchmen delivered annual apologies (and procured watering rights) on the hoof. When I attended the 614th occasion, there were cows not only at the misty frontier stone but also ambling along the steep hairpin bends to the scarp. Cows are not sacred in the Pyrenees but they enjoy the right, it seems, to drive in the middle of the road.

The French now offer cash in lieu of livestock, although a tutelary clutch of dun-coloured steers was present among the music-makers and folklorists who saluted the gauche formalities with which the meeting of opposite numbers began. The mayor of Isaba, the biggest of the Spanish communities, presides over the incantations in honour of eternal peace between France and Spain (the part spoke for the whole, up here, long before the whole spoke for the parts on the Island of Pheasants). The dignitaries were doubtless full of mutual esteem – who respects a mayor more than a mayor? – but the distinction between the Spaniards, in their *hidalgo* outfits, and the Frenchmen, in their Republican sashes and Fernandel-like suits, was as abrupt as a slap in the face. The Frenchmen are doomed to pay the annual price of their ancestors' sins not only by remitting the price of the cows but also by eating a Spanish meal. When they return, after enduring Iberian generosity for several bibulous hours, they are reminded of the gastronomic wisdom of not straying from home ground. How can it be that a mark on a mountain delineates the land of those who can cook from that of those who, however copiously, can only serve food? (There are, of course, exceptions: I had the best *paëlla* of my life in the Restaurant Tauro in Port Bou, the 'wrong' side of the Mediterranean frontier.)

By the time you have recrossed the peaks and descended into the Vallée d'Aspe, in the Béarn, the vexed issue of the Basques is left to westward. No heavy contention appears to blight the social or political climate. Yet the little town of Oloron-Ste Marie (a refuge for Resistance fighters in the war) is at one end of an issue which typifies the bureaucratic and economic comedy of modern Europe. The railway line used to pass down the valley, along a very picturesque

The spectacular station at Canfranc built in 1915 in the Spanish Pyrenees

route, into Spain, where the grandiose station of Canfranc, built in 1915, belittles the more practical proportions of the S N C F's station at Oloron. The line functioned, modestly, for half a century, but then, twenty years ago, Something Mysterious happened. A night train, manned by a scratch crew, somehow stalled and ran backwards down the line. It failed to take a bend, smashed through a bridge and ended in the River Aspe. The damage was scarcely irreparable, but it has never been repaired. It is alleged that the French deliberately sabotaged the line, for economic reasons, although the means appear to have derived from Ealing comedy. The rupture has taken on symbolic significance since Spain's adhesion to the Common Market. Macro-economic considerations suggest that a new line, through the centre of the Pyrenees, could hardly fail to be beneficial to both sides and to the local communities, which are now being depopulated, but the rust continues to thicken. The question of *réouverture* requires more than funds from Brussels or acquiescence in Paris: the *fueros* of Aragon, a Spanish province with certain ancient, quasi-sovereign privileges, grace its local assembly with transit authority. Aragon wants both a new road *and* a better rail link. In default of both, it will sanction neither. The valley of the Aspe is thus reverting to nature and the spectacular station of

Canfranc, with its 365 windows and its grassy marshalling yards, takes on the trappings of ghostliness.

Ghosts abound in the Pyrenees. The Romantics discerned liberty in mountains. Imitating Petrarch, they considered themselves nearer to God, or the Life Force, on a peak than in a cathedral. Long before Shelley and Byron traipsed up to the Mer de Glace, the ancient Anatolians put a seat for the gods on top of Mount Sipolos in case any passing Olympians wanted a rest. Western minds have been less solicitous of divine comfort than of punitive purposes, at least in the Pyrenees. The fortress of Portalet was designed for uncushioned prisoners rather than dozy divinities. Since the eleventh century this Procrustean pile, carved from the cold rock of a narrow pass, has been a byword for inhospitality. Its proximity to the Spanish border added irony to hard-heartedness when members of the Resistance were locked up in it during the last war. Léon Blum and others of his government were among the prisoners who spent sunless months at Portalet. At the Liberation Philippe Pétain, their erstwhile gaoler, was sent to the same cells by General de Gaulle, who specialized in grim humour. The old marshal, having been obliged to climb the fortress's five hundred steps, acknowledged that he could understand Blum's indignation. Portalet's bleakness seems to defy any happy metamorphosis of the kind which has often turned the sombre castles of Spain into attractive Paradors, but there are rumours even here of plans to convert the Piranesi-like penitentiary into a hotel. What symbol will the Michelin men devise to indicate a suitable halt for masochists?

The mountains are full of secret roads, along which, even in the darkest times, traffic could pass. Not all the forts and revenue men, not all the frontier guards nor – during the war – the German occupying forces, could choke the flow of refugees and contraband, of heroes and scoundrels. Escapers and *passeurs* have their engraved tribute just outside Tarascon-sur-Ariège. The monument has a gim-crack modernity – metal birds fly stiffly above metal hands clutching at bars – but it commemorates the singular bravery of those who faced danger alone, or in very small groups. Tourists eat indifferent picnics behind the memorial screen. Those who have never heard the yap of pursuing hounds or feared for their easy lives can only tread in the footsteps of the brave and be grateful not to be tested in their fire.

Early in my writing life, I edited the manuscript of a British agent who arrived near Pau after a hazardous journey through occupied Europe. He was penniless and threadbare, but found reliable friends who brought him to the verge of the mountains. His shoes were worn out and they could supply only a pair of *espadrilles* (a speciality of the region, of course). In mid-winter, he was taken by a *passeur* past the furred and booted German border guards to begin the cold crossing. He had to kick foot-holes in the ice as they went over. By the time Jacques was safely across the frontier (Fascist Spain rarely betrayed Allied personnel), he had severe frostbite. He lost several toes and was lucky not to fare worse. Eventually he was able to travel on to Madrid, where he was taken in to see the British ambassador, Viscount Templewood, who – as Sir Samuel Hoare – had been one of the advocates of Appeasement. His Excellency looked at his lame visitor and observed, 'I sometimes think you people are more trouble than you're worth.'

The landscape in which Jacques was hidden and through which he climbed has often concealed fugitives. In the early thirteenth century in particular, the eastern half of the Pyrenean frontier was riddled (as their enemies might have said) with the Christian heretics who were known as Cathars. The caves above Tarascon, where Resistance fighters huddled, were an old sanctuary for them. The word 'Cathar' derives from the Greek *katharos*, or clean. The Cathars' cleanliness was, above all, spiritual. The sect disdained man's mundane existence and were urgent for detachment from the world, the flesh and the devil who – in their doctrine – was responsible for both. The Cathars' zeal for the afterlife was equalled only by the official Church's eagerness to despatch them to it.

The Cathars rejected the Roman clergy and its hierarchy. Their own ministers were known as 'Perfects', men already in the state of other-worldly purity to which the whole sect aspired (the laity tended to postpone the renunciation of the flesh and its compensations until the proximity of death elevated their sights). The Cathar or 'Bogomil' creed is said to have originated in the Balkans; it was a mixture of Manichean gloom and homely decency, a sort of Mediterranean Methodism perhaps. The official Church was outraged at their do-it-yourself simplicities, just as the Cathars were at the sumptuous palaces and pampered practices of ecclesiastical princes. Pope Innocent III declared a crusade against them and the usual righteous pogroms were soon undertaken. Simon de Montfort, the father of one of the traditional founders of English parliamentary government, was a keen scourge of the infidel. The Cathars' other name, the Albigensians, derived from the town of Albi, one of their bastions. As the crusade swept through Provence, the Albigensians were driven from their red-brick towns and forced against the mountains. Their last resorts were the remote fortresses, such as Roquefixade and

Montségur, where their communities preferred hardship to conformity. In these spiritual tower blocks the Perfects ministered to an obstinately primitive and unaggressive flock, while the Church Militant laid siege below. The hilltop castle of Montségur was the Masada of the Cathars: they resisted valiantly for months, until the French general was forced to commission a detachment of six hundred Basques to scale the heights and, in due course, render them accessible to Christian justice. The two hundred and fifteen Perfects who declined to recant were burned to death, along with their intransigent charges. It is said that the sloping field to the left of the refreshment kiosk was the scene of the *auto-da-fé*. There is something sadly typical in the commissioning of one set of marginal people in order to exterminate another.

It seems most improbable that so unworldly and unacquisitive a group as the Cathars should have accumulated great wealth, but their enemies alleged that, the night before Montségur fell, four Perfects escaped with a huge treasure. The myth of Cathar gold persists in the region and offers toothsome opportunities for Sunday journalism. (George Sims wrote a thriller, *Rex Mundi*, on the subject of Rennes-le-Château, a haunted fastness where dark secrets are said to abound.) Poverty was almost certainly the mundane condition of nearly all Cathars. We should know little of their shattered world were it not for the efficiency of those who set out to destroy them: the Inquisition was as bureaucratic as it was officious and it kept thorough records. The discovery of some of its files by Emmanuel Le Roy Ladurie resulted in a famous instance of resuscitation.

Montaillou was (and is, just) a tiny village in a rugged area tight against the Pyrénées Orientales. Its fourteenth-century residents led lives of almost unimaginable obscurity and hardship, but they come vividly to life in Ladurie's sociological text: you can almost smell them, which is not an experience for the squeamish. To bathe once a year was evidence of a certain effeteness. Not the least surprising fact of Montaillou life six hundred and more years ago was the mobility of its jobbing shepherds. The search for pasture and for work took flocks and men across the mountains into Catalonia, as well as down into the valleys where the Count of Foix (rather than the king of France) was the dominating lord. Transhumance – as Fernand Braudel's great history of the Europe of the Philip II reminds us – involved prolonged treks and rare stamina as the flocks were taken, at risk from tempest and brigands, from summer to winter pasture, and back. While it is true that the medieval (and

Overleaf The fortress of Montségur, the last refuge of the Cathars

post-medieval) peasants were more concerned with their own *coin* than with any 'national' issue (even today the French countryman uses the word *pays* to refer to his native heath, not to France itself), it would be unwise to suppose that the men of Montaillou were unfamiliar with the world beyond their village.

Only a crust of wall above the colourless modern village betokens the Inquisition's suspect community. Yet the thoroughness of the documentation allows us a voyeur's access to the manners and morals of the time. The biggest lecher in the place was the village priest, who could be said to have given *droit de seigneur* a new sense. Pierre Clergue led a double life which made him a sort of clerical Kim Philby: he worked for the Inquisition and took backhanders from the Cathars. His main concern seems to have been the reinforcement of his family's power. There are new and substantial Clergue tombs in the graveyard outside the charmless, new church, so he could be said to have achieved his enduring purpose. Clergue cured souls and helped himself to bodies with an energy which lacked scruple but excites a certain appalled admiration. The Inquisition's zeal for interrogation was not limited to matters of doctrinal orthodoxy. One of the witnesses is recorded as confessing, 'I fornicated with public prostitutes; I made dishonourable suggestions to married women, and even to virgins. I was sometimes drunk; I told lies; I stole fruit.' He failed, one notices, to burn anyone at the stake. Only good men confessed to that.

As you move eastwards along the Pyrenees, the anomalies of the frontier increase. The negotiators on the Island of Pheasants were perhaps less concerned with fine print as the regions under consideration receded from them. Having settled the broad principles, the French were, one may guess, eager to get the signatures on the paper. They had, after all, largely imposed their will. Their main concern to the east was to secure their rights to Languedoc-Roussillon, as it is now known. Considerable tracts of it had been in fee to the Spanish Crown until Richelieu's success (and Olivares's disastrous Catalonian policies) rendered Philip IV incapable of holding it. The detachment of part of Catalonia from its Spanish allegiance – Perpignan had been Perpinyá – was the last substantial transfer of real estate in Franco-Spanish history. In the light of that triumph, the French could afford to allow the Spanish to pull some local wool over their eyes. The result is that the little backwater of the Val d'Aran remains Spanish, although the main range of the mountains could be said to lie to the south of it. There is a curtain of high hills between the valley and France, but the serious crags stand between it and Catalonia, whose inhabitants use it for summer holidays and winter sports. The Val d'Aran has its own language (a mutation of Catalan) and a certain militant parochialism: I met a local mayor who, if he lacked the separatist fantasies of ETA, was keen to preserve the authenticity of his own commune. ('Aran', one learns, is actually the Basque world for valley: this is the valley of the valley.)

There are frontiers within frontiers all along the Pyrenees. In the 1930s, a patronizing British traveller could call Andorra 'a corner of Arcady'. It had been a poor but independent state since 1278. The remoteness of its main valley gave it immunity from both secular and ecclesiastical ambitions. At the time of the Treaty of the Pyrenees the bargaining powers decided, whether from magnanimity or indifference, not to alter the arrangement whereby the bishop of Seo d'Urgell, in Spain, and the Count of Foix were the 'co-princes' who guaranteed Andorran sovereignty. (When the Count of Foix-Béarn became Henri IV of France, in 1589, his dyarchal rights had been absorbed by the French Crown, but Andorra was unaffected.)

Vladimir Nabokov once spoke of the most beautiful of the laws of nature, 'the survival of the frailest'. His sense of irony might have been tickled by the fact that the French Crown perished and Andorra survived, although it scarcely retains the polychromatic delicacy of the butterflies of which Nabokov was principally thinking. Twenty-five years ago, the co-principality still had its shepherds and its beauty. Snowbound in winter, prettily inaccessible in the brief summer, it was a staging post for smugglers (tobacco was then a speciality) and a suitable subject for pastoral. Today, only human sheep are to be found within its cluttered borders. Thanks (if thanks are due) to the clouds of carbon monoxide rising from traffic and central heating, snow scarcely settles on the slopes above the old town. In fact, the place reveals scant antiquity: it has been ripped apart to make way for the duty-free emporia on which the ghastly prosperity of the inhabitants depends. Only the parliament house and the law courts supply a certain dignity.

The venality of Andorra should not be read for softness. Only 8 per cent of the residents are said to be of native stock, but a few powerful families are still in command. They are as reticent as they are ruthless, and as rich as they are unapproachable. A journalist who dared, in merely questioning tones, to challenge their authority had his house mysteriously dynamited and found it prudent to decamp to Toulouse. The conversion of a musical comedy state into an international tip for tax-free merchandise may appal the ecologist, but it seems to be very much to the taste of the Andorrans. In theory, neither Spanish nor French visitors ought to be able to get away with the quantities of 'bargains' with which their vehicles are loaded, but a certain complaisance is to be found at both ends of the valley, although enormous customs houses testify to the millions of crass pilgrims who come this way. The boom began when Spanish tourists, languishing under Franco's hermetic economy, came to town to buy 'luxury' articles. The first was a simple Duralux glass, not an obvious candidate for Aladdin's cave but a delectable rarity in a time of austerity. The Andorrans may have been simple people, but they were never fools: they had always played the markets between France and Spain and now they became the market itself. The Romantics thought it easier to find God in the mountains; the cynics can now find Mammon with equal convenience. There are said to be more petrol stations to the acre here than anywhere else on earth.

The bonanza may have its term, although the Andorrans have been playing the middle against both sides for so long that locals are fairly optimistic. Nevertheless, the E C looks with an unamused eye on the double loophole which the co-principality offers to those who do not regard the payment of V A T as a moral imperative. Just as the Roman Church was not disposed to wink at the mountainous insolence of the Cathars, so the officials who implement the Treaty of Rome are reluctant to countenance exception. The spiritual intolerance of the Middle Ages is ridiculous in the eyes of those who see nothing funny in economic dissidence. It is, of course, a nice irony that the salaries of the men in Brussels who are seeking to reduce the 'anomaly' of Andorra are themselves 'extra-territorial' and tax-free.

Andorra is by no means the smallest, although it is certainly the most flagrant, exception to the tidiness of the frontier as a result of Cardinal Mazarin's diplomacy on the Island of Pheasants. (Richelieu was dead by the time the profits were being extracted from his policies.) The French determination to maintain access to their new Catalonian territory impelled them to insist that the villages of 'Rossello' (now Roussillon) should be made over to them. The Spaniards conceded what they could not refuse, but they did have the nerve to contest the French claim to a place called Llivia, not far from the Mediterranean littoral and well to the north of the Pyrenean massif. Their reasons were legalistic, but irrefutable: Llivia, unlike neighbouring places, was not a village but a municipality, deriving its charter from Roman times, when it was named for the wife of Augustus. The French have not accepted the point in particularly good part (Llivia is not indicated on any local signpost), but the town remains a Spanish enclave within metropolitan France. One drives to it along a few miles of no man's track, although there are neither cultural nor economic dividends to be derived from visiting its lonely Hispanic eminence (the local museum asks you for fifty pesetas to examine the reconstruction of a Victorian apothecary's shop). Llivia offers no lurid advertisement for *Hispanidad* and there is small risk of its being inundated with refugees from the surrounding French Catalonia.

Yet the eastern wing of the mountains has been a place of tragic migration and enforced exodus for as long as the descending mountains made it a corridor for the defeated and the desperate, as well as a tempting breach for conquerors from the south (Hannibal's elephants lumbered this way). At the end of the Spanish Civil War, half a million defeated Republicans tramped across the border to be disarmed and often abused by the officials of the French Republic which had done conspicuously little to succour them and which now interned them, on winter beaches, with pusillanimous sympathy. Arthur Koestler's *The Scum of the Earth* provides the best literary account of the cold comfort which awaited the anti-Fascists. There is, however, no shortage of witnesses to tell you of those cruel years. Many of them have become French citizens, but their allegiance is, above all, Catalan. Catalonian fervour stops short, on the whole, of the murderousness of ETA, but it does not lack heat. Spanish refugees formed the majority of the 'French' resistance to German occupation during the war and they continued the fight against Franco after 1945, when their hopes of democratic help in the Caudillo's eviction were disappointed by considerations of *Realpolitik*.

In 1940, the flow of refugees changed direction. If half a million Spaniards had fled north from Franco's firing squads, a new wave of fugitives was fleeing central and northern Europe in the wake of the Panzers. Of those who reached the Spanish border in 1940, none was more manifestly a man of civilization than Walter Benjamin, who arrived in Portbou that summer. Benjamin, a Jewish scholar who had been an ornament of the Frankfurt School. Disbanded by Hitler, the Frankfurt intellectuals had been the think-tank, so to say, of the Weimar Republic. Its professors had been hated by the Nazis who detected in their speculative ingenuity all those elements of Jewish Jewish culture which they wished to destroy. Benjamin combined a Marxist world-view with unreliable worldliness. He now hoped for sanctuary, at least temporarily, in a country where Reds were anathematized. He was travelling with a group of refugees whose papers, it was said by the Spanish frontier police, were not in order. Turned back, Benjamin and his friends went to a waterside hotel (now blanched into conformity with the usual brochured style). The apostle of European high culture – he was a Jew who had rejected the Zionist appeals of his friend Gershon Scholem to come to Palestine – took poison in the night and was discovered dead in the morning. The Spanish authorities, whether from shame or because a new edict had arrived from Madrid, allowed Benjamin's companions to proceed to safety. Local rumour claims that Benjamin was done to death by the Gestapo, but there seems little doubt that he was reduced to despair by the frontier he was either too scrupulous or too guileless to cross save by official channels. By a curious alphabetic coincidence, Walter Benjamin's name lies adjacent, in the regiment of the dead, to that of Rabbi Benjamin, another Jew but one who, it seems, had all the adventurous resource lacking in the scholar. Rabbi Benjamin left Spain in the twelfth century and travelled as far as China. One man's insurmountable frontier is another's point of departure.

Walter Benjamin's experience warns against too panglossian a reading of the prospects for European unity and the universal rule of law. In 1992, not only will Andorra have to cope with the unaccommodating provisions of the Treaty of Rome but the whole of the EC will move towards a homogenized consensus. The customs barriers will come down and we shall, in theory, be waved through to a fraternal future. How eagerly will Europeans abandon their ancient allegiances and suspicions? Will the French speak well of the Spaniards? Will the Basques and the Catalans speak well of either? '*Il n'y a plus de Pyrénées*,' said Louis XIV after the bridges had once again been removed from the Island of Pheasants; '*Il n'y aura plus de frontières*,' Brussels announces. We may drink to a dream of European solidarity, as we may to universal justice, but I confess to an inclination to sip a furtive toast to loopholes and anomalies. Rules, like prison bars, should never be beyond all conceivable bending. *Fiat justitia*, by all means, but let us also honour the escapist's hope of somehow being able to step across a threshold where the writ of universality stops short. Let us hope, even if we cannot legislate, for the persistence of some ancient *fuero*, some papal indiscretion, some diplomatic wheeze which will prevent even the most benevolent authority from enjoying the very last word.

RONALD EYRE is a theatre director, opera producer and broadcaster. His most recent productions are *Peter Grimes* for Opera North and Ronald Harwood's play *The Dresser* for the Shochiku Company in Tokyo. He wrote and presented the series *The Long Search* and *Seven Ages* for BBC television.

NADINE GORDIMER is an award-winning novelist who lives in South Africa. Her novels include *The Conservationist*, which won the Booker Prize, *Burger's Daughter*, *July's People* and *A Sport of Nature*. Collections of short stories include *Something Out There*, *A Soldier's Embrace* and *Selected Stories*. *The Essential Gesture*, essays on writing, politics and places, was published in 1988. A new novel, *My Son's Story*, will appear in 1990.

NIGEL HAMILTON is the author of the official biography of Field-Marshal Montgomery of Alamein in three volumes. The first volume won the Whitbread Prize for the Best Biography of 1981 and the last the Templer Award for the best contribution to military history in 1986. He is currently writing a comprehensive life of President John F. Kennedy, to be published in 1992 to coincide with the seventy-fifth anniversary of his birth.

CHRISTOPHER HITCHENS is Washington columnist for *Nation* magazine and for *Harper's*. His books include *Cyprus*, *The Elgin Marbles* and a collection of essays, *Prepared for the Worst*. He wrote and narrated the BBC documentary *The God that Failed* and presented the documentaries *My Britain* and *The Enchanted Glass* for Channel 4. His study of the special relationship between Great Britain and the United States, *Blood, Class and Nostalgia*, is published in July 1990.

FREDERIC RAPHAEL has written seventeen novels, two biographies and three volumes of short stories. His most recent novel is *After the War*. His screenplays include *Darling* and *Two For the Road* as well as (for television) *The Glittering Prizes*, *Oxbridge Blues* and *After the War*. He is also a translator and essayist and a Fellow of the Royal Society of Literature.

RICHARD RODRIGUEZ is a writer and a journalist. He works as an associate editor with Pacific News Service in San Francisco. His first book, *Hunger of Memory*, was an intellectual autobiography. *Mexico's Children*, a book about the memory of Mexico in California, is due to be published in late 1990.

JON SWAIN worked as a foreign correspondent in Cambodia and Vietnam between 1970 and 1975. Since 1975 he has worked for the *Sunday Times* travelling extensively in Asia and Africa. From 1987 he has been based in Hong Kong as the Far East correspondent of the *Sunday Times*. He has won many press awards for his coverage of the wars in Cambodia and Vietnam.

JOHN WELLS is a writer, actor and director. With Richard Ingrams he writes the 'Dear Bill' letters for *Private Eye*. He wrote and appeared in the title role of *Anyone for Denis*. He has contributed regularly to the *Spectator* and the *Daily Telegraph Magazine*.